Revolt
U.S.A.

Revolt
U.S.A.

BY LAMAR MIDDLETON

Essay Index Reprint Series

BOOKS FOR LIBRARIES PRESS
FREEPORT, NEW YORK

First Published 1938
Reprinted 1968

To Evelyn

LIBRARY OF CONGRESS CATALOG CARD NUMBER:
68-29232

PRINTED IN THE UNITED STATES OF AMERICA

CONTENTS

ILLUSTRATIONS

Revolt
U.S.A.

Revolt
U.S.A.

IT IS A CHERISHED TRADITION WITH US, AND one about which we are more articulate and vehement perhaps than any other, that the temperament of the American stems from the readiness of his forebears to rebel. As a nation we had our origins in rebellion. When the immoral British became insupportable, we virtuously ousted them; and the Civil War, from one standpoint, was also an example of our quick impatience with injustice. We have accepted the word of most educators in the United States, buttressed by a formidable array of historical novelists, that our national character began with this predilection to revolt, that it has shaped our government, our reflexes, our manners and morals. It explains our resiliency as a people—a mass of 130 millions which, for example, will embrace Prohibition ardently, and after thirteen years repudiate it; and it explains our immunity to the scourge of defeatism that is endemic in Europe. Rebellion, in other words, is the rock on which stands the American tradition of liberty.

This is, of course, a pleasant view of ourselves. Reading our history in short perspective, there seems to be considerable surface evidence to support it—from Bacon's rebellion down to the farmers' strikes of a few years ago. It would be, as indeed it has been, a fairly simple task to write a beguiling tale of America from which the reader would conclude that since about 1676 we have been in constant, magnificent revolt against injustice: the inevitable inference is that we have earned our place in the sun today by a righteous and consistent intransigeance.

Such an agreeable portrait, however, must be recognized as something of a caricature when our principal rebellions are examined individually, instead of being lumped together as related parts of one protracted revolt by a homogeneous people.

In such an examination, in any consideration of the social and political circumstances prevailing at the time of a given uprising in the United States, it must be admitted, I think, that none of these rebellions sprang from a characteristic peculiar to us as a people. Rather they occurred because of our want of homogeneity, because of our inconsistencies, often because community inertia gave an opportunist precisely the psychological field in which revolt might be nurtured.

One of the most stubborn and naïve ideas in our national creed is that Americans are, and always have been, a people easily distinguishable from others. If not directly, that conception is implanted in us by implication, certainly, from our first to our last years of formal schooling, and by much of our subsequent reading.

By some special magic, we learn, the American as a national underwent no period of social gestation, nor of political evolution, but about a generation before the Revolution he and his brothers suddenly appeared on the scene, a people who overnight had been happily dowered with unanimous views upon the body of principles that make up democratic government. Indeed, much of the aura with which we surround the Constitution comes from a muddled conviction that it must be an invulnerable declaration of wisdom because all the delegates at Philadelphia recognized its shining virtue. Our historical curriculum does not accent the uncomfortable truth that the Constitution was a succession of compromises, most of them reached in bitterness.

Were we, in fact, so unified a people as is commonly believed, the question would inevitably arise, What, then, has there been for us to rebel against? Apart from the issues of the Revolution and the Civil War, what could a people so much in agreement, so similar in outlook, find as pretext for violence and bloodshed? This book answers with nine of those rebellions, the major ones in our history (excepting the Revolution and the Civil War). But the writer has been concerned not only with the facts of these uprisings but with what they connote of our national character.

Examined before a rebellion, during its height, and afterward, we are a people of whom this, I believe, may fairly be said: we have little unanimity, we are astonishingly credulous, and we have small stomach for prolonged violence. These conclusions do not square with the wistful belief aforementioned—that rebellion is inherent in the American temperament, and that we are a people with unequivocal convictions of social right and wrong.

However disillusioning it may be to the ubiquitous man-in-the-street, the fact is that an "American" never existed in the eighteenth century, if indeed he has achieved national entity in the twentieth. Even now he is far less recognizably a national than, say, the Frenchman or the Pole—or any of those implausible aliens who, we are fond of believing, are forever unable to agree upon the sort of government they want.

Yet that vaguely inferior and indolent European, together with his women, in the 150 years of our life as a nation has shown himself far readier to do battle in the street than has the American. He seems also, incidentally, to have lacked the self-consciousness in insurrection that characterized most of the rebellious rank-and-file in the United States. The majority of our "rebels," as well as the leaders themselves, who followed Herman Husbands, Daniel Shays, Ethan Allen, David Bradford, Thomas Dorr and the rest acted, even when risking their necks, as though abashed and in dread of ridicule.

Several of our rebellions give eloquent testimony of the disunion not only in the nation generally, but in the communities affected. The Whiskey Insurrection is a case in point. A Federal tax on whiskey and on stills appeared justifiable to the New England States, where there was no economic profit in converting grain into spirits. But to four Pennsylvania counties the levy was anathema, a piece of discriminatory legislation as iniquitous as the Stamp Act. The unsympathetic eastern States thought the controversy in western Pennsylvania had been provoked by a rabble of irresponsible farmers over-fond of their whiskey. That, of course, was not true. But it was true that the farmers had valid cause for complaint, that they had as advocates men of the calibre of Albert Gallatin, and that they deserted their leaders and capitulated to the Government the instant an armed clash became probable. In main outline, the progress and collapse of the War of the Regulators, of Shays' Rebellion, and of Dorr's Rebellion followed the same unheroic pattern.

No one will claim that virtue always attaches itself to any people in rebellion against civil and military authority. If the achievements of American insurrection are not a noble saga, it may well be due to an innate canniness stronger—if less inspiring to contemplate—than any passion we may have for independence, for any enlightened decentralization of government. But the story does show that we have no real desire to remedy wrongs by direct action that is physically dangerous, whatever our school histories may imply. And it seems further that we have a higher, not a lower, boiling-point than most nations—doubtless because materially we possess more.

In rebellion, I have said, we are an extraordinarily credulous people. But before we steeled ourselves to insurrection we endured a fabulous lot of economic abuse and Constitutional infringement. If we have not always been a supine people we must own, certainly, to a remarkable capacity for absorbing punishment without recoiling. Even the most enthusiastic historian of American trade-unionism, for example, will hardly claim for it a consistent militancy.

I am reminded of an incident in Paris a few years ago which shows the almost joyful spontaneity with which even the cautious, pragmatic Frenchwoman will rebel against the

combined might of her government. The Stavisky fraud involved several pawn-banks in the south, hundreds of miles
from the capital. The various forgeries had no effect, or at
most a microscopic one, upon her purse. Yet so infuriated
were she and hundreds of her neighbors over the connivance
of a few members of the Chamber of Deputies that the women joined the mobs of men, to throw marbles into the
Place de la Concorde, to bring down the horses of the Gardes
Mobiles, blithely indifferent to the machine-gun bursts raking the adjacent Rue Royale. (More persons lost their lives
in that minor French uprising, incidentally, than in any
American equivalent, excepting two.) The wildest imagination cannot picture a group of New York women facing
riot-guns at Washington, in front of the House of Representatives, because a Chicago bank, with the cooperation of
several Congressmen, failed for several millions.

It might reasonably be assumed that a story of rebellions
in the United States would show at least a progression and
pace common to them all. Were this so, if in fact all rebellions
had at the start and in early stages certain determinable
symptoms, there would be place here for an invaluable
primer for kings and dictators, premiers and presidents. Perhaps fortunately that is not so—Jefferson among others suspected that rebellions might have beneficial effects as a social
cathartic. Here, in any event, such rebellions as we have
suffered have been nearly unpredictable until the eve of their
outbreak. Where one set of factors in one social or economic
latitude bred an uprising against government, almost the
identical factors in another locality resulted in little save
querulous protest. More evidence of our heterogeneity.

18

This dissimilarity may be seen more clearly if one glances at the leaders of these nine uprisings. Bacon was a young man of the ruling class in seventeenth-century England who had a personal hatred for Berkeley, the Virginia Governor, but had no passion for any but a monarchist regime. Essentially the Mathers were two New England bigots who believed in autocratic rule by their church, that is, by themselves. Husbands, the eloquent stooge for the North Carolina Regulators, was a Quaker whose interest in insurrection was strictly literary and non-combative. Daniel Shays, a soldier of the Revolution, was a man of physical courage, no education nor positive convictions. Ethan Allen, originally a land-speculator, was an adventurer stricken with acute monomania. Bradford was a country lawyer and petty opportunist. Turner was a deluded Negro. In conviction and disinterestedness, an amateur soldier, Dorr of Rhode Island, is to my mind the most plausible of the lot, save Debs, and it should be recalled that Debs regarded the Pullman strike as extremely unwise.

None of them can serve as the prototype for an American insurgent leader—as a national character he does not exist. The only common aspect in these outbreaks is that, excepting the Green Mountain contretemps, all were fiascos, that none came even close to accomplishing the object for which it was launched. In Europe local rebellions, putsches, and mutinies have led repeatedly to a successful coup-d'état, although often to a regime more oppressive than its predecessor.

There are two reasons why this country is unlikely, in the predictable future, to have another dose of Jefferson's social purge. The first is that, as centralization of power has increased (and under recent and imminent legislation is increasing), the physical force and the legal implements of Washington combine into a formidable threat to rebellion, however compelling a cause the rebellion may have. The second—even if the first were untrue—is that our diffuse society no longer breeds individual martyrs—going to war *en masse* is not the same thing. We have become a people humiliatingly disciplined, docile and submissive.

A nation with ear glued to the radio and eye riveted on the weekly magazines will not erect barricades in the street in our time.

1677

BACON'S REBELLION

"—AND GOD DAMN MY BLOOD, I CAME FOR A commission, and a commission I'll have before I go! I'll kill Governor, Council, Assembly and all, and then sheathe my sword in my heart's blood!"

The histrionic phrases are not theatre. Nathaniel Bacon means what he says; the black-haired young man is on the brink of a massacre. Behind him, six hundred infuriated Virginia planters, farmers and their men are deployed over the Jamestown green facing the State House, their firearms at the ready.

The words are hurled at the corpulent, bewigged Sir William Berkeley, who confronts Bacon and his men. Behind the envoy of Charles II is his Virginia Council, frightened at the imminence of death a trigger-instant away. The idle and the curious flanking the square are stunned into silence, now abruptly shattered by the treble clatter of firelocks.

Bacon: "Make ready——"

The Governor capitulates. "You'll have the commission— you shall!" The Governor makes his own dramatic flourishes. He showers every epithet he knows on the younger man's head, then rips open coat and shirt. "Here! Shoot! 'Fore God, a fair mark——shoot!"

Bacon looks over his shoulder. He ignores the invitation, and another to resolve their differences by the sword. It costs him nothing to be magnanimous. He has won his point, at the point of several hundred guns. He knows he will receive his officer's commission to set out against the Indians.

The square relaxes. Bacon's men ground their arms. "Sir, I come not, nor intend, to hurt a hair of your Honor's head, and as for your sword, your Honor may please to put it up; it shall rust in the scabbard before I shall desire you to draw it."

Bacon was born January 2, 1647, at Friston Hall, Suffolk. Little is known of his adolescence and young manhood. His education was the formula swallowed by all youths of patrician blood in seventeenth-century England. He left St. Catherine's College at Cambridge with a master's arts' degree at twenty-one—an embarrassingly late age for the times—and then studied law in London.

He was no scholar, despite his direct line of descent from Lord Bacon. But one quality suggested that he might not remain a complacent member of upper-class society: he had more curiosity about the world than most of his acquaintances. One summer, two years before he left Cambridge, his father, Thomas Bacon, won the consent of John Ray to include Nathaniel in the tour of a selected group of students "to many Forraigne Partes." Ray was perhaps the most cele-

brated naturalist of his day. At nineteen Bacon visited the
Netherlands, Germany, France and Italy. Such apparent
lack of insular outlook, of indifference to any land save
Albion, was not fashionable, but otherwise he was orthodox
enough. Anyway, he could point in extenuation to the
travels of his uncle and namesake, the elder Nathaniel Bacon,
who since 1650 had lived in Virginia, and had once served
as President of the Council. Given the younger Bacon's education and antecedents, nothing but accident could keep
him from a career in public life in England.

Such an accident was his dissatisfaction with the allowance
of £150 given him by his father. The son, when twenty-
seven, had married Elizabeth, daughter of Sir Edward
Duke, and had need of more money, although a memoir-
writer of the last century (the Unitarian William Ware)
remarks that "he had married more than he inherited." The
elder Nathaniel gave his son £1800, and pointed to the west.
Nathaniel, Jr., took the hint, and late in 1674 he arrived at
Jamestown, at the mouth of the James River.

The uncle, Nathaniel, had been in the colony of Virginia
since 1650, had served as president of the Council of State,
and was still a member of that body when his nephew arrived with his bride. He was well-to-do, influential and reac-
tionary, and because he was childless it was popularly supposed that the young arrival would be his heir. This belief
was also popular with the nephew. With what was left of his
patrimony, and with the aid of the avuncular Bacon ("a
Rich Politick man"), the new colonial bought two properties. One was a homestead at Curl's Neck, on the James
River about twenty miles below Richmond, and forty miles

above Jamestown, the capital. The other plantation occupied a district within the present-day Richmond known today as "Bacon's Quarter Branch." Overnight he became a
country gentleman in the Virginia tradition—then distinctly
a royalist one.

Neither portraits nor engravings of Bacon exist, and pos-
thumous description is of the sketchiest. In 1675, soon after
his arrival in Virginia, he was twenty-eight; but, it was
written of him a year later, he appeared "about four or five
and thirty." Three years later a body of royal commissioners,
dispatched from London to make a report for Charles II on
the rebellion and its brutal aftermath, was more explicit, although their portrait was an "official" one.

"He was a person whose erratique fortune had carryed
and shewne him many Forraigne Parts, and of no obscure
Family . . . He was indifferent tall but slender, blackhair'd
and of an ominous, pensive, melancholy aspect, of a pestilent,
prevalent Logical discourse tending to atheisme in most
companeyes, and dangerous hidden Pride of Heart, despising
the wisest of his neighbors for their Ignorance, and very
ambitious and arrogant."

In a few months, the elder Bacon in Virginia maneuvered
the appointment of the younger to the Council. If this was
nepotism, there was undoubted sense in it: the population
of the colony was less than 40,000, of which more than
2,000 were slaves, 6,000 others "servants"—less menial than
it sounds today—and the rest landless freemen. The planters,
all freeholders, were in the extreme minority, and there was
no abundance of educated men to serve either on the Council or in the House of Burgesses.

It is not to be thought that Governor Berkeley especially welcomed the young man to the Council. Among other things he frowned upon Bacon's profanity—Nathaniel, Jr., was prone to such sulphurous locutions as "damn my blood" and even, upon the aforementioned occasion, "God damn my blood!" The Governor, however, had hopes that young Bacon might join his uncle in the bloc of rich planters on the Council which supported Berkeley against the common run of settler-farmers. And the Governor, moreover, was indebted to the elder Bacon, who had stood with him in offering asylum to the supporters of Charles I after the civil war in England. The young man's readiness to invoke God was scarcely sufficient reason to suspect Bacon of being the firebrand he proved to be.

The Virginia of the day was overripe for revolt, and it is astonishing that revolt did not occur before 1676. At the time of Bacon's arrival, the colony was destitute; in that fact, and particularly in the absence of energetic steps to improve affairs, lay the root of trouble.

In 1651 and 1660 Parliament had passed the Navigation Acts, restricting colonial exports to English vessels sailing to British ports. The effect of this was to force the colonists to sell to home monopolists at a time when all England was living on war-rations, and a pipe was a dispensable luxury. The price of Virginia tobacco, virtually the currency of the colony, fell to much less than cost. Further contracting Virginia trade, the Navigation Acts forbade the sale in England of grain raised in the colonies. The colonists' was an intolerable position: they could not export their wheat and rye to the Mother Country, they were forbidden to sell it elsewhere, and they were forced to sell their tobacco in her almost non-existent market. Meanwhile they were burdened with steadily mounting taxes—the recurrent motif throughout the history of revolution and rebellion in America.

A century before the phrase became a battle-cry, here was taxation without representation. Fifty years before, in 1624, the Virginia Assembly had declared that the Governor could not levy taxes against the will of the Burgesses, the ostensible representatives of the people. But under Berkeley's governorship that enactment had fallen into desuetude, since he had not permitted new elections since 1662. For fourteen years, by means of one "adjournment" after another, the Assembly remained the same, a group of "grandees," as the small farmers said in Virginia, hand-picked by the absolutist Governor.

The basic colonial tax was upon the "tithable polls," i.e., on all males over sixteen, and it was strictly a per capita tax, not based on property assessment. The tax on the planter with a thousand acres was substantially identical with that levied on the colonist tilling a hundred acres. (By 1670, six years before the explosion, the ageing Berkeley had so lost sight of economic and political realities in the colony, or had so confused himself with Charles II (or, possibly, with God), that he propelled through the Assembly a manifestly illegal act restricting the vote to land-owners). The poll-tax paid for the nominal expenses of government. But "nominal expenses," in the eyes of the puppet Assembly, included such perquisites as a man-servant and two horses for every Burgess, salaries for committee-clerks, and a substantial sum for liquor. (Without a good daily liquor supply it was apparently unseemly to enter the State House at Jamestown.)

Evidently it was felt in London, in 1672, that the Virginians might endure a great deal more. Charles II, engrossed in Nell Gwyn, impatiently signed away the entire colony for a period of thirty-one years to his cronies the Earl of Arlington and the Lord of Culpepper (the latter a cousin of Bacon's) in return for forty shillings a year. This fantastic concession was kept secret two years; then, in 1674, the "proprietors" began to assert their rights. They descended upon the colonials, some of whom paid the lords off rather than resort to the courts to clear their deeds. But the demand for redress grew—the colony, already insolvent, would not face thirty-one years of tribute to the pair of "Lords Proprietors." Governor Berkeley, always unable to speak an outright affirmative, was persuaded at length to send a commission of protest to London. But the colonials must pay the "normal" expenses of that deputation; and *normal*, said he, meant a sum requiring an extra sixty pounds of tobacco per head. Beyond this piece of stupidity it might seem human ingenuity could not go.

But there was more.

In 1675, Governor Sir William Berkeley was sixty-five. One may suppose that he was losing his hand at chicanery, his fine Italian hand grown palsied. He was no longer covering his tracks in his private trade with the Indians, forbidden under the colonial articles; "notwithstanding Which," Bacon charged, "our present Governor monopolized a trade with the Indians, & granted licenses to trade with them for which hee had every 3rd skinne, which trading with the Indians has proved soe fatall to these pts of the world that I feare wee shall bee all lost . . . acquainting [our] most inveterate Enemy with our manner of living and discipline of warr; has also brought them generally to the use of our firearms with such dexterity . . ."

It is plain that Berkeley, surrounded by the rapacious civil officers sent over by the King originally to mollify the colonists, secretly gave them permission to trade in furs, firearms and liquor with the Indians, in return for one-third of the profits. There is a considerable literature devoted to this American colonial governor and Cavalier, the playwright incidentally of a tragi-comedy, *The Lost Lady*. Here it is pertinent to note that he was first made Governor of Virginia in 1641, after serving as a "gentleman of the privy chamber" of Charles I, and that his first administration was popular—the colony's leaders were then all royalists, and delighted in referring to their executive body, for example, as "His Majesty's Royal Council." A Cromwellian fleet deposed him in 1651, but the colonists returned him to office after the Restoration. Charles II confirmed the election; and thereafter, until the detonation set off by Bacon, Governor Berkeley used his office to fill his pockets. Politically he had once had skill and finesse. Berkeley was the complete royalist, set against any but the tightest British tradition, demanding homage first to His Majesty, next to himself and, if the colonial supply were not then exhausted, to God (distinctly not the God of the Puritans or the Quakers, however, whose worshippers he had booted from Virginia). Perhaps one act alone describes his outlook. Berkeley forbade the establishment of a printing-press in Jamestown, "as making people too censorious of their superiors."

In the Virginia cauldron, then, there were at least five elements any one of which might have soured the brew. There was the crippling effect of the Navigation Acts upon trade, particularly upon the sale of tobacco; there was the palpable injustice, as well as the illegality, in the method of taxation; there was the disappearance of universal male suffrage; there was the swindle perpetrated by Charles II in his grant to Arlington and Culpepper; and there was Governor Berkeley's cupidity and his intransigeant attitude toward the colonists' simplest grievances.

But there was a sixth—the outbreak of depredations by the Indians. There is a certain ironic justice in the fact that it was the Indians, in the illicit traffic with whom the Governor was profiting, who revealed Berkeley's hand.   .

The geographical picture in 1675 may be readily understood by a glance at any map of Virginia. Since about 1607 the colonists had sought to entrench themselves along the shore of Chesapeake Bay and the shores of the rivers to the east, where in Bacon's time the large plantations were concentrated. If one draws a vertical line through Richmond from the Potomac on the north to the Carolina line, the territory east of that line would represent approximately all the settlements of the whites in 1675.

It would also embrace, however, a number of Indian encampments, although the tribes were retreating west of that line. The Susquehannocks, the Doegs, and other tribes left their old hunting-grounds sullenly, as might be expected, but for thirty-five years prior to 1675 a degree of armed

neutrality had prevailed. The French had yet to begin inciting the Indians against the British, at least to any such
degree as occurred fifteen years later. The colonists, their
women and children, had forgotten the savage yell—the
paralyzing preface to the tomahawk. They were out of
temper, certainly, but their ire was directed at Berkeley and
the battening Burgesses, not at the Indians. Fighting the
land to obtain the scantiest subsistence and to pay their taxes,
many of them felt a fatal sense of security from the redskin.
Surely, the greater menace was the Governor.

In the spring of 1675, when Bacon had been several
months in the colony, the Indian struck—without regard for
the niceties of military etiquette, without any warning to the
enemy (in contemporary accounts the Indian is indiscriminately the "savage heathen;" Bacon was fonder, in capital
letters, of the "Barbarous Heathen," a label which occurs
resoundingly in the proclamations, edicts, etcetera he wrote
during the twenty weeks of his campaign).

In the thirty-five years of surface peace, the colonists had
been gradually pushing the Indian back, in Virginia as elsewhere. His own trails aided the white infiltration into his
hunting- and trapping-grounds and the rich bottomlands
where he planted his maize, pumpkins, beans and tobacco.
But since Berkeley's first term as Governor, starting in 1641,
the colonial penetration in the colony had not been greatly
resented by the Indian. The peaceful invasion was effected
under the anaesthetic of a trade that most of the tribes regarded as eminently satisfactory. In exchange for furs, of
whose European value he was totally ignorant, the Indian
had been regularly given bright worthless knicknacks,

blankets, or, if he had sufficient furs, fire-arms, shot and liquor. A very sudden result of his degradation by white influence, apparent throughout the colonies, but particularly so in Virginia and Massachusetts, was his return to a level of savagery from which he had long since progressed.

But in Virginia, at last, the Doeg and Susquehannock chiefs saw that they were not only stripping the country of beavers and other furs for the whites, but were also losing the land. And in compensation the whites were not offering more in barter. They were more chary, in fact, with their guns, they demanded more for their blankets, their trinkets, and they even reduced the amount of spirits that had once been the reward of a good season's trapping. The banks of the rivers and small streams in southeast, northeast and central Virginia, which once had known only Indian villages and encampments, were dotted now with the cabins of the colonists, who had no respect for Indian snares and nets. The continued retreat upstream in their skin-boats and bark canoes must stop. The Governor's agents with whom they traded, the real object of their rage, were scattered, difficult to find; a target for revenge much readier at hand was the new settler, who had a minimum of protection from their arrows, scalping-knives and tomahawks. After the long period of quiet, he would not expect attack.

Had the settler been more observing, however, he would have been warned. That was the opinion of Thomas Mathews, a planter and a member of the Assembly, son of a former Governor of the colony, to whom certain natural phenomena in the year 1675 appeared ominous. As one indication of forthcoming trouble, he wrote, a large comet was to be seen every evening for a week, rushing in a stream of fire over the western horizon. Then again, there was the flight for sveral days of vast bodies of pigeons which settled on the trees at night in such numbers that their weight broke the branches; and this very thing had occurred in 1640, the year of the last massacre. And as a final omen, there were "swarms of fflyes about an inch long, and big as the top of a man's little finger, rising out of spigot holes in the earth."

But evidently such infallible warnings had no meaning for the colonists.

Stafford County lies in northeast Virginia. To the west and south the gentle hills descend to the Rappahannock, and to the east is the broad Potomac. On a Sunday morning in April, a party of colonists, making their way to church, passed the farm of a herdsman named Robert Hen. They found him lying across the doorstep in a lake of blood, and although tomahawked he was still alive. Near him lay a dead Indian—the proverbial good Indian. The herdsman had strength only to cry out "Doegs! Doegs!"—this the name of a less friendly tribe. ("From this Englishman's bloud," Thomas Mathews informs us, "did by degrees arise Bacon's rebellion, with the following mischiefs which overspread all Virginia." Elsewhere the narrator refers to the "mischiefs" as a "horrid action." Evidently Mathews was a man whose style was one of severe restraint.)

In Virginia, as elsewhere among the colonies in that day, such a spectacle ordinarily meant that other white men would be attacked. The little party raised the alarm, and

Colonel Giles Brent and Colonel George Mason, the commanders respectively of the horse and foot forces of Stafford County, immediately organized a posse of thirty men, and gave chase. About twenty miles up the Potomac they crossed over to Maryland, after firing indiscriminately on every Indian they saw. At dawn they divided forces, and soon thereafter Brent killed the king of the Doegs and took his small son captive. Mason had fired at another Indian cabin, and received a return fire, when one of the tribe rushed outside to say, "We are Susquehannocks—friends!"

But the tribes, aroused, continued to murder on both sides of the river, and continued also to be murdered.

To quell the Indians, the Maryland government gave Major Thomas Truman a force of militia with orders to expel the Susquehannocks from an old fort near the present site of Washington. Virginia was asked to assist, and Colonel John Washington, great-grandfather of George Washington, went out to join Major Truman. Between them the two colonies had a force of about a thousand men. They besieged the fort seven weeks, and in that time they killed five or six of the Indian chiefs who had come out from the fort to parley. The colonists' excuse when upbraided by Berkeley was that they recognized in these Indian "great men" the murderers of white settlers. In retaliation, about fifty of the besiegers were killed. Seventy-five of the Indians escaped one night, and as a memento they killed ten of the sleeping white men before they fled. The Indians headed southwest for the James River, and they marked their progress by murdering white men, women and children as they passed. En route the Susquehannocks incited other Indians, and almost overnight the Virginia woods were alive with red men craving revenge. The colonials went into the fields with their weapons beside them, small, exposed families sought the protection of larger ones, and palisades and redoubts were built around these centers.

But the Indian was set on a reign of terror. He had had enough of the Virginia colonist, of Berkeley "the white god." In January of the new year (1676), a strong raiding-party descended with triumphant yells on several rich plantations bordering upon the upper Potomac and Rappahannock. Between thirty and thirty-five white men, women and children were treated to the scalping-knife, and finished with the tomahawk. A few of the whites were first tortured, tied in frames that were bound to posts.

An Indian war of major proportions appeared inevitable. The settlers were gradually forced to abandon their farms, which the Indians promptly pillaged and burned. After the devastating Potomac raids, it began to be feared that the red-skin might try to recapture the fertile Cavalier country east of Richmond. To the colonists' alarm, the Doegs and Rappahannocks apparently had settled their differences, for warriors of both tribes were spied in the same bands that were swooping on the farmers, levelling their families with the tomahawk, and razing their buildings and crops with the torch.

The sudden flood of protests, petitions, pleas for aid that poured in on the Governor threatened to keep him away from his decanter. But Jamestown was a comfortable distance from the bloodshed. Such complaints as these Berkeley waved aside:

"That great quantityes of tobacco has been Raised for the building of fforts [Surrey County complained] & yet no place of defense in the County sufficient to secure his Majesties poore subjects from the ffury of fforaine Invaders." And from Isle of Wight County, "Also wee desire that there be a continuall warr with the Indians that we may once have done with them."

For several weeks the Governor continued to ignore these and other pleas from the alarmed colonists, although each day brought reports of new massacres to the capital. There were such open challenges directed at Berkeley as "no bullets pierce beaver skins" and "rebel forfeitures would be loyal inheritances." Berkeley's dalliance was so evident to the colonists, every hour in fear of their lives, that the suspicion that he had dealt privately with the Indians—and was reluctant to antagonize them—turned to conviction. Shortly after the Rappahannock and Potomac raids, he made matters worse for himself by recruiting a punitive expedition under Sir Henry Chicheley, and then disbanding it, declaring that no defensive measures could be adopted legally until the meeting of the Assembly in March.

This obstacle did not deter the Indians. Horrors mounted.

Dominated by Berkeley, the Assembly when it convened undertook to establish forts on the upper reaches of the rivers and along the frontier. These forts, which the colonists complained were "no more than mousetraps," were to be erected by means of another tobacco impost, constituting "a great grievance, juggle and cheat" and a "design of the grandees to engross all of the tobacco into their own hands." This riposte Berkeley chose to ignore.

Since the Governor would not protect their lives, the colonists devised their own measures. The movement began near Merchant's Hope Plantation, in Charles City County (near the mouth of the James River), where Mathews reports that the inhabitants "beat up drums for Volunteers to go out against the Indians, and, and soe continued Sundry dayes drawing into arms." He expresses astonishment that the authorities, by which he means the Governor, permitted "soe dangerous a beginning and going on."

Sometime before April of 1676, the Indians, retreating to the James River after one of these forays, crossed Bacon's plantation at Bacon's Quarter Branch, and killed his overseer. His rage over this loss seems altogether disproportionate, since it was what happened elsewhere nearly every day. But the overseer's "bloud he vowed to revenge, if possible."

And Bacon exclaimed, "If the redskins meddle with me, damn my blood I'll harry them."

Henceforth is seen a Bacon become, in the space of a year or less, a Virginia patriot burning with outrage, a man horror-struck at the atrocities of the "Barbarous Heathen," a man inflamed over the injustice and oppressions of Berkeley.

There is something wrong with the picture. Bacon was twenty-nine, not the age when a man turns zealot. Hitherto his letters to friends in England were ordinary enough. But shortly after his overseer's murder, he is writing that "finding that the country was basely, for a small, sordid gain, betrayed, and the lives of the poor inhabitants wretchedly sacrificed," he "resolved to stand in this ruinous gap"and to expose his "life and fortune to all hazards."

Thomas Mathews in his "Appendix," written much closer to the time of the rebellion than any other works, save the letters of Bacon himself, remarks that it was recognized by contemporaries that Bacon had "run out his patrimony," and "wanted patience to wait the death of his oppulent cousin." This, the Appendix continues, "made him suspected of casting an eye to search for retrievement in the troubled waters of popular discontents."

Bacon recognized that the situation early in 1676 had every element to make for a spectacular coup against Berkeley—except leadership. The loss of an overseer to a young aristocrat only recently arrived in Virginia, meant little personally; as a (conscious or unconscious) peg for righteous indignation it was invaluable. In his position, without genuine roots in Virginia, he must have been witless not to seize the opportunity. Certainly it took courage, however selfish a courage, to seize that chance, but to assert that he was without motives of self-interest is to deny Bacon the native shrewdness that was his small share of genius.

While the colonists were "beating up drums" in Charles City County, four planters in Henrico County, directly west, were discussing the "sadness of the times and the fear they all lived in." They were Captain James Crews, Henry Isham, Colonel William Byrd, commander of the Henrico County militia, and Nathaniel Bacon, all owning plantations in the neighborhood of what is today Richmond.

Crews, so the tale goes, explained that the day before, across the river in Charles City County, he had suggested to the recruiting leaders that Bacon—a member of the Governor's Council—was an ideal man to lead an independent expedition against the Indians. Isham and Byrd (who later saved his career by making his peace with Berkeley) concurred. Bacon, the youngest of the quartet, the least established in the community, was suddenly more than ready to be persuaded.

That acute prescience of Lord Bacon's descendant was his death-warrant. But it was his warrant also to a considerable fame. Urged by the trio, catching fire from their earnestness, he agreed that the following day he would inspect the volunteers at Merchant's Hope Plantation.

At this stage, he describes his feelings:

"Now, the Governor having placed me here in a position of trust [the Council], I thought it my duty to discharge my conscience in it, by introducing a looking-after the welfare of the people, they being poor, few and in scattered habitations on the frontiers and remote parts of the country nigh these Indians, who falling upon us (as well as other parts) and killing, amongst the rest, my Overseer, and laying desolate a plantation of mine to my great loss of cattle and all my crop . . . I resolved to march out upon the Enemy with what volunteers I could then gett, but by so doing found that I not only lost the Governor's favor, but exposed my verry life and fortune at home as well as abroad."

Mrs. Bacon is similarly grieved. Writing to her sister in England, she refers to the "sad condition . . . occasioned by the troublesome Indians, who have killed one of our Overseers at an outward plantation which wee had, and we have lost a great stock of cattle, which wee had upon it, and a good crop that wee should have made there, such plantation Nobody durst come nigh, which is a verry great loss to us."

When, the next day, the volunteers of Charles City County saw him approaching, the troops shouted "A Bacon! A Bacon!" Bacon consented to lead the men, and then and there by acclamation became the "General of the People." He enrolled volunteers, whose arms were, if anything, inferior to those which hundreds of Indians had procured through Berkeley's connivance. And here Bacon used an amusing dodge: he set down his recruits' identities "upon a large paper, writing their names circular-wise that their ring-leaders might not be found out." Then, "having conjured them into this circle," Bacon "gave them brandy to wind up the charm."

According to Thomas Mathews the volunteers numbered some three hundred, but when the time arrived for action, a few weeks later, Bacon writes that he marched "with about 70 men onely which engaged and stood by me (the service being too hott for the rest)."

The orthodox view that Bacon was heedless, swept away by his fine frenzy, as it were, for a Virginia free of Berkeley, does not square easily with his next and cautious move. He made application to Berkeley for a commission. The Governor replied evasively. "Being from time to time denied," Bacon explains, "I resolved to stand up in this ruinous gap; rather . . . than basely desert my post, & by soe bad an example make desolate a whole country, in which no one dared to stir against the common Enemy, but came flying from the Enemy and crowded together like sheep, leaving their plantation and stock a prey to the Enemy."

At this point, Bacon gets mad—that is the only word for it. Thus, in June 1676: "I'll hurry them, commission or no commission!" From Charles City County he goes north to Kent County, which had also suffered from the Indians, to find more volunteers, not so simple a task at a time when landowners are concerned primarily about their crops, and during the daytime, at least, can forget about the tribes.

Altogether, the force numbered three hundred. Bacon tired of waiting on the Governor, and there was a good deal of sentiment to support him.

"This day lapsing," Mathews relates, suggesting that Bacon's message to Berkeley was more an ultimatum than a request, "they marched into the wilderness in quest of these Indians." In this first venture into the field, with his force finally reduced to about seventy, Bacon emptied an Indian stronghold on the upper James of a small party of Indians.

The Indians were entrenched on a small island near the south shore. After an hour of siege, Bacon realized that firing into the woods covering the island—and covering the Indians—was a waste of ammunition. The only means of dislodging the enemy was a frontal assault, since there was no way of outflanking the island force. It shows the confidence which Bacon inspired that his followers agreed to that hazardous approach in the open, against an invisible and amply protected foe who had firearms as well as arrows.

They waded to the assault, miraculously dodged the

clouds of arrows, the bullets, and fell on the Indians, giving them no time to escape in their canoes. Eleven of the white men lost their lives.

He writes that "I . . . returned with a greater victory from sharper conflict than ever yett has been known in these pts of the world." He adds that he killed "about 100 men and 2 of their kings, besides women and children." This gave "great satisfaction to the people," which was probably true. Mathews, a neighbor of Bacon's, rather minimizes the foray, but the Virginia State Library has an anonymous manuscript which says that Bacon and his men had a fairly severe battle.

He returned to the lower James a hero.

To Berkeley, this was insurrection. Legally it certainly was insurrection; Bacon acted without commission or other authority. When the force advanced, and the Governor heard of it, he plastered Jamestown with a proclamation that all were rebels who did not return in three days. That was fairly effective; it reduced Bacon's numbers by nearly five-sixths.

Then Berkeley took the field to arrest his upstart Councilman. Soon he learned that a few days before, on his return from the first Indian battle, Bacon had been "elected" to the Assembly, that almost all of York Peninsula was ready to acclaim him as their leader against the Governor. The Governor judged it discreet to return to Jamestown with his small mounted party. Before leaving the Falls of the James, where he had awaited Bacon, he entertained Mrs. Bacon with a description of the forthcoming hanging of her husband as a man "rude, dissolute and tumultuous." Bacon was promptly expelled from the Council, and even his uncle supported the Governor. But the latter, after his abortive expedition, had reappraised sentiment, and he thought it wise at last to dissolve the fourteen-year-old legislature.

In reply to the Governor's charges of rebellion and treason, Bacon himself issued a manifesto; how and where it was printed is unknown. He has the Patrick-Henry touch:

"If virtue be a sin, if piety be 'gainst all the principles of morality, if goodness and justice be perverted, we must confess that those who are now called rebels may be in danger of those high imputations, those loud and several Bulls would affright innocents and render the defence of our brethren, and the inquiry into our sad and heavy oppressions, treason. But if here be, as sure is, a just God to appeal to, if religion and justice be a sanctuary here, if to plead the cause of the oppressed, if to aim at his Majesty's honor and the public good without any reservation or by-interest, if to stand in the gap after so much blood of our dear brethren bought and sold . . . be treason, Lord Almighty judge and let the guilty die!"

Bacon, now back at his plantation at Curl's Neck on the James, prepared to leave for the capital to represent his Henrico County constituency at the June meeting of the House of Burgesses. But on Mistress Bacon's insistence, he consented not to go alone—Berkeley would be too ready to clap him into irons, if the Governor felt that the people would tolerate it. So Bacon, accompanied by forty men bristling with arms, boarded a small sloop to make the trip down-river.

A mile above Jamestown he dropped another. The youthful rebel leader, usually pictured as the impetuous hero, would not take unnecessary risks: from Sand's Point, opposite which they had anchored, a messenger was sent to Berkeley to demand whether he, Bacon, might take his seat with the Burgesses.

The Governor answered plainly. A shore battery sent a shot after the sloop. Meanwhile Bacon, under cover of night, went ashore to consult with two friends, Richard Lawrence —an Oxford graduate and a member of the House, whom the Governor despised as an "aesthetical and scandalous person"—and William Drummond (to Berkeley "that perfidious Scot"), a onetime governor of a North Carolina colony.

They warned the rebel that Jamestown was on the brink of rebellion, that the conflict between Berkeley and the Council on the one hand and Bacon's supporters on the other was severe. If he proceeded to enter the capital openly, Berkeley would certainly toss him into jail, and furthermore unless Bacon set sail forthwith up the James, the Governor would attempt to seize the sloop.

At least momentarily checked, Bacon returned to his sloop, and began to move upstream. In a few minutes he found his way barred by the Governor's cruiser, *Adam and Eve*, which fired across his bows and forced him to heave to. The rebel was arrested, and, with his escort, brought to Berkeley at the State House.

He was now at Berkeley's mercy, and his bodyguard was in irons. The Governor did not dare punish him drastically, in view of the popular support behind Bacon; yet the young insurrectionist must be made to recognize publicly that with the Governor rested the supreme authority (although the newly elected House of Burgesses was less pro-Berkeley than its predecessor of fourteen years). For his part, Bacon recognized his own position—and he acted as any wily realist might in the circumstances.

The old Cavalier, frigidly: "Mr. Bacon, have you forgotten to be a gentleman?"

Bacon: "No, may it please your honor."

Berkeley: "Then I'll take your parole."

Bacon was released on his own recognizance, and went to stay with Lawrence—remaining within Berkeley's easy reach—until the Governor should determine the penalty.

At this point Bacon's uncle interceded to ask the Governor whether, rather than risk the possible consequences of subjecting the rebel to draconian punishment, he would accept an apology and recantation, to be read by the culprit to the Burgesses. For good measure, and as a sop to Berkeley's vanity, the elder Bacon proposed that his nephew read this apology on his knees.

Berkeley agreed.

It is not known what Bacon thought of this proposal, but it is known that he accepted it. He did not intend repining in jail over some academic point of honor.

Berkeley brought the new Assembly to order. "If there be joy in the presence of the angels over one sinner that repenteth," he declared "there is joy now, for we have a penitent sinner come before us . . . Call Mr. Bacon."

Thus Bacon, kneeling before Berkeley, and in full view of the Assembly:

"I . . . do hereby most readily, freely and most humbly

acknowledge that I am and have been guilty of divers late unlawful, mutinous and rebellious practices, contrary to my duty to his most sacred Majesty's governor . . . his Majesty's most worthy governor and captain-general of Virginia . . . And I do hereby, upon my knees, most humbly beg of Almighty God and of his Majesty's said Governor . . . gracious pardon and indemnity . . . And I do hereby promise, upon the word and faith of a Christian and a gentleman . . . I will always bear true faith . . . and demean myself dutifully—" it continued in this vein for ten minutes of bliss for Berkeley.

Henceforth the tempo of the rebellion against Berkeley quickens. The Governor promised to restore Bacon to the Council eventually if he would "live civilly 'till next quarter-court." The rebel, however, was restored to his seat the same day, and his bodyguard pardoned. This was doubtless due to the elder Nathaniel Bacon, who is supposed to have written his nephew's apology.

The accounts agree that Bacon, continuing to live with Lawrence, learned from the latter that Berkeley had struck a magnanimous attitude solely to disarm the rebel, and that the Governor was preparing, after Jamestown had sufficiently calmed, to seize him. In the sessions of the new legislature, Bacon was the initiator of several measures aimed at defense from the Indians. So popular was he, in fact, that Berkeley was forced to promise Bacon a commission in relatively explicit terms, one of which was that he would lead a force of a thousand militia. But manifestly the Governor had no intention of entrusting that much power to a man becoming every day more of an idol.

Lawrence, according to Thomas Mathews and others, uncovered a Berkeley plot to assassinate Bacon.

The conspiracy was of the simplest. Since Bacon was not believed to be in fear of his life, now that he had made amends to the Governor, he would not be guarding against ambush. The tale was that Berkeley proposed keeping the Assembly in session until after nightfall. The home of Lawrence, Bacon's host, was on the outskirts of Jamestown, perhaps a third of a mile from the State House. The road, scarcely more than a cow-path, leading to it was made darker by its passage through thick woods. If Bacon were found in the morning, at some point midway home, with an arrow protruding from his shoulder-blades, it would be reasonable to conclude he had been killed by some vengeful Indian.

The plot, whether fact or not, was all the pretext the rebel needed.

Bacon left Jamestown at night on horseback—the arresting party next morning thrust sabers through all the beds in the Lawrence ménage lest he be hiding beneath. He stopped near the head of the James, in the "up-country," and told residents of the conspiracy against his life, of the Governor's refusal immediately to grant him a commission. Almost overnight—he was that persuasive—he had gathered about him six hundred armed men from plantations, lowland manor-houses and log-cabins. In two days he was within a day's march of Jamestown, which had word of his advance.

Berkeley, no coward, countered by posting four heavy guns at Sandy Beach, the one land approach to the capital, and by issuing a call for the militia of York and Gloucester counties. The response to that summons was so half-hearted that less than a hundred men obeyed the Governor, and the vanguard of these was easily disarmed by Bacon's men when it arrived at Jamestown. After stationing patrols to cover the main thoroughfares, Bacon drew up his men in parade formation on the sward facing the State House.

The House of Burgesses was in turbulent session inside; outside, the capital was alive with excitement. Bacon sent an aide to Berkeley with a defiant message calling for his commission forthwith. At length the white-haired Governor came out to the green with all the Council, expended every epithet he knew on Bacon's head, and offered to settle their differences by the sword.

"Sir," Bacon declared, "I come not, nor intend, to hurt a hair of your Honor's head, and as for your sword, your Honor may please to put it up; it shall rust in the scabbard before I shall desire you to draw it."

Berkeley, here losing control of himself, tore open his shirt, and cried, "Here! Shoot me! 'Fore God, a fair mark—shoot!" Bacon's retort was, "God damn my blood, I came for a commission, and a commission I'll have before I go! . . . I'll kill Governor, Council, Assembly and all, and then I'll sheathe my sword in my own heart's blood!"

After these histronics, turning to the petrified Councillors, Bacon insisted on the need "of preserving our lives from the Indians, inspecting the public revenues, the exorbitant taxes, and redressing the grievances and calamities of that deplorable country"—his program, in a few days, had become far more ambitious than chastisement of the redskin.

Then, turning his back to face his troops—"Make ready, and present!" The order to fire was an instant away when a terrified Burgess screamed from a window, "You *shall* have it, you *shall!*" referring to the commission.

Thus, at the point not of a pistol but of several hundred guns, Berkeley was forced to capitulate. Next day the commission was sent to Bacon, together with blank commissions for some thirty officers. Pressing his advantage, the rebel forced the Governor to sign a letter to Charles II, absolving Bacon of treason and approving of his conduct (although Berkeley was able to disclaim the document before it arrived in Whitehall).

Bacon soon had other employment for his forces than intimidating the Governor. He was dictator without portfolio in the capital, but that fact made no impression on the Indians beyond the limits of the town. Twenty-three miles away, on June 25, 1676, they descended upon two settlements bordering the York River, and massacred eight Virginians. Bacon set out with a thousand men, and en route to the York River disarmed the main body of the Gloucester County "loyalists," some of whom he impressed into service with their horses.

In rebuttal, a group of Gloucester men sent the Governor a petition demanding protection from Bacon. Berkeley, however feckless, did not lose a moment, and grasped the incident as a pretext again to issue a proclamation branding Bacon as a "Traitor and Rebel" (July 29); and he promised Gloucester petitioners to protect them from the "outrages

and oppression to which they have lately too much submitted, by the tyranny and usurpation of Nathaniel Bacon, Jun., who never had any commission from me but what, with armed men, he extracted from the Assembly, which in effect is no more than if a thief should take my purse, and make me own I gave it to him freely . . ."

The rôles of Berkeley and Bacon, on paper at least, now seemed reversed—the Governor was the protector, the young man the oppressor. Berkeley, awaiting aid from England, called for recruits, ostensibly to suppress the Indians, but, of course, actually to put down the threat of civil war.

The rebel, meanwhile, plodded on toward the Falls of the James, expecting to meet the Indians. He had not proceeded far when a messenger arrived with the news of Berkeley's second proclamation and with the report that the Governor, in Bacon's rear, was raising forces in Gloucester County.

Bacon summoned his men, addressing them as "gentlemen and fellow-soldiers," and explained that they must turn their "swords to our own defense," pitting brother against brother, instead of attacking the Indians immediately.

"But they are all damned cowards, and you shall see they will not dare to meet us in the field to try the justness of our cause—and so, we will down to them."

The response was a shout of "Amen! Amen!"

The column faced about toward the town of Gloucester. Berkeley meanwhile had appeared there to harangue a crowd of twelve hundred, and to call for volunteers, since the petition suggested they were loyal to Charles II and hence loyal to His Majesty's representative at Jamestown. But Berkeley's appeals lacked sparkle, and when suddenly word came of Bacon's advance, no one pledged support to the Governor. The crowd melted, and Berkeley fled back to Jamestown. The handwriting was clear: he would also be forced to flee the capital. In a small sloop, with Lady Berkeley, he was "wafted over Chesapeake Bay thirty miles to Accomac."

En route back, Bacon's scouts captured a man who claimed to be a deserter from Berkeley's force. At a field court-martial, he was found guilty as a spy by a tribunal of leaders that did not include Bacon. He intervened, however, and summoned his officers. If one would put in a favorable word for the prisoner, he would spare his life. None was uttered, and the convicted spy was bound to a tree and shot.

The first stop was at Middle Plantation (now Williamsburg), where Bacon reviewed the situation. Berkeley had decamped, and he, Bacon, was governor *de facto*. Drummond advised deposing Berkeley by simple proclamation, and appointing Sir Henry Chicheley his successor. But this Bacon refused to do as too extreme and dangerous. First he issued a pronouncement declaring himself and his men loyal subjects of Britain; second, he published a list of grievances — one of which pointedly dealt with Berkeley's beaver-trade with the Indians; third, he called for a meeting of the people's leaders, at Middle Plantation, on August 3, when he demanded they sign a pledge to rise in arms against the Governor, if the latter sought to attack Bacon.

At first this was thought too much; it smelled of treason to the Crown. At the moment that Bacon's demand seemed about to be refused by the majority, a "messenger" arrived, breathlessly and providentially, to state that the Indians were advancing on York Fort, then filled with the helpless, and to add that the Governor had stripped the post of all its artillery. In the emergency, the leaders rushed to support the young Cromwell. They signed the pledge.

There is more than a suspicion that the entire scene at Middle Plantation was stage-managed by Bacon. The force did set out after the marauding Indians, but not for several days which were required to draw up a "Declaration of the People" and a "Manifesto." These were despatched to London. Here again the tune is the criminality of Berkeley, and the loyalty of the colonists to Charles, although at this time Bacon was asking his intimates whether they believed five hundred Virginians could defeat an expeditionary force from England, for, he notes, "there is a report Sir William Berkeley hath sent to the King for 2,000 Red Coates."

Bacon, after killing several hundred Indians, considered the next step. Keeping only one detachment, he returned the others to their homes, and prepared for the work of forming a government. With this task he was well under way when word came that his elderly nemesis was once more active—the irrepressible Berkeley had returned to Jamestown with seventeen ships and six hundred men recruited in the Accomac country across the Bay. The bait had been twenty-one years' exemption from all taxes, a distribution of all the property of the traitors, and pay of twelvepence a day while with his Majesty's colors.

Berkeley on September 8 entered a Jamestown very nearly deserted, and among his first acts was to seize all of Lawrence's property, which the Governor scrupulously noted included "a fair cupboard of plate." He fortified the capital, and pronounced a death sentence on all Baconians.

The response of the young general, still on the James River, was to resummon his troops, but he could not gather more than three hundred men, still weary and footsore from their Indian pursuit. On September 13, the force reached Green Spring, the Governor's country-estate outside Jamestown. On Berkeley's property he drew them up—"so few, weak and tired" in his words—and shouted, with an oratorical technique now perfected, "Come on, my hearts of gold! He that dies in the field, lies in the bed of honor!"

Immediately outside Jamestown, on Sandy Beach, he threw up earthworks, and set up a siege of the capital by holding this one land approach. Berkeley's ships in the river, and his soldiers perched on the palisades surrounding the town, rained lead on Bacon's position. Safe behind the earthworks, the men could be indifferent to the fire, which they returned with interest. After three days the Governor ordered an advance in the open. It was forcefully repelled, and in the withdrawal Bacon's men seized two pieces of artillery. When it appeared that Bacon could maintain the siege indefinitely, and that the prospect of plunder was remote, Berkeley's men began to desert.

The Governor fled Jamestown a second time, with twenty men silently dropping down the river to Bacon's rear. When that night they looked back, they saw that the sky danced with red. Bacon had put the capital to the torch, Drummond and Lawrence supporting his determination to leave Berkeley without a capital by setting fire to their own dwellings.

The State House, a "fair and large church," twelve new brick houses, and a half dozen frame buildings were razed. Before the State House collapsed, Drummond salvaged the colonial records. Berkeley, a refugee again on the eastern shore of Chesapeake Bay, remarked dourly that Bacon "burned five houses of mine . . . They say he set to with his own sacrilegious hand."

Bacon returned to Green Spring to rest his men. (The Governor complained later that his "dwelling-house was almost ruined; his household goods, and others of great value, totally plundered; that he [later] had not a bed to lie on; two great beasts, three hundred sheep, seventy horses and mares, all corn and provisions taken away . . ."

Bacon sought an exchange of prisoners—Berkeley had seized several rebels sent to pursue him when first he escaped across the Bay, and had hanged one of Bacon's lieutenants, a Captain Carver. The Governor ignored the offer.

His men refreshed at the Governor's expense, Bacon turned northeast for Gloucester County to consolidate his position. He established headquarters at the home of Colonel Augustine Warner, Speaker of the House of Burgesses. Thence he started in pursuit of a Colonel Brent, reported heading a force of a thousand Berkeley loyalists in Rappahannock County. When Bacon's men neared, however, Brent's troopers threw down their arms. Back in Gloucester, the rebel tried to persuade the townsmen to take the oath he had drafted at Middle Plantation. Although there was visible objection to the pledge to bear arms, if necessary, against "Red Coates," should Berkeley procure them, about six hundred in Gloucester threw in their lot with Bacon.

He now planned a tour of northern Virginia, to discuss the colonists' needs in the hinterland, as well as an expedition across the Chesapeake further to bedevil Berkeley. He fully believed the Governor would then flee to England, and that he would succeed him as president of the Council.

Almost certainly this would have occurred, with or without the approval of Charles, had not Bacon encountered an unexpected foe—malaria. He had contracted that fever in the fetid air of the swamps below Jamestown during his siege of the capital. Shaking with marsh fever, alternately hot and cold, nevertheless he remained on his feet for two days after the first attack, weakly directing preparations for the expedition north. Then mist rose before his eyes, he began to babble, to mistake Lawrence and Drummond for his uncle and Berkeley. Lying in bed in the Gloucester home of a Major Pate, one moment he was ordering a charge against an Indian stronghold, the next an assault on a vast army of Redcoats, and calling throughout for his wife. Before he fell into a coma, with Pate, Drummond, Lawrence and others disposed about the bed, in remote delirium he was "enquiring ever and anon after the arrival of the Friggats & Forces from England, and asking if his Guards were strong about the house."

At last he was calmed, assured by all that they were ready to repel either British or Indians. A few hours later, the night of October 1, Bacon died.

The day following, everywhere in Gloucester there was talk that he had been poisoned, supposedly by some agent of Berkeley's. Some of the early chroniclers believed it, although the evidence is slim. But there was one mystifying circumstance. Lawrence and other intimates claimed the body immediately and hurried with it out of Gloucester. They left no record of how they disposed of the body, nor their reason for secrecy. One story is that his grave lies a mile and a half from Major Pate's home (now known as Bacon's Fort), beneath eight ironstone rocks that today resemble a tomb, but this is so much a theory that historical societies have not made researches. Another is that Drummond and Lawrence bore the body west to the James River, where they constructed a coffin, weighted it with stones and sunk it midstream. One explanation for their haste was that they feared the body might be exhumed from the grave if Berkeley knew its site, and hanged from a gallows—a pleasantry to which the corpse of Cromwell had been subjected seventeen years before.

Although it had widespread support, Bacon's rebellion was peculiarly a one-man show. When the leader died, it collapsed for want of his impetus and drive. And when word of the rebel's death crossed the Bay, Berkeley was quick to send a party, under Major Robert Beverly, to feel out the situation. The major seized Colonel Hansford, one of Bacon's officers, together with some twenty men, and took them to Accomac. Hansford had "the honor to be the first Virginian that ever was hanged"—the Governor is disposed to heavy satire—but it was conceded officially that he was "a valiant stout man, and a most resolved rebel." Soon thereafter one Captain Wilford, an Indian interpreter and a knight's son, fell into Berkeley's hands, and he also swung as a traitor. A Major Chesman, also brought in chains to Accomac, died in prison "of hard usage."

Berkeley then sailed for York River himself, with his force in several ships. Here and there, as the rebellion weakened, more of Bacon's lieutenants were captured. At York, Berkeley executed four men. Drummond was caught in Chickahominy Swamp, half-starved, and taken to Middle Plantation.

"Mr. Drummond," Sir William greeted him, bowing his lowest, "you are very welcome. I am more glad to see you than any man in Virginia. Mr. Drummond, you shall be hanged in half an hour."

And Drummond, totally unconcerned, "What your Honor pleases."

In his report of the execution to Charles II, Berkeley described Drummond as "a Scotchman that we all suppose was the original cause of the whole rebellion . . ." Captain Crews, one of Bacon's earliest supporters and the first to urge him to lead an independent excursion against the Indians, went the way of Messrs. Carver, Hansford, Drummond *et al* —a total of at least twenty. Lawrence escaped Berkeley's rope, but was believed to have drowned trying to escape the Governor's men.

On January 22, 1677, Berkeley summoned the Assembly to meet at Green Spring—Jamestown was little more than ashes. The members petitioned him to shed no more blood. Meanwhile, Charles II, learning of the hangings, complained irascibly that "the old fool has hanged more men in that naked country than I have done for the murder of my father," and despatched a royal commission of three to report on the affairs of the colony. To settle the atmosphere, Charles offered to pardon all "rebels" who would swear allegiance to the crown within twenty days. Berkeley amended this to except a number of ringleaders, and brought on his head the ire of the King, who, in another proclamation, declared that the Governor's action was "so different from ours and so derogatory to our princely clemency" that it was of "no validity."

So, embittered by the conciliatory policy of the commissioners, Berkeley was forced to return with them to England to plead his own case before the King. Lady Berkeley was unbending to the last. To show her contempt for the King's envoys, she appointed the common hangman as *pro tem* driver of the coach which conveyed them from Green Spring to the British flagship—presumably in this fashion heaping upon them some subtle opprobrium. The commissioners returned to their monarch with a voluminous report, "A True Narrative of the Rise, Progress and Cessation of the Late Rebellion in Virginia, Most Humbly and Impartially Reported by His Majestyes Commissioners Appointed to Enquire into the Affairs of the Said Colony."

They tell the tale that Berkeley died of chagrin, unable to have an audience with Charles. He died, whatever the cause, July 13, 1677.

Of Bacon's courage there can be no doubt. However limited the material about him, his advance on Jamestown proved his fearlessness, and his ability to imbue other men with disregard for death. He was imperious, but it is seen repeatedly that his judgment was not blinded by his temper —he had a precautionary acumen far beyond his years. That he fully expected and wanted to become Governor, sometime in 1677, whatever measures England might launch against him, seems a certainty at this distance. Even in what relatively little is known about him, he shows himself the accomplished realist: it is not credible that he did not fully anticipate the governorship, and indeed if necessary would have seized it as his merited reward. He had youth, but he had it jointly with the reflective bent of age. He had a certain ready idealism, but an acute eye for the main chance, the personal opportunity. Apart from the man himself, retrospectively the chief interest in his rebellion is that it is, in miniature, the Revolution of a century later.

1689

THE ANDROS INSURRECTION

IT IS EARLY THURSDAY AFTERNOON, BUT THE tortuous streets of Boston near the waterfront at that hour are alive with people shouting "Secession!"—a word new to the American continent. Apart from some twenty companies of soldiers, many in the crowds are armed with muskets or with clubs, and their numbers swell as hundreds pour into the town from Charlestown across the harbor. They are following a column at the head of which is a portly but patrician figure, a man somewhere in his fifties, whose hands are chained. He follows, bewilderment and astonishment on his face, in the footsteps of a diminutive and gleeful drummer-boy. From the houses flanking the narrow streets epithets rain on the prisoner's head, but no physical harm is done him.

The prisoner is Sir Edmund Andros, the governor of the vast Dominion of New England, and the date is April 18, 1689. The events of that day have since become known as the Andros Insurrection. Here is the first popular advocacy of States' Rights, a phrase to become a provocative slogan in the years immediately before the Civil War.

The clamoring, gesticulating throngs push up the hill to the Royal Council Chamber, where Andros is ordered imprisoned on Castle Island, with twenty-five of his aides. Boston is plastered from one end to the other with the proclamation that a council of safety will supplant the Governor and his Council.

Andros has been seized because of popular indignation generated by the publication of a "Declaration of the Gentlemen, Merchants, and Inhabitants of Boston, and the Country Adjacent," authored by Cotton Mather, whose father, Increase Mather, is sometimes regarded as one of the agent-provocateurs of the revolt. The "Declaration" was solemnly read to Andros by the younger Mather before the Governor was sent to jail. It summarized the colonists' grievances against the Governor, who was, despite a few blunders, more or less the hapless bystander.

They complained:

1. That Sir Edmund Andros was involved in "an horrid Popish plot" which had as object the extinction of the Reformed Church by "such as were intoxicated with a Bigotry inspired into them by the great Scarlet Whore";

2. That he was in part responsible for the revocation of the Massachusetts charter, in October 1684, which substituted a President and Council for the former popular Assembly;

3. Of the injustice of the Navigation Acts, which had much the same effect on New England trade as they had on the Virginia colony;

4. That the appointment of Andros, in 1686, as Governor gave him arbitrary powers to make laws and impose taxes

as he pleased, backed up by soldiers from Europe, and "not without repeated menaces that hundreds more were intended for us";

5. That Andros and his Council heaped "Preferments principally upon such men as were strangers to and haters of the People," that these "horse-leeches" from New York extorted stupendous fees for the probating of wills, for warrants, etcetera;

6. That in effect the colonists were slaves who "have been treated with multiplied contradictions to Magna Charta," while "pickt and packt juries have been very common among us";

7. That, contrary to the custom of the colony, the inhabitants had to "lay the hand on the *Book* in swearing," instead of swearing merely with uplifted hand;

8. That despite land-title guarantees given them by Charles II, in 1683, by which no freeholder's property could be attached, the colonists had been told repeatedly "that no man was owner of a Foot of Land in all the colony," and that to safeguard themselves they had to pay excessive sums for additional patents, and their rents were raised illegally;

9. That the few honest members of the Council were seldom admitted to those sessions where skullduggery was the order;

10. That the Massachusetts colonists had been embroiled in another Indian War, and that "the whole war hath been so managed that we cannot but suspect in it a branch of the Plot to bring us low" (moreover, the complainants were nettled that the army of "our poor friends and Brethren" was under "popish Commanders");

11. That Governor Andros, in the face of an expected attack from the French in Canada, had not taken adequate measures to defend them, and that in consequence they were in danger of being "given away to a Forreign Power."

In view of this indictment, the Boston leaders declared they had decided to "seize upon the Person of those few Ill Men," until William III and Parliament decided what punishment and action were suitable.

However severe the strictures in the four-page bill of complaint—it is replete with charges of "Popery" and the machinations of "Papists"—the fifteen signers showed a satirical concern for the personal welfare of Andros. In a covering message read to the Governor, by that hour in chains, they explain that "being surprised with the Peoples sudden taking of arms . . . and tending your own Safety, We judge it necessary you forthwith surrender . . ." This was the answer to Andros' demand for an explanation of the "tumultuous arming" in Boston.

To bring into historical focus the end of Andros' rule over the Dominion of New England, it is well to go back to 1685, a little more than four years before the insurrection, when the Duke of York succeeded to the throne as James II.

Whatever the political and administrative failings of Charles II (James' predecessor), that monarch had recognized the military advantage of a consolidation of his American colonies into one royal province. There were also, as will be seen, pressing civil reasons, and these, with the military considerations, were so compelling that it was fairly beside the point that Massachusetts, for example, cherished its independence, or that New York was jealous of its relative autonomy. The military factors which favored a consolidation were, first, defense from the Indians, who naturally struck at those colonies whose militia was weakest; and, second, the threatening presence of the restless and ambitious French in Canada. The major civil purpose was the creation of some order out of the political hodge-podge that the colonies presented: after 1652 Massachusetts—a chartered corporation—governed New Hampshire and Maine; Plymouth was an independent colony without charter, and others of the seven colonies had their own governments whose authority stemmed directly or indirectly from the Crown. Inevitably, the jealous authorities clashed over areas of jurisdiction, and in London, Charles' headaches were unending (if mitigated by a yearly income of $6,000,000).

In 1684, the year before his death, Charles decided to act. The most vociferously independent colony was Massachusetts, which virtually ignored the Navigation Acts, ignored Parliament, and was almost an absolute Puritan theocracy in which non-Puritans had no vote and were, in effect, pariahs. Charles revoked its charter, suppressing the Assembly. The ensuing howl was deafening, particularly from the Puritan ranks.

In 1686, after James had become king, he followed precedent, and abolished the Assembly of New York, of which he had been proprietor as Duke of York, and despatched Colonel Thomas Dongan as Governor.

The colonists saw what was coming. The King's next act was to appoint Sir Edmund Andros, who had served previously as his ducal deputy in the colony of New York, as Governor of a consolidated Dominion of New England. Although he permitted Virginia its Assembly, none was to be allowed the Dominion. Authority was to be vested in the Governor and forty-two councillors, appointed by the King from leaders in the several colonies. Andros had power to make laws and impose taxes with the advice and consent of a majority of the councillors—but any five would constitute a quorum. To most of the colonists this seemed a blatant violation of Magna Charta, and no amount of ingenious pleading makes it otherwise. Eight of the councillors, or nearly a fifth of the entire membership, represented the interests of New York. No book or pamphlet might be printed without Andros' approval, but press censorship was not then regarded as immoral, and it was, in fact, a device long employed by Puritan leaders in Massachusetts.

Although the consolidation was, of course, enormously unpopular with the colonists, it had one consoling aspect for the two largest colonies: if New York, through its councillors, might meddle with the affairs of Massachusetts, the latter could also have its hand in the affairs of New York. For the rest, the colonies were blind to the potential military and administrative benefits in the merger.

Ready to set about enforcing the unpopular project, Andros arrived from England at Boston in December, 1686. He had to cool his heels until the arrival of his commission from James, which was duly "proclaimed with great parade" from the Boston Town House. The powers it bestowed upon Andros were certainly extreme.

Typical phrases in the commission:

FOY sc.

"And we do hereby give and grant unto you fful power and authority to suspend any member of our Council . . . And we do hereby give and grant fful power and authority, by and with the advice and consent of our said Council, or the major part of them, to make, constitute, and ordain Laws, Statutes, and Ordinances . . . also to execute Martial Law in time of invasion, insurrection, or war . . ."

Although in the first draft of Andros' commission provision had been made for a representative Assembly, James deleted that section later. In 1676, a decade before, when Andros was his agent in New York, James had expressed the opinion that "an assembly would be of dangerous consequences; nothing being more known than the aptness of such bodies to assume privileges destructive to the peace of the Government."

Two weeks after the receipt of his commission, Andros left Boston for New York, to establish his authority there. He had meanwhile appointed Captain Francis Nicholson as Lieutenant-Governor, and a friend of long standing; James Graham of New York, was made Attorney-General of the Dominion. In New York the Governor, although well-known to the colony for his service under the Duke of York, found no warmer welcome than he had at Boston, for here too the Assembly had been dissolved.

But Andros, armed with a commission giving him dictatorial powers, by 1688 ruled over a territory more than one-fourth the size of England—all the New England colonies together with New York and, after 1687, New Jersey.

At this time Andros was just fifty. His career up to this point may be sketched briefly.

He was born in 1637, the son of Amice Andros, a master of ceremonies to Charles I, and Elizabeth Stone, of the feudal aristocracy of Guernsey. At twenty-three he was appointed "gentleman in ordinary" to the Queen of Bohemia. At twenty-nine, he had won a major's commission, and had led an infantry regiment against the Dutch in the West Indies. Partly owing to the influence of the Earl of Craven— a relative of his wife—he was appointed landgrave in Carolina, in 1672, receiving some 48,000 acres—although he proved indifferent to that grant: the life of a country gentleman had no allure for the soldier. Two years later he was appointed lieutenant-governor (or ducal deputy) of all the Duke of York's territories in America. This embraced New York itself, just restored by the Dutch, who had seized the settlement the year before; New Jersey, Delaware, Martha's Vineyard, part of Maine and a claim, at least, to all of Connecticut west of that river. It was a magnificent post for a man not yet thirty-seven.

Andros added to his prestige at home not only by his protection of New York from Indian attack, but by despatching aid in emergencies to Rhode Island, Massachusetts and Maine. A knighthood was inevitable, and it was given him in 1678. But his record as agent in New York for the Duke was not an unblemished success. A group of merchants in New York charged him with making false statements of the tax revenues. In 1680 the Duke summoned him to London for an explanation, and set one John Lewen to checking Andros' accounts. The Lewen report was unfavorable to the Duke's agent, but he vindicated himself in London, where York was satisfied that, if Andros lacked finesse, he was not wanting in honesty.

For the next four years little is heard of him. In 1685, a few months before he returned to America as governor of the newly-formed Dominion, he was appointed lieutenant-colonel of the Princess of Denmark's regiment of horse.

Engravings of him exist. The face is strong, the nose straight but full, a mouth firm but not cruel, mildly protruding eyes that are over-large and skeptical—more a Bourbon than an English face, but at all events distinctly in the autocratic mould. The records indicate that he was brusque and impatient—his background bred little tolerance with democratic instruments—but he was not prone to the choleric violence of, say, a Berkeley. Primarily a soldier, he seems to have had little comprehension of colonial economics, which was one reason for his downfall in New England; and he had little understanding or patience with Puritan ascetism (the Mathers were shocked that he worked on the Sabbath). It was perhaps the height of tactlessness that he permitted and attended the occasional Episcopal services in Boston's Old South Church, the stronghold of Congregationalism and anti-Romanism. But judged against the records and characteristics of other colonial governors in America, Sir Edmund Andros is not far from the head of the class.

It is one of our national conceits to believe that the pre-Revolutionary colonial was some peculiarly "American" animal, to be distinguished from a mere Englishman or other alien. In the light of our subsequent war for independence this is understandable, but it is, of course, nonsense. The bawling that arose after the New England colonies were consolidated into the Dominion was largely due to the fact that the colonials did regard themselves as Englishmen, and as such, were entitled to representation, to the vote, to the whole body of civil principles and the philosophy embraced in Magna Charta. Massachusetts was more vociferously independent of the Crown than were the other colonies—Virginia, for example, was predominantly royalist—but at no time in the seventeenth century was there a serious movement for separation. States' rights, and secession from the Dominion of New England, yes; but not a clean break-away from the Mother Country.

Publishing the powers under his commission, and employing them effectively, were two different matters, as Andros soon learned. The revocation of some of the colonial charters required more than a decorative scrawl from the King's pen.

Andros' appearance at Hartford, in October 1687, is a New England classic. With some hundred men and a deal of fanfare, Andros appeared before the General Court, and demanded the surrender of the charter—its literal physical relinquishment. Governor Robert Treat and members of his Council launched into long-winded and academic discussion of the King's right to revoke the Charter, and succeeded in forcing Andros and his restive entourage to listen to their oratory for several hours in the Indian-summer sun. Meanwhile, there were a dozen schemes afoot to get the Charter and hide it. Treat and his associates felt that, while Andros might declare the Charter void by simple decree, they could salvage something for the colony's future by preserving the scrap of paper; they felt it could not be said that the Charter had been revoked if it still existed in physical fact.

At last the debate was removed to the courthouse. There the Connecticut colonials continued their equivalent of a filibuster, talking endlessly and irrelevantly until nightfall forced the lighting of candles. By this time the Councillors were themselves on the point of exhaustion, and Andros' patience was ended.

In apparent capitulation, the Council conceded that submission to the King's demands was unavoidable, and the cherished Charter was laid upon the conference table. The Dominion Governor arose wearily to pick it up. At this point the candles were extinguished. When they were relighted, and after apologies from Treat, the document was missing. The councillors, of course, denied vehemently any knowledge of or part in a fairly obvious sleight-of-hand performance. Some years later it was learned that the document had been secreted in the hollow of the so-called "Charter Oak," a tree seven feet in diameter, since blown down (souvenir fragments of it are scattered throughout Connecticut). After Andros' downfall, the Charter conveniently reappeared, and the British courts conceded that it had never been vacated legally, although the colony had given in to Andros.

But much sterner opposition to the Governor was forthcoming. King James' commission had given Andros authority to levy taxes with the "advice and consent" of the Council—again taxation without representation. To avoid conflict, if possible, Andros maintained the former basic rate, approximately a penny a pound. In 1688, the new assessments were announced, and the first Massachusetts county to mutiny was Essex, in the north. With the exception of Marblehead, Newbury and Salem, every town refused to pay, while the selectmen of Ipswich resolved that the rates "did abridge them of their liberty as Englishmen," since they had been deprived of an assembly.

Andros acted promptly on this first outbreak of insurrection, planning to set an example. He was over-severe. The twenty ringleaders of Ipswich were arrested, charged with "publishing factious and seditious votes and writings," a charge perilously close to treason, and sent to jail. After a few days of solitude, hardtack and water, most of the Ipswich "insurrectionists" sued for the Governor's pardon, and pledged themselves to enforce the taxes. The court levied fines of disproportionate size. Andros, by prompt action, had suppressed a revolt of potential danger. Even to his unlegal mind taxation without representation was a violation of Magna Charta, and he saw that his judges were in no unassailable position when they retorted to the protesting colonials, "You must not think that the laws of England follow you to the end of the earth."

That is precisely what most of them did think, not unreasonably.

His efforts to extract quit-rents provoked growling criticism of the whole land system. The hostility that arose over quit-rent controversies was not altogether Andros' fault, since he was largely powerless to control the rent increases demanded by landowners three thousand miles away. More often than not, the small farmer leased his acres from another, much larger lessee who paid his rent to the British holder of the original grant or other title. The colonial farmer, for example, in good faith signed a lease with the larger lessee, the latter also acting in good faith. When the English owner without notice demanded an increase, the large lessee passed it on to the tenant-farmers. Against such boosts they had no protection, particularly the tillers of a few acres, and they had no contact directly with the grantor overseas. Moreover, the large lessee in the Dominion was not disposed to forward collective complaints abroad, since by so doing he imperiled his own lease. He applied to the courts when the small farmers would or could not pay the increases, and the courts had rarely any alternative but to order evictions. The judges and other court officers, whose income depended on fees, were not likely to nolle-pros these suits.

If this were not complication enough, the Indians could be depended upon to make Andros' post an unpleasant one. In April of 1688, he went to Portsmouth and to Pemaquid, where he repaired the fort. Captain John George of H. M. S. *Rose* was assigned to cruise up the Penobscot River to learn what he could of one Baron de St. Castine, a Frenchman who some years before had received permission to settle there among the Indians. St. Castine, a safe distance from Boston, elected to believe that "to settle" included the privilege of trading with the Indians. And trading, he reasoned further, surely included barter with guns and ammunition. This, of course, was not permitted the colonials, and it was even a more heinous offence in a foreigner. The Frenchman, Captain George reported, had established a warehouse on the river, dangerously stocked with guns and ammunition which he was selling to the Indians. St. Castine exercised a good deal of influence over the Canadian-frontier Indians, the Captain added, by reason of his marriage to the daughter of a chief. From these messages, Andros rightly suspected that St. Castine was on the point of inciting the Indians against the British. He decided he would investigate himself. In St. Castine's absence the station was seized, its ammunition and guns sent to the Pemaquid fort. Next Andros made a tour of the colonies as far south as New Jersey, and at Albany he halted for a powwow with the chiefs of the Five Nations. He sent a warning to the governor-general of Canada to remove his garrison at Oniagra, and that French official, intimidated by the military resources at Andros' hand, readily obeyed. Andros was blunt, but he was effective.

In his absence from Boston, however, the councillors succeeded in provoking Indian tribes in the north, whose temper now had a particularly low boiling-point. At Saco an officer seized twenty Indians whom he believed guilty of attacks on the settlers, and sent them in chains to Boston. In retaliation, their relatives on Casco Bay imprisoned several colonials as hostages. In nervous negotiations for an exchange of prisoners, three Englishmen were killed. Andros, at Albany, convinced that his councillors were so bungling matters that an Indian War was imminent, ordered the Indian captives freed, and he hurried on to Boston.

When the Indians, coming closer to home, burned New

Dartmouth and Newtown, Andros raised a militia force of seven hundred, and when Major-General Winthrop declined to lead them, claiming illness, the Governor elected to command the force himself. He marched north, and apportioned the men among eleven new garrisons. They fell on the Penobscot settlements: St. Castine fled, and the Governor returned to Boston, leaving the militia in command of a few regular-army officers.

There were pressing reasons for his return post-haste to Boston.

While at Pemaquid, he had received from James II a circular, addressed to all the colonial governors, which presaged the overthrow of the last of the Stuart kings. James warned his representatives in America "to take care that upon the approach of any fleet or foreign force, the militia . . . be in such readiness as to hinder any landing or invasion that may be intended to be made." The King claimed to have "received undoubted advice that a great and sudden Invasion from Holland, with an armed Force of Forreigners and Strangers, will speedily be made upon His Majesty's Kingdom of England."

This was a chilling reference to William, Prince of Orange. England was weary of James' belligerent Catholicism.

Three thousand miles away, in Maine, Andros lost no time in relaying the warning to all the coastal settlements within his jurisdiction; his proclamation is dated January 10, 1689. That was manifestly not only his duty, but it was the way of precaution. It is, however, indicative of the Boston Puritan sentiment of the day that Andros was roundly criticized for his proclamation in a pamphlet published two years after he was deposed—"The Revolution in New England Justified, And the People Vindicated . . ." by Edward Rawson and Samuel Sewall. In the course of this denunciation, it is complained "that Sir E. A. with others whom the People in New England seized and secured, did, after notice of His Present Majesty's [i.e., William III] intended descent into England to deliver the Nation from Popery . . . to their utmost oppose that glorious design. . . ."

—Andros, in other words, was supporting the machinations of Rome from a small fort in Maine.

He arrived back in Boston early in March to be confronted with a foolish charge that he had negotiated a secret treaty with the Indians by which he was to support them in attacks on the colonials. He turned his back on the complainants, and left the charge to the courts; but the atmosphere was now grown electric.

It clarifies the picture at this point—the eve of the insurrection—to glance briefly at Increase Mather and his eldest son, Cotton Mather, lords and masters of the Puritan theocracy and, in Massachusetts, the unofficial chief officers of state. There is a literature of appalling extent devoted to this pair of divines, but here may be considered only their active part in the uprising against Andros.

Increase Mather had openly entered politics in 1684, when the Massachusetts Charter was revoked by Charles. Hitherto he had exercised his influence mainly by indirection. The following year he was elected president of Harvard, a post which added to his political influence. From the pulpit of Old North Church, he exhorted Boston citizens not to submit to the King, to demand re-establishment of the Assembly—a body that had been strictly controlled by the Puritans. He sailed for London, in 1688, to present to James II the Congregational petitions for a return to the last charter. He almost missed the ship in consequence of charges of libel brought against him by an Andros supporter, but at sailing-time was safely smuggled aboard, evading a process-server by minutes. He had five interviews with James before the latter's abdication, and, soon after the triumphant arrival in London of William II, he achieved an audience with that ruler. Mather was without official status, but William was inclined to believe that Mather spoke the views of most of the Protestant colonials. The King, however, not to agitate the Dominion chemistry, had ordered a circular sent to the governors in which he called for the preservation of the *status quo*, except in cases of Papists holding office. Had it reached Andros, the circular might well have proved fatal to Puritan plans for an uprising, since it would have given royal sanction to Andros' continuance in office after the downfall of James. And any concerted move against the Governor, in that event, could be interpreted by the courts only as rebellion or treason. To Increase Mather and the Puritan leaders at home it was dangerous that Andros should know that his position was still legal after James' flight; it was to be preferred, in fact, that even word of the abdication should not reach the ears of the Stuart loyalist until too late. The Governor, however, learned of the abdication from his lieutenant-governor, Nicholson, in New York, some time before it was announced officially at Boston, on April 4, 1689.

The circular did not reach Andros, as a result of a White-hall backstairs intrigue devised by Mather with the aid of Sir William Phips, the Massachusetts agent in London, who had the paper held up in London. Mails between England and America often were two to three months in transit. That accomplished, Increase Mather in letters home began to stir up his colleagues in Boston to overthrow Andros in the name of William and Mary; he argued that it could and should be made to appear that the leaders had, in effect, saved Massachusetts from remaining loyal to the Catholic James by deposing his chief appointee in the Dominion.

In Boston the atmosphere was kept tense by Cotton Mather during his father's absence at court. There were incendiary rumors that Andros planned turning over the Dominion of New England to Louis XIV of France, with whom James had found asylum. The propaganda was expert, for that day, and it was effective because the Puritan rank and file were a credulous lot.

Much was made of the Governor's imprisonment of John Winslow, who had brought to Boston a copy of William's Declaration from The Hague (his acceptance of the British throne), and had refused to produce it, although Andros was within his rights in demanding that its contents be made known. Then it was observed that when the succession to the throne did become known in Boston on April 8 the Governor did not order an official celebration, as had been done in other colonies and in the British West Indies. If this were not damning enough, Cotton Mather and others charged that Andros had despatched most of his troops to Maine, purposely leaving Boston exposed to Indian attack, or to the French. Moreover, and perhaps more immoral than anything else, the militia in the north was commanded by "Popish officers," under whom they were reported about to mutiny. The case against Andros was circumstantially convincing to the man in the street. Increase Mather, writing from London, instructed his brother divines "to prepare the minds of the people for a change," citing a recent opinion of the British Attorney-General, Sir Henry Powys, that the revocation of the Massachusetts charter five years before had been illegal. How Mather and Phips persuaded Powys to this judicial reversal no one knows.

But that one phrase alone—"to prepare the minds of the people for a change"—was incitement to riot. Andros was not unconscious of his very real danger. To Captain Brockholes, in command of the garrison at Pemaquid, he wrote on April 16 that "there is a general buzzing among the people, great with expectation of their old charters, or they know not what." It is a question whether at this juncture he was paralyzed by indecision, or whether he thought it beneath his dignity to take notice of the conspiracy against him.

Toward the end of April "a Strange Disposition entered in the body of our people to assert our Liberties against the Arbitrary Rulers that were fleecing them"—the phrase is by Samuel Mather in his *apologia* for his father's part in the insurrection. That disposition was scarcely "strange," since it was the direct result of the unrest created by the two Mathers. The "principal Gentlemen in Boston," i. e. the Puritan leaders, met with Cotton Mather to discuss the report of a mutiny and desertion of a company of militia in

Maine. They resolved that if the mutiny appeared to be leading to a general uprising against the Andros government, leaders among themselves "would appear in the head of what action should be done . . . that by their Authority among the People the unhappy Tumult might be a little regulated." This artless pretext for an uprising against Andros they announced in a public declaration.

The report of the mutiny among some of the militia in Maine was confirmed, and a number of disgruntled soldiers arrived in Boston on April 17. Andros called out his regular-army officers to round up the deserters preparatory to marching them back to their posts. Andros denied knowing of any cause for the soldiers' sudden disaffection; there had previously been protests, however, elsewhere in the Dominion over the pay of fivepence daily. But the situation was beyond Andros' control. The deserting mutineers called upon the Boston and Charleston militia to join them against the Government, and Andros says that there were suddenly "about two thousand horse and foote . . . being wholly a surprise"—although his astonishment could not have been so great since he admits he knew that "several of His Majesty's Council in New England . . . combined and conspired together with those who were Magistrates . . . to subvert and overthrow the Government."

The mutiny of the militia was a godsend to the forces against Andros. They needed more of an emergency, as a pretext for action in the streets, than such academic issues as the revocation of the charter in 1684, or the legality of the Governor's commission from James II. By early forenoon of the next day, the public temperature had reached such a point that Andros decided to gag Cotton Mather by arresting him for preaching sedition. But events moved too fast.

Leaders of the militia mutiny before noon descended on the frigate H.M.S. *Rose,* fearing she might train her guns on the town, and seized Captain George. Andros, meanwhile, raced to Fort Hill on the south after reports had come that mobs in both ends of Boston were in arms, and converging on the Council Chamber. The fort dominated the avenues of approach by land and sea. In quick succession, the mobs, after arresting the naval commander, seized two court justices, Edward Randolph, secretary of the Dominion and a member of the Council (who had accused Increase Mather of inciting revolt), the sheriff, the jail-keeper, and others.

At this stage, one of the Puritan leaders, Nathaniel Oliver, sent a message to Andros in the fort pointing out the danger if he did not surrender himself and Fort Hill. The Governor refused to surrender. But to avoid bloodshed he consented to go to the town-hall, "to advise on ways of quieting Boston." The Governor's "consent" was superfluous; he had no sooner begun to parley with Oliver's emissaries than he was placed under arrest.

While the mobs were swelling around Fort Hill, Andros in the townhall was confronted by the immediate leaders of the uprising—Cotton Mather, four other Puritan ministers, five of the Dominion Councillors, and several well-to-do merchants. The Councillors, responding to demands of envoys from the mob, ordered Andros to enforce the capitulation of the fort. He again refused. The leaders lost patience with his conception of duty.

A pistol was placed to Randolph's head, and he was conducted to the fortress to announce that Andros had ordered its surrender. The garrison obeyed the fake command. A similar message was conveyed by Randolph to Castle Island, the fort in the harbor. There the Governor's force suspected a ruse, and the militia refused to leave that stronghold until the following day, when convinced that the other garrison had put down their arms. They consented to open the gates, if their liberty was guaranteed; and a pledge to that effect was readily granted. The moment the fort was vacated, the soldiers were clapped into jail.

Compared to Randolph and others, Andros fared well. He was imprisoned on Castle Island, where, his jailor reported, "He was well satisfied with his Entertainment at Least to outward appearance, and by his discourse." He was permitted the run of the island, and could even walk upon the walls, provided he remained in sight of his captors.

To end the danger—not the fact—of rioting and pillaging, after two days a council of safety was organized with a membership of twenty-two. The former Governor (before the charter revocation), the former deputy governor and thirteen ex-magistrates consented to rule in the "spirit" of the old charter, until orders came from England. It was, in effect, another Governor-and-Council administration, except that now the Puritans were returned to control.

Word of the revolt against Andros spread quickly throughout the Dominion. Plymouth returned to its former colonial regime, Connecticut returned to office the men holding posts before the Hartford fiasco, and Rhode Island acted similarly. New Hampshire and Maine returned to the jurisdiction of Massachusetts. In New York, where the threat of a French invasion via Canada was increasing daily, Lieutenant-Governor Nicholson was unable to find agreement over the form of a new government, and he hurried away to England for advice, abandoning Andros to his prison in Boston Harbor. In his subsequent report to the Lords of the Committee for Trade and Plantations, the captive Governor asserted that "by the encouragement and persuasion of those of the Massachusetts, the several other provinces and colonies in New England as far as New Yorke have disunited themselves, and set up their former separate Charter, and by that means the whole revenue of the Crown . . . is lost and destroyed." He also claimed that by the withdrawal of the militia from Maine and the recall to Boston of the coastal frigates, British property in Maine and most of New Hampshire had been destroyed by the Indians, and several hundred settlers killed or taken as hostages.

Andros did not intend to remain supinely in prison if there was the slightest chance of escape. His patron James II might have fled England, but nevertheless Andros was certain he could find military support in New York, if he could make his way there. While waiting for that moment when his guards might relax their vigilance, he lived in hopes that Nicholson, his lieutenant-governor, would march on Boston and demand his release of the Council of Safety, in the name of the Crown. But Nicholson had no such intention.

Andros had been imprisoned only a fortnight when he attempted his first escape. During that fortnight his conduct evidently had been such, his outward disinterest in freedom so pronounced, that his captors had come to accept his *parole-d'honneur* at face value; to Andros, however, a gentleman's agreement was void if one of the parties to it was a rebel. By tacit consent he was permitted to exercise out of sight of the guards, which was not so material a concession since he could not wander far on the fortified island.

In some manner he obtained a woman's dress, cape and hat, either from one of the island commandant's household servants or, more probably, smuggled to him from shore. Shortly after dark the portly figure of Sir Edward Andros waddled down to the landing-stage in search of a ferryman to row him ashore.

He nearly succeeded. In the dark, the Governor looked like a washerwoman returning home for the night. Then, with freedom within sight, one member of the watch noted the incongruity of the military boots protruding from beneath the skirt.

Laughing, they led him back to the fort, and increased the guard.

Andros waited more than three months for another opportunity. It was useless to resort again to disguise. On the night of August 2 he succeeded in bribing a guard at the landing. By the next morning, when he was missed, the Governor had almost reached Rhode Island, where he hoped to be safely outside the jurisdiction of Massachusetts. But in that colony he waited overlong for a ship to take him to London or to New York. He was seized by the militia, and again returned to Boston Harbor.

An order from William, dated July 30, 1869, for the removal of Andros and his companions in jail to England ("take care that they be civilly used") did not arrive at

Boston until February the next year. At home, finally, Andros and his co-defendants were soon acquitted. The former Dominion head served as Governor of Virginia during 1692-97, and he took to that colony the charter of William and Mary College. Thereafter he disappears from the scene in America.

Late in October, 1691, more than two years after the uprising, William, over Mather's protest, granted a charter to Massachusetts providing for two legislative houses, consisting of the former Council, acting as the upper body, and beneath it the assembly. Laws could be vetoed by the Crown-appointed Governor, and of course also by the King. The underlying reason for Mather's complaint was that, although the Dominion no longer existed, the former rule by churchmen could not survive in a new system where suffrage was extended to all males with freeholds worth forty shillings yearly, or with property valued at forty pounds. So far as the colonial rank and file in Massachusetts were concerned, the new regime meant no more than another minority rule: before 1684, they had had over them rule by churchmen; during 1686-89, the span of Andros' regime in the Dominion, they had known a more or less absolute administration by the Crown, acting through a governor; after his downfall, the suffrage qualifications had the effect of concentrating political power in the hands of the landed aristocracy, strong in Maine and New Hampshire, which were now included in the new Massachusetts charter.

The Andros rebellion was the first in America where a movement for secession had strong support, although it was not a separatist movement from England, and was launched, moreover, by a clique. Ironically, it was fostered by a group of zealots who did not want religious liberty for others, and whose philosophy of government was autocratic rule by the theologically pure.

THE WAR OF THE REGULATORS

THE SHERIFF OF ORANGE COUNTY, IN WEST-central North Carolina, one day in 1765 rode to the cotton-patch of Herman Husbands, a Quaker, to demand payment of tax-arrears. A more than usually stiff member of the Society of Friends, to whom little was humorous in life, Husbands replied with a short, bitter laugh.

He would pay his taxes, he said, when he was assured the money would find its way directly to the county treasurer. And he had other complaints to make: the tax-rate, the extortionate court fees, and the dishonesty of county officials. The astonished sheriff scratched his head, climbed back on his mare, and, trotting back to the county-seat, wondered to what his world was headed if farmers could pronounce impertinently how and when they would pay taxes.

Husbands' refusal to pay had the effect of cementing sentiment in many districts of his own and nearby counties. Many settlers cheerfully followed his lead. In their collective refusal to pay was the birth of a group that adopted the name Regulators. They were organized first in Orange County, in 1766, largely as a result of the encouragement given them by Husbands, who stood ready to express their complaints in the form of "advertisements," petitions and resolutions, scores of which were to flow from his pen. They had first considered calling themselves "The Mob."

But the Quaker, soon to be expelled from the Society of Friends for marrying outside it, never formally joined the Regulators, although his association with them remained close up to the end. His reluctance to join was due to his Quaker's abhorrence of violence, to which he correctly believed the Regulators inevitably headed. Nevertheless, for more than six years he was the Regulators' most vocal and influential advocate, hunting a remedy for the economic troubles of the so-called "back counties." The records testify that he was "sober, intelligent, industrious and prosperous; honest and just in his dealings." There were reports that he was related by blood or marriage ties to Benjamin Franklin. He had some correspondence with the Philadelphian, who, at this time, was serving as the London agent of the Pennsylvania Assembly. Husbands gave circulation in the back counties to scores of various "patriotic" pamphlets sent him by friends and agents of Franklin in Philadelphia.

A less austere figure, but an equally influential one in the evolution of the Regulators, was Rednap Howell. He was a lanky school-teacher, a sparse, sandy-haired man from New Jersey, and a brother of the governor of that colony. The settlers of Orange and adjacent counties became accustomed to seeing him plodding over their grassy valleys on his ancient horse, and they accepted with enthusiasm copies of the political doggerel he composed. Rednap became the unofficial bard of the Regulators, who were the earliest equivalent of the vigilantes known a century later to California and Nevada. His scribbled verses set the disgruntled back counties to singing songs, some of them bawdy, directed against all the officials from the Governor, the envoy of His Majesty George III, to the lowest sheriff or court clerk. To the recent immigrants to the west, many of them Quakers, all these officials were venal; that their misdeeds were commemorated in song gave them, among the angry settlers, a degree of publicity and a factual complexion that no amount of formal protests and petitions would have achieved.

Thus:

> "When Fanning first to Orange came
> He looked both pale and wan,
> An old patched coat upon his back
> An old mare he rode on.
> Both man and mare wa'n't worth five pound,
> As I've been often told;
> But by his civil robberies
> He lined his coat with gold."

Edmund Fanning, the subject of the foregoing doggerel, was only one of the villains in the piece, although a major one, since he was a powerful superior-court judge, a colonel in the militia, a member of the Assembly, and, if some of the ballads are to be believed, a gentleman of excessively flexible morals. Another of the Regulators' chief enemies was Governor William Tryon, an ambitious royalist. Ranged with them were the older English settlers, who had established traditions, and, of more profit to them, occupied the fertile eastern part of the colony; it was generously dotted with their large plantations and estates. They had no liking for the newcomers in the Appalachian foothills to the west; in their eyes these were an uncouth and cantankerous lot, who, moreover, did not belong to the Church of England.

With respect to taxes, the settlers' grievance was first over the poll-levy, that inequitable device which had been one of the contributory causes to Bacon's rebellion in Virginia. As in that colony and in Massachusetts, so in North Carolina: the small farmer in the undeveloped counties was made to pay as much as the well-to-do farmer and planter in the east. An income tax simply based on ability to pay was heresy.

There were ample grounds for the charges of dishonesty in the methods of collecting taxes. Such an experience as the following (taken from the records) was commonplace. A sheriff with a tax-bill appeared at the back county farm of Abner Smith. In that frontier region there was little English money in circulation, there was virtually no gold nor silver, and trade was conducted mainly by commodity barter. Abner, without notice of the sheriff's coming, had not sufficient cash on hand. When he asked that political harpy to accompany him to the money-lender in the neighborhood, the official refused, and nailed an attachment to some part of the property equal, in his eyes, to the amount of the tax due, or to all the property. When Abner, an hour later, obtained the money and galloped in pursuit of the official, he learned that the sheriff had taken some obscure route back to the county-seat, a trail impossible to follow. When the settler arrived there, he found his property had been sold to a friend of the sheriff for less than half its value. That in many cases collusion could not be proved between the sheriff and the buyer still did not make it any less true. Further to infuriate the settler, the law entitled the sheriff to a fee of 2/8d for his pains in impounding the property and swindling the farmer. The sheriff's legitimate income came from such fees.

And the sheriffs, who were freeholders appointed by the Governor, were fertile in ideas how to increase their incomes at the expense of the settlers. They persuaded the Assembly at New Bern to pass a law entitling them to an additional fee for calling at rate-payers' homes for taxes when farmers had not brought in their taxes to designated localities during January and February. Referring to the law, Husbands observed that the sheriffs and their deputies were remarkably fond of remaining on their posteriors.

Another reason for the refusal, in 1766, of several frontier counties to pay their taxes was the well-known reluctance of the sheriffs to turn over their collections promptly to the county treasurers. Even Governor Tryon, to whom the Regulators were no better than thieves and highway robbers, admitted that "the sheriffs have embezzled more than one-half of the public money ordered to be raised and collected by them." Two years later an official investigator reported that the sheriffs of several counties were in arrears more than £49,000. The office of county treasurer was an elective one, and the incumbents, fearing the political ill-will of the sheriffs, whose posts were appointive, were not inclined to alienate men who might be influential at election time.

But however bad the tax situation was—and only two

years before the North Carolina colonists had refused flatly
and violently to submit to the Stamp Act (the immediate
genesis of the Revolution) — the chief reason for the widen-
ing discontent was the extortionate fees. For the poorer settlers in the western counties, there was no way of circum-
venting these charges. A contemporary pamphlet entitled
"The Nutbush Paper" cites the common example of a small
farmer against whom a judgment had been found for five
pounds owed to a merchant. To enter the judgment in a
docket and issue a writ of execution, the court clerk as-
sessed costs of 41s.5d. against the debtor — a perfunctory,
clerical operation, a matter of thirty seconds. Since the
farmer could not pay, the clerk was entitled to collect by
demanding the debtor's labor for twenty-seven days at 18d.
a day. Meanwhile, the farmer's wife was scarcely eating, his
children were under-nourished, his acres lay fallow, and the
merchant had still to be paid. After the twenty-seven days'
labor for the clerk, the farmer was made to work nineteen
days to pay the lawyer who had drawn up the farmer's admission of the debt, after which followed another nineteen-
day period of labor to pay off the sheriff who had served the
court clerk's notice of judgment. Thus, after more than
two months of forced labor, the farmer was privileged to
return to his home and starving family, to witness the sale
of his cows and horses for a trifling sum to discharge his
debt to the merchant and to "satisfy these cursed hungry
caterpillars that will eat out the very bowels of our commonwealth if they are not pulled down from their nests in
a very short time."

Those who had followed Husbands' lead were Welsh,

Scotch-Irish, English and a few German settlers, a hard, strong-principled, rather inflexible group of small farmers. Many of them had immigrated to escape one or another form of oppression on the other side. Here, after surviving unending hardships, they saw their microscopic profits being wrested from them by office-holders who cared nothing for their struggles with the land, and not far ahead of them they saw imprisonment for debt. In the face of the continued abuses, in the absence of any sign of redress, a violent reaction among them was inevitable. If the colony acting together the year before had proved it could successfully defy the Crown by disavowing the Stamp Act, it was conceivable that one part of the colony could successfully defy the local authorities. Husbands' refusal to pay over his tax into the prehensile hands of the sheriffs was precisely the example that Orange County wanted.

A call written by Husbands was read and posted in the county court, asking each district to despatch delegates "at some place where there is no liquor (at Maddock's Mill, if no objection), at which time let it be judiciously inquired whether the free men of this country labor under any abuses of power or not."

That the court even permitted the call to be read suggests that the authorities at Hillsboro, the seat, recognized that some concessions had to be made. To refuse permission might have given the appearance of official guilt. Moreover, when the court was in session, and farmers from scattered localities were in attendance, it was customary to permit the reading of announcements of interest to citizens. Subsequently it was nailed beside notices of horse-sales, auctions, property transfers and banns. Nevertheless, to move directly into the enemy's camp, into one of the courts charged by many of the settlers with corruption, was certainly the part of boldness.

But apparently the danger, if any, was not recognized by the officials. One of them, indeed, a county justice and assemblyman named Thomas Lloyd, conceded publicly the "reasonableness" of the summons to a meeting to consider "any abuses or not." Speaking for the court, he declared the officials might consider sending a delegate to the meeting.

Husbands, pleased with the absence of opposition to the reading of the summons, returned to his home to note in his diary that "this Method will certainly cause the Wicked Men in Power to tremble; and there is no danger can attend such a meeting, nor nothing hinder it but a cowardly, dastardly spirit."

On October 10, twelve delegates appeared at Maddock's Mill, representing as many small communities. They waited some time for an ambassador from the officials. At length a messenger arrived with a message, signed by the county court, which stated that no representative would be sent because, upon a rereading of the "call," it was noted that the phrase read ". . . let it be *judicially* inquired whether the free men of this county labor under any abuses of power or not." Obviously, the message added, the delegates at Maddock's Mill had no judicial powers to inquire into anything, much less into the conduct of the elected or appointed officials.

The message proved a red flag at the meeting. Husbands swore that the summons, as written by him, had employed the words "judiciously inquired" and not "judicially inquired." The delegates agreed that the officials were quibbling, if one of them (probably Fanning) had not actually falsified the posted document. But that which chiefly enraged the men at Maddock's Mill was a postscript to the message warning the delegates that Colonel Fanning, then an assemblyman, regarded the meeting as insurrectionary.

However infuriated the delegates were at the absence of an envoy from the officers of the court, the message had the effect of clearing the air and sharply delimiting the sides in the conflict. Here was an open and clean break. Without debate, it was resolved that the farmers would meet at least once annually to review the actions and the qualifications of men in office. The somewhat naïve hope was expressed, in Husbands' account of the meeting, that the officials would consent eventually to submit their tax records to these civilian gatherings for "regulation."

To the officials this was heresy. The view that officeholders were obligated to give an account of their stewardship to their constituencies was farcical to the Orange County bureaucracy. But the delegates at Maddock's Mill were in earnest. It was significant that they referred to themselves in their resolution as "said regulators." Their immediate objective was the expulsion of Fanning from the Assembly.

Under the impetus of that meeting, the loosely organized group began to grow. In the spring of the new year, 1768, the number of Regulators was brought to nearly one hundred by two acts of the Assembly, two measures which could not have been better calculated to incite insurrection.

One was the passage of the aforementioned law by which, if taxpayers did not appear at county-seats in January and February to pay the past year's assessment, the sheriffs were entitled to a substantial fee for calling at the homes of delinquents. The effect of this was to add yet more to a tax burden long since felt to be intolerably oppressive on the small farmer. The other piece of legislation, equally short-sighted, was approval by the Assembly of an appropriation of £15,000 with which to build for Governor Tryon a mansion at New Bern suitably imposing for an envoy of George III.

Husbands could not contain his fury.

While the Quaker laid plans for another meeting, he received a request from farmers of Sandy Creek, also in Orange County, for advice how most effectively to organize in opposition to the sheriffs' exercise of their new prerogatives. His answer was that they should join with the group that had met the year before at Maddock's Mill. As a bid for support, the second meeting was held at Sandy Creek.

It developed that the Sandy Creek settlers were more radical than those from Husbands' neighborhood, and at the outset the former showed impatience with any measures short of violence. They argued there was no effective manner of preventing a sheriff from holding a forced sale but by beating him. The more moderate wing, influenced by the Quakers, at length brought away from the meeting a compromise agreement, but it lacked little in vigor.

That agreement, exploding in the faces of Governor Tryon, Colonel Fanning and the authorities generally with the force of an ultimatum of war, provided that:

"We, the subscribers, do voluntarily agree to form ourselves into an association, to assemble ourselves for conference for *regulating* public grievances and abuses of power, in the following particulars, with others of a like nature that may occur: (1) We will pay no more taxes until we are satisfied that they are agreeable to law, and applied to the purposes therein mentioned, unless we can not help it, or are forced; (2) We will pay no officer any more fees than the law allows, unless we are obliged to do it, and then to show our dislike and bear open testimony against it; (3) We will attend all our meetings of conferences as often as we conveniently can, etc.; (4) We will contribute to collections for defraying necessary expenses attending the work, according to our abilities; (5) In case of differences of judgment we will submit to the judgment of the majority of our body."

The first clash occurred in April. Regulator leaders in a third meeting, conforming to their intention of "regulating public grievances and abuses of power," had requested the sheriff of Orange County to send them a list of recent tax-payments, together with a statement of disbursements by his office—this was their first condition to further payment of taxes. The request, peremptorily phrased, was not enthusiastically received, and the statement was not immediately forthcoming, although the Regulators contended with force that tax payments and disbursements were all part of the public records.

When the settlers' patience had about ended, an under-sheriff precipitated mob action. He had the temerity, or the stupidity, or both, to seize the mare, saddle and bridle of one of the Regulators to satisfy payment of a small judgment. The under-sheriff was acting within the law, and any plan of reprisal was suspended until the disposition of the case was known. When it was learned that the official had sold the seized property for four dollars to another official, there was no further hesitation.

Seventy Regulators, first gathering outside the county-seat, galloped into Hillsboro, appropriated the horse after paying the judgment, and returned the mount to its original owner. Thence they proceeded to the courthouse, and after haranguing the sheriff for his dalliance in submitting the list of tax-payments, trussed him up behind the building. Riding out of town, several of the band fired shots into the roof of Fanning's house as a reminder that their anger was not restricted to the sheriff. (Husbands, not a member of the raiding party, explained afterward that the parting fusillade was provoked by the appearance of an armed man at Fanning's door, threatening to fire on anyone who approached.)

In addition to his other offices at the time of the raid, Fanning was colonel of the Orange County militia, its commanding officer. The Hillsboro incident, the firing of shots into his home, the humiliation of the sheriff, could not be countenanced. The only construction he could place upon the foray was that of rank insurrection. Apart from that, Fanning had been personally insulted, his authority flouted. He received word of the raid at Halifax, where he had been attending superior court. To Lieutenant-Colonel John Gray, at Hillsboro, he sent ahead orders to mobilize a punitive force of seven companies of militia, and he dispatched a report of the raid to Governor Tryon at New Bern. It charged the

insurrectionists with almost every crime save rape. He declared the insurrectionists had sworn to pay no more taxes,
which was not true—they had sworn not to pay them to
the sheriffs; that they had sworn to kill any and all tax-
collectors, which also was not the fact; that they had conspired to nullify the execution of court writs, wherein there
was some truth; and that they desired to summon all the
county officials before "the bar of their shallow understanding," which was more rhetoric than indictment.

The militia colonel until now had been inclined to mini-
mize the importance of the Regulator movement, if it could
be called a movement; he seemed to believe the protests,
resolutions, "advertisements" and the rest were inspired by
Husbands and a handful of malcontents in remote districts of
the county. But he changed his mind when a messenger arrived with disturbing word from his lieutenant-colonel at
Hillsboro.

Gray, obeying orders, had circulated the mobilization
order for seven companies of militia to report for immediate
duty at the county-seat.

Scarcely a hundred men had responded. Most of these
declared they would elect to pay fines rather than engage in
any campaign to arrest Regulator leaders. If this was not
mutiny, it was near to it. In view of the militia's disaffection,
Gray added, he had thought it wiser to temporize with the
Regulators until such time as reinforcements might arrive.

Through the intervention of the Reverend George
Micklejohn, Gray agreed to meet leaders of the Regulators
on May 11. Fanning, becoming alarmed, sent a second report to the Governor, explaining that he had heard the in-

surgents planned to surround Hillsboro on May 3 with reinforcements from Anson, Rowan and Mecklenburg counties
where, he hastened to say, the revolt had had its inception—
he did not wish Tryon to know that the uprising had been
born in the heart of his own bailiwick. And, he added, the
traitors planned to burn the town if their demands were not
met. Of this last there is no existing evidence. The Council
at New Bern, acting on the Governor's recommendation,
promptly declared the Orange County movement an insurrection, and Tryon sent Fanning a proclamation to post in
the county-seat.

The Regulators met on April 30. They selected twelve
delegates to represent them at the parley May 11; not all of
them were enrolled Regulators. Their instructions were to
procure the tax-lists of the two former sheriffs, to obtain a
statement of the taxes collected the past year, and a copy of
the fees permitted by law. Meanwhile a petition bearing four
hundred signatures, among them those of many non-Regu-
lators (including Husbands), was drafted for submission to
the Governor in case the county officials, after the forthcoming meeting, should be obdurate.

At this point Fanning, whose strong suit was not political
finesse, decided to anticipate trouble by creating some himself. He felt relatively secure in the light of the Council's
ready action and an offer by Tryon to come to the seat of
trouble himself if need be. On the same day that the Regulators met to elect deputies, the Governor's secretary arrived
at Hillsboro, and posted the proclamation "desiring all Rioters to disperse . . . and on their Refusal, commanding officers to aid and assist to disperse them." Fanning, who might

better have remained out of sight, organized a posse of twenty-seven men, the majority of them under-sheriffs, bailiffs, and court-clerks despised by the farmers, and set out for Sandy Creek.

Arrived there, he ordered the sheriff to arrest William Butler, one of the leaders of the Regulator force that had recovered the mare at Hillsboro, and Husbands. They were jailed at the county-seat, and Butler was threatened with hanging if Husbands escaped; it was thought this might serve to dampen the Quaker's ardor. The charge was inciting rebellion, and after their arraignment before a peace justice they were returned to their cells, tied hand and foot, and now informed they would hang immediately. The Quaker Husbands was frankly terrified.

So, he relates, "it came into my mind that if I made Colonel Fanning some promise he would let me go. So on my motion he was sent for, and signified to me that he had been asleep, and was called and told I wanted to see him, and he had come to see what I wanted with him.

"Says I, if I may go home, I will promise not to concern myself any more whether you take too large fees or not. &c. It took with him, and, after humming a little, he repeated over what I must promise . . ."

The pledge extracted from Husbands is reminiscent of that which Berkeley forced upon Bacon in Virginia nearly a hundred years before. The colonial authorities of the day seemed to place a good deal of confidence in formal recantations—or political apostasies may have fed their pride. Husbands agreed, at Fanning's dictation—

"—never to give your opinion of the laws, not frequent

assembling yourself among people, nor show any jealousies of the officers taking extraordinary fees; and if you hear any others speaking disrespectfully, or hinting any jealousies of that nature of officers, that you reprove and caution them, and that you will tell the people that you are satisfied all the taxes are agreeable to law, and do everything in your power to moderate and pacify them."

Husbands did not walk from jail, as he soon learned, with the stature of the people's hero. He had been quick to recant when faced with danger. He continued to remain outside the rank and file of the Regulators. He boasted that, in signing the foregoing, he had tricked Fanning, the brilliant lawyer, into an admission of "officers taking extraordinary fees," but that academic triumph made no impression on the farmers. Butler, on the other hand, when threatened with summary hanging, declared that his life would be a small contribution to the cause.

Husbands, in any event, signed the absurd pledge in order to get his freedom. As it developed, there was no need of his signing the retraction, since the colonel was anxious to be rid of him. When Fanning learned that some seven hundred Regulators and sympathizers, hearing of the incarceration of the two men, were en route to Hillsboro to storm the jail and free them, he backed down. Most of the farmers had been informed of the arrests by runners who raced overnight from one home to another, and now many of them were armed. Fanning wasted no time setting the two men at liberty to head off the mob.

Thus a collision was avoided. When the forces reached the outskirts of Hillsboro, they were confronted by the Governor's secretary, who relayed a message purportedly from Tryon that "if they would petition the Governor, he would Protect and Redress them against unlawful extortions, or Oppressions of any Officer in the County; Provided they would Disperse and Go Home."

Husbands wrote that "no sooner was the Word spoke, but the whole Multitude, as with one Voice, cried out, Agreed. That is all we want; Liberty to Make our Grievances known."

Husbands' association with the Regulators was not ended, but he had been greatly frightened. He despised violence, but he was provoking a situation that could be controlled only by a man of more force, more courage and fighting capacity. Returned to the insurgents, "some of them insulted me [saying] that if I did not join them now, they would let the Governor do as he pleased with me." He planned to sell his land, and in fear both of Fanning and Tryon on one hand, and the Regulators on the other, he fled to the woods for two weeks.

At the next session of the court, the charges of inciting rebellion against Husbands and Butler were continued, not because of any dearth of evidence against the men but doubtless because the Governor did not dare risk another popular march on the county-seat at that time.

Since the Governor's secretary had declared that Tryon would consider a petition and "Protect and Redress them against unlawful extortions," the Regulators' next move was to draw up that document. Husbands, Rednap Howell, Butler and other leaders hoped that at last they would get a sympathetic hearing. They set to work.

The first obstacles were raised in their own ranks. Younger and more extreme Regulators had tasted violence in the Hillsboro raid, and they pointed to the fruits of direct action: the wrong done to one of their number had been righted (by the return of his horse), the sheriff had been suitably chastised, and, most important of all, the militia had shown themselves reluctant to fight the Regulators. This faction suggested that the charges to be relayed to the Governor, with the open threat that they would take the law into their own hands if correction were not soon forthcoming.

The extreme Regulator wing was opposed by the moderates led by Husbands. As was to be expected, the moderates were chiefly those who had the most to lose. They were also the men upon whom pressure of one sort and another was brought to bear by the officials, sometimes working through others. The court justices made themselves felt through the ministers, but in most instances the pressure applied was less subtle. Husbands was openly threatened with the finding of a new indictment charging treason, punishable by death, supplanting the lesser charge of incitement to rebellion. Others were told that immediate and full payment would be demanded on their notes, mortgages and other obligations, or warned of a boost in rents on their acreage, if they continued critical of their lords and masters.

A note of comedy was furnished by Colonel Fanning. He came forward with an offer to draft the Regulators' petition himself on the ground that, as a lawyer and a member of the Assembly, he was more at home in the use of the parliamentary phrase. But the Regulators declared themselves satisfied with the flamboyant style of Husbands.

The document eventually drafted, after bursts of argument pro and con had exploded over Husbands' head for three days and nights, was something of a compromise between the two factions. The threat of direct action was implied only, and as a sop to the ministers, who were between two fires in the controversy, the petition asked pardon for any past acts unwittingly "contrary to the King's peace and Government." The remainder of the document, however, was unfaltering. There were twenty specific charges of extortion against the sheriff, his deputies, the court clerk and registrar, and they were supported by as many affidavits.

Instead of expressing sympathy with the settlers' complaints, or suggesting arbitration between them and the county officials, Governor Tryon replied with a denunciation and, in effect, a challenge to battle. First he declared his secretary had had no authority to pledge his consideration of any petition from men acting in defiance of the laws of the colony. Second, the Regulators' meetings were treasonable, since devoted to conspiracy against the State. As a final insult, he added praise for the loyalty of Colonel Fanning, and commendation of those Orange County militiamen who had answered the mobilization order, "for their prudent and splendid behavior." A postscript remarked that the Council had approved the terms of his reply.

The Governor's response was so much salt on their wounds. It was evident to the Regulators that the Governor had disavowed the pledge relayed by his secretary because it was now convenient to do so; before, he had been playing for time to consolidate the militia against them in neighboring counties. So far as the Regulators' explicit charges were concerned, they were dismissed by Tryon with a note that they would be "duly considered."

In adjacent Anson County, meanwhile, settlers had caught the fever of direct action from the Regulator movement in Orange County. As the Sandy Creek group had asked the advice and support of the original Regulators, so now did those in Anson County. There a band of small farmers, in April 1768, appeared at the county courthouse to petition the justices to hear specific complaints of extortion against the sheriff and other officials. Their right to read or file the complaints was denied without explanation.

The men—the "Anson banditti," in the Governor's words—left the courtroom quietly, and held council on the village green. There they took heart when reminded of the success of the recent raid into Hillsboro. The men marched back to the courtroom—and emptied it. The court clerk was soundly flogged, the justices were warned that legitimate grievances must not be ignored, and then were literally chased from the bench. Before riding out of town, the farmers left behind a signed resolution that, following the precedent of Orange County, they would pay no more taxes to the sheriff, they would recapture all property seized for non-payment of debt, and they would contribute to a fund to defray costs of lawsuits provoked by their acts. This had become the approved Regulator technique.

Except for the fusillade at Hillsboro, the "Anson banditti" had acted even more drastically than their friends in Orange County. They had prevented a court from exercising its functions, much in the vigorous fashion employed by Captain Shays and his supporters in Massachusetts less than two decades later. One of the results of the Anson County raid was identical with the post-Hillsboro fiasco. Governor Tryon ordered Colonel Samuel Spencer to call up the militia in Anson County to bring in the ringleaders.

Nothing came of the halfhearted gestures to comply with Tryon's order.

In July, Tryon went to Hillsboro to attend the county-court sessions, where he hoped by his personal intervention to be able to persuade the insurgents to pay their taxes and to cease their violence. But by this time the Governor's ready promises of consideration meant nothing to the Regulators. He began to grow worried when a thousand settlers, not all of them Regulators, met about twenty miles from Hillsboro. Tryon, believing they might advance on the town, summoned the militia, but found he was unable to collect more than four hundred men. He then sent word again to the Regulators that their method of seeking redress was criminal and treasonable. He promised, however, to dismiss the militia if, by August 25, the Regulators selected twelve men to raise £1,000 as a surety bond for Husbands and Butler, who were to be tried on the old charge of incitement to rebellion at the impending court session. He added as another condition that the Regulators must promise to make no attempt to rescue the two defendants from the court.

The Regulators refused to send any bondsmen to Tryon, and protested that they had never thought of employing force to remove Husbands and Butler from the jurisdiction of the court.

The Governor began a tour to increase his forces by raising the militia in the adjacent counties. He had unexpected success, partly due to his ingenuity in winning the support of Presbyterian and Baptist pastors, who were, at least in principle, opposed to violence: and it was violence, and hence insurrection, that the Regulators employed, Tryon insisted. When he arrived back at Hillsboro on September 21, the Governor had a force of 1,461, with "two small companies of gentlemen." Compared to the Regulators' strength, it was a formidable body; and moreover it was officered by six lieutenant-generals, two major-generals, three adjutant-generals, two majors of brigade, seven colonels, five lieutenant-colonels, four majors and thirty-one captains; it fairly bristled with epaulets. Most of those with commissions were members of the Assembly.

Against this array, a force of some 3,700 ill-equipped farmers was helpless. They assembled a half-mile from Hillsboro and sent word to the Governor asking on what terms their submission would be accepted.

The plea was humiliating, but the Regulators had no choice except to sue for peace when confronted with a force the size of Tryon's command. In any pitched battle they could not hope for success. With fingers crossed, they submitted to the Governor's terms, which were that they put down their arms, swear an oath of loyalty to the Government, and pay their just taxes. Amnesty was granted by Tryon to all but thirteen of the Regulator forces. Early the next month, the militiamen had all been sent back to their farms.

The atmosphere was such in the Hillsboro courtroom that Tryon for once determined upon diplomacy and leniency. The charges against Husbands and Hunter, and those against the thirteen Regulators who had led the force outside the county-seat, were suspended. This was a bid for concurrence of the Regulators in the disposition of charges they had brought against Colonel Fanning and lesser officials.

Thomas Lloyd, comparatively friendly to the Regulators, was one of the justices presiding at the trial of Fanning, which began in a courtroom packed with insurgents. The Governor, however, took no risk of a repetition of the chastisement handed out to court officials at Anson, and militiamen and bailiffs were disposed in force around the room.

The charge against Colonel Fanning of malfeasance in office, of extortion in the collection of fees, was supported by a number of witnesses, and by some of the affidavits which had previously been sent to the Governor. It was heard by a jury on which, of course, no Regulators served. Despite the witnesses and their affidavits, the jury returned a verdict that the colonel had merely "erred involuntarily." The jury could not find that Fanning had ever had conscious intention to defraud. For its deterrent effect, however, the Assemblyman was fined a penny each on five counts.

The trial was a farce. Far from lessening the Regulators' opposition in Orange, Anson and Rowan counties, it merely stiffened it, and increased the resentment further afield. For the present, however, it was decided not to employ direct action, since the farmers might not again be able to avert an open battle with the militia. They resolved to try for reforms by political means.

The Assembly had been dissolved in 1769 by Tryon's order, and here might be an opportunity to obtain representation in that body, which hitherto had been almost unanimously ranged on the side of the Governor and the officeholders generally. Orange, Anson, Halifax and Granville counties returned completely new delegations to New Bern —Husbands among them. Pending the meeting of the lower legislature, the several strongly Regulator counties drew up a joint petition to the Assembly.

The leaders, however, had not altogether abandoned direct action. When an Orange County Sheriff, John Lea, sought to serve bench warrants on several Regulators, they laughed at him, and then thrashed him.

The Assembly met in October, but it was again dissolved by Tryon because of his dissatisfaction over the passage of several resolutions dealing with Crown relations. The new election was held in March 1770.

Husbands was reelected. Fanning was defeated, and it appeared that the Regulators in Orange County, at least, had won a substantial victory. But the presence in the lower house of Fanning, one of Tryon's staunchest supporters, and his presence also at Hillsboro, were important to the Governor. Tryon changed the status of Hillsboro to a borough, and engineered the colonel's return to the Assembly as its representative. Nevertheless the new Assembly, under the impetus supplied by the Regulator members, was in a fair way to enacting a mass of corrective legislation, reducing taxation and costs of litigation, when renewed violence broke out at Hillsboro.

There the leaders had given up hope of relief. They had petitioned the Governor, the Council, and the Assembly with no success. They were too impatient to wait for any dubious benefits that might come to them in the course of time from the new Assembly. It was decided to address a petition directly to the Superior Court, and once again to recite their grievances. Several of the phrases in that document were an augury of what was to come:

"Our only crime with which they can charge us is vertue in the very highest degree, namely, to risque our all to save our country from rapine and slavery, in our detecting of practices which the law itself allows to be worse than open robbery . . . As we are serious and in good earnest, it would be a loss of time to enter into argument on particular points . . ."

The Superior Court met at Hillsboro September 22. The day and night before, groups of Regulators had seeped into the county-seat, purposely not arriving in large bodies for fear that militia from outside counties might be hurried to the town if Fanning were to become nervous over a concentration of insurgent strength. As it was, the court opened in an atmosphere freighted with apprehension. The officials realized suddenly that there were fully 150 Regulators in the town, and that none of them had the countenance and manner of the idly curious. There was no hope of summoning up the militia in a few hours, and Governor Tryon was several hundred miles distant at New Bern.

The clerk, calling out the first case on the docket, was interrupted by the spokesman for the Regulators, who had determined to take the initiative. He was James Hunter, the future "general" of their forces, who walked up to the bench and tossed up the petition to Justice Richard Henderson. The court stated that other business had precedence, but it would consider the petition two days hence. In view of the Regulators' temper at that moment it is fairly surprising that the justice's ruling was accepted without protest, particularly since it afforded Fanning time to prepare for trouble.

Most of the Regulators remained in Hillsboro for the two days. They had time to plan what steps to take if the court took no action on the petition.

On September 24 the court reopened, the room again crowded with Regulators. This time they did not wait for the clerk to open the proceedings. An unidentified Regulator walked up to Justice Henderson, and declared that he and his companions were aware that the bench had no intention of submitting the petitioners' charges to the grand jury.

To this challenge the justice remained silent. He was next told that if the court did decide to act as the only means of averting public disorder, the present jury must be dismissed and an impartial one summoned.

The threat of "public disorder" forced the court to a semblance of action. Justice Henderson, sparring for time, remarked that it would require a certain delay before another jury could be impanelled, even supposing it were found that there were legitimate grounds in law, in the petition, for prosecution. He was well launched into an academic dissertation when, looking up, he realized that the Regulators were rapidly leaving the courtroom.

Led by Husbands, Rednap Howell and James Hunter, they gathered outside the courthouse.

In a few minutes, all were mysteriously supplied "with switches or sticks." They could prevent anyone's leaving or entering the building. When a lawyer, John Williams, who enjoyed the favor of the court, began to mount the steps the Regulators knocked him down, and beat him. He finally escaped. If the court would not act on their petition, it would not be permitted to act on anything. The mob next fell on William Hopper, deputy attorney-general of the colony, and gave him a taste of their "switches." Three petty officials were given "cow-hide correction very severely." Then the cry went up for Fanning.

The colonel was inside the court-house, seeking shelter with Judge Henderson. When the Regulators burst into the room, Fanning dashed to the bench, desperately hoping his pursuers might consider the court as inviolate as a church. But he was pulled down, dragged to the street by his heels, beaten and bounced on the cobblestones; but by a "manly exertion miraculously broke holt and fortunately jumped into a door that saved him from immediate dissolution." He was soon forced from that refuge, but at length permitted to return home on his promise to surrender himself the next morning.

A number of other officials fled the town—"took to the woods to escape like treatment," the Boston *Gazette* noted. Justice Henderson, powerless to subdue the mob and himself paralyzed with fright, adjourned court unceremoniously, and escaped from Hillsboro at night. The Regulators now decided to improve on their previous gesture directed at Fanning's house, and razed and smashed everything inside it, carefully excepting the store of liquor. A satirical note was sent Fanning offering to pay damages of approximately £1,500, if he would return the fees he had extorted from the farmers. To that offer Fanning replied that he "only wanted revenge, and revenge I will have" (but three years later he was suing the Assembly unsuccessfully for the loss of his property). Afterward the Regulators denied that in wrecking the dwelling they stole a large sum of money.

If hitherto Governor Tryon's reprisals had not amounted to much more than threats and bluster, the Regulators now had forced his hand. The disorders at Hillsboro, the assaults on court officers and the destruction of property, were open rebellion against the constituted authorities. But the Regulators, it appeared certain, craved a showdown, and they felt strong and reckless enough to face the militia.

The following day they returned to Hillsboro, seized the court docket, set up a dummy court, and passed judgment themselves on the cases pending. Typical of their marginal notations on the docket were "Fanning must pay," "damned rogue," "judgment by default, the money must come of the officers," and other expressions that were, according to a pro-Tryon account, "teeming with billingsgate and profanity." The same account (by Marshall De Lancey Haywood) cites a report that the mob cut down the decomposed corpse of a Negro who had been hanged in chains, and propped it up in Judge Henderson's chair as a token of respect.

Fanning surrendered the next day, and there was talk of hanging him. But the moderates prevailed, and he was released on his promise to take the road leading out of Hillsboro and continue running until lost to view. It led, as might be expected, directly to the Governor.

Because of the sympathy for the Regulators existing in the west of the colony, Tryon ordered every county there to muster its militia to determine the number who were loyal to the Government. This seemed imperative to the Council, since every day came new reports that the Regulators planned a march on New Bern to force the Assembly to submit to their demands for relief. The report was preposterous, since only the year before the Regulators had capitulated at the first demonstration of militia force, but evidently the Assembly had grown panicky after the second raid on Hillsboro. And the nervousness was not limited to the legislators. The capital heard reports that the Regulators, failing satisfaction, were preparing to burn New Bern, after the manner of Jamestown in Virginia—and for much the same reason.

There was some faith in these frightening tales because of sporadic violence. At Granville, Justice Henderson's house, barn and stable were destroyed by fire, and rightly or wrongly the insurgents were charged with incendiarism.

In the fall (1770) session of the Assembly, Husbands showed that the suspension of the sentence against him had not softened his feelings toward either the Government or Tryon. The latter demanded of him why farmers of Orange County, with whom the court had dealt leniently, continued to withhold payment of taxes to the sheriff.

They owed his Excellency, Husbands admitted, the equivalent of so much butter, but "as that was apt to stick to the fingers, to prevent waste they had sent their taxes by their representative, who was ready to pay it to the treasurer, if I could get the proper receipt." With this, Husbands tossed a bag of specie on the table facing Tryon.

The boldness of Husbands' act provoked an uproar in the Assembly. His sarcasm was an attack not only on the honesty of the sheriff of his county, but it was also interpreted by many in the lower house as a reflection on the probity of the Governor. However dramatic as a protest against tax abuses, the gesture cost Husbands a measure of support in the Assembly, thus far less anti-Regulator than it had ever been.

The effect of the incident on the Governor was a decision that Husbands must be suppressed. Apart from the Quaker's impertinence, this was not the time to have it appear that the Regulators were willing to pay their just taxes. Tryon had already suffered a political setback in a recent opinion from the colonial attorney general. That official, asked whether the Hillsboro raiders could be charged with treason, replied that they could be indicted only for rioting and possibly, since they had insulted the court, with a misdemeanor.

Husbands soon felt his loss of a personal following in the Assembly. Almost overnight he became the target for a variety of charges in a move to impeach. First the Assembly found him guilty of publishing a "false and seditious libel" against Justice Maurice Moore, of the Superior Court, to whom the Quaker had obliquely referred as one of the "Wicked Men in Power." Next a now hostile majority of the lower house found him guilty of falsely testifying before the Assembly's Committee on Grievances to extortionary acts with which the Regulators had charged Colonel Fanning. Third, he was charged with uttering the seditious threat that, if arrested, he would bring down on the heads of the Assembly a force of hundreds of Regulators to tear down the jail. He was not bluffing.

The charges were deemed sufficient to oust him, and that with considerable enthusiasm. Nevertheless, this was not punishment enough. The lower house, elaborately considerate of Husbands' personal safety, and of the safety of the community, dispatched a resolution to the colonial chief justice which urged Husbands' arrest. The justice complied, after reports were given him that the Regulators, hearing of Husbands' difficulties, were massing in Orange County to march to his relief.

He was charged with treason. He was in jail for six weeks before the grand jury acted, refusing to return an indictment. On the day of his release, the Regulators were actually marching in a body on the capital. They were headed off at Haw River, but Husbands' long imprisonment was added fuel in Orange and the surrounding counties.

Both the Council and the Assembly now suffered acutely from nerves. The lower house rushed through a new riot law (the "Bloody Act") which made of anyone ignoring a court summons for sixty days, an outlaw, and therefore one who could be killed with impunity. Also it authorized the attorney-general to try cases of riot in any district court he pleased, thus permitting him to arraign a defendant before a jury favorably disposed to the Government.

On the day that the bill was passed, to endure for one year only, word arrived that the Regulators, two hundred miles distant, were massing men, provisions and wagons at Cross Creek for an advance on New Bern. Immediately, Tryon was voted £500 to protect the town. The terror that news invoked was such that three days later (January 2, 1771) the lower house passed a number of bills incorporating many of the reforms demanded by the back-county farmers. But that gesture toward relief was too late; and Tryon, disgusted with Husbands' release, was spoiling for a fight. Like Andros, he was more the soldier than the civil administrator.

During the spring the Governor hurried preparations for an advance on Hillsboro to arrest the leading Regulators under the new law. He planned two columns, one of Cape Fear militiamen under General Hugh Waddell, to march to Salisbury in Rowan County, there joining a second column under Tryon marching directly to Hillsboro from New Bern. But first there was the problem of raising the man-power. In Bute County, for example, not one volunteer came forward. Elsewhere companies came forward without arms, a palpable trick to avoid service. But the Governor made some headway by offering a bounty of forty shillings, and on April 23 the eastern column set out from New Bern, and picked up several militia detachments en route to Hillsboro. Tryon arrived there, meeting no opposition, on May 9, with 151 officers and 917 men.

General Waddell was less fortunate. On the same day, May 9, he forded the Yadkin north of Salisbury, to learn that ahead of him was a large force of Regulators. The commanding officer summoned his aides, from whom he learned that nine youths in Indian disguise had fallen on a party bringing ammunition to Waddell from South Carolina, and had burned the powder. They reported, besides, that the Regulator force ahead of them was evidently superior to the

Government column, both in number and equipment, and that a large number of militiamen had become increasingly reluctant to fight as they neared the Regulator country. The majority had been recruited in Anson, Rowan and Mecklenburg counties. In the face of these discouragements, General Waddell turned back, reforded the Yadkin, and retired to Salisbury. A scout made his way successfully around the Regulators, reported that the enemy had cut them off from joining him at Hillsboro. He gave Waddell's strength as 48 officers and 236 men, together with an artillery company.

Governor Tryon did not hesitate. With his force he started out on May 12 to rescue Waddell. That necessitated a march of seventy miles through the heart of the Regulator country. Two companies were left behind to guard Hillsboro. The next day he reached the banks of the Haw River, and was joined there by twenty-three mounted men. On May 14 he reached the west bank of the Alamance River. After resting two days he formed his battle formation in two lines about 200 yards apart, and advanced to meet the Regulators, encamped five miles beyond.

Although a number of his men had deserted, and others had flatly refused to fire at Regulators, Tryon's force was about 1,200. The number of Regulators facing him was about 2,000, but the evidence suggests that not more than half were armed. They had no effective leadership, and not the slightest knowledge of military strategy. Most of them, including their leaders, believed that their numbers and their firmness would overawe Tryon, would intimidate him into negotiations. Few were aware of their real danger. They doubted that any pitched battle would occur.

Husbands, hopeful of a settlement, had accompanied the force into the field, together with one Reverend David Caldwell. That the Regulator leaders expected to negotiate with the Governor is indicated by a petition from them that the minister had conveyed the day before, May 15, to Tryon asking him again to hear their grievances and to return "a speedy and candid answer." The commander promised a reply the following day.

The reply reached the Regulators as Tryon was moving toward them.

To prevent an "Effusion of Blood," he demanded that within an hour the Regulators ground their arms, "surrender up the outlawed Ringleaders, and submit yourselves to the Laws of your Country, and then rest on the lenience and mercy of Government." Dr. Caldwell again interceded with the Governor, but could get no further concession for "the Obstinate and Infatuated Rebels."

The emissary hurried back—by this time scarcely a mile separated the opposed forces. He advised the leaders to scatter the men to their homes. Breathless, he shouted at them:

"The Governor will grant you nothing! You are unprepared for war! You have no cannon! You have no military training! You have no commanding officers to lead you in battle! You have no ammunition! You will be defeated!"

Neither the leaders, headed by Hunter, nor the rank and file apparently understood the full meaning of Tryon's reply, which in effect was an ultimatum. Many of the men on the field had come along as spectators, curious to watch a bloodless meeting between opposed leaders. The more perceptive pastor "sadly left the scene." And Husbands, also realizing that blood would flow in a few minutes, galloped off the field, not stopping until he reached Maryland; he knew that Tryon would not hesitate to hang him on the spot as an example to the country. As though expecting some additional word from the Governor, the Regulators waited calmly, the men falling to wrestling and firing at targets. The first they knew of the proximity of Tryon's men was an artillery volley over their heads.

Contemporary accounts of the "battle" vary, but most of the writers agree that the Government volley frightened away all but three hundred of the Regulators. Panic seized the others. Those who remained advanced toward Tryon "bellowing defiance and daring their opponents to advance," while others "bared their breasts."

When the Government fire became general, the Regulators dodged behind trees and rocks, Indian-fashion. In a charge by a small party, the Regulators seized two cannon from a column commanded by Fanning, and turned them against the enemy, but they were forced to retreat when unsupported by their main body.

Half an hour later Tryon ran up a white flag of truce, and his drums beat the signal for a parley—a few moments before, one account relates, a Regulator bullet had ripped through the Governor's tricorne. The white flag and the bravura of the drums were abracadabra to Hunter and his untrained men. They maintained their fire, outnumbered at least four to one. In the absence of any responsive flag or cessation in their fire, Tryon concluded (according to his order-book) that the Regulators would give no quarter.

After another half-hour, Tryon led a charge with his

mounted troop, the militia at the double behind him. The dwindling band of Regulators gave ground slowly, for one or two minutes, then fled into the woods. With them were Hunter, Butler and Rednap Howell. That was the end of the Battle of Alamance Creek.

The casualties: the "loyalists," 9 killed, 61 wounded; the Regulators, 9 killed, number of wounded unknown.

Of fifteen taken prisoner, a carpenter named James Few was executed on the field, on the insistence of Fanning that the man had participated in the destruction of his home (friends of Few claimed that his mind had been deranged when the colonel seduced his fiancée). On June 18, at Hills-boro, six prisoners were found guilty of treason, and hanged the next day in the presence of Tryon's troops. One of them, James Pugh, (whose sister married Husbands), began a diatribe against Tryon as he teetered on the gunpowder barrel which served as a scaffold; an officer booted it over to halt the harangue.

Eventually six others condemned to death were pardoned by the King upon the intervention of Governor Tryon; Tryon was content with the execution of the seven. All the others, except Husbands, were pardoned on taking the oath of allegiance, a total of more than 6,000 in Orange, Rowan, Anson and Mecklenburg counties. Husbands received a pardon after the close of the Revolution.

Two years before the "battle," Tryon had been promised in London the governorship of New York when that post became vacant. After the uprising was suppressed, feeling against him continued so hostile that the transfer was made available immediately. The New York governorship was, in a sense, a reward for upholding royal authority in North Carolina, but it was insufficient recompense in Tryon's eyes. In letters to England he complained that he should have received a baronetcy at least. Fanning went north with him as secretary. In the Revolution, five years away, Tryon and Fanning both fought with the British, and were wounded, and after the hostilities the latter served as governor of Prince Edward's Isle. There charges of tyranny were lodged against him, but dismissed eventually by a London commission of inquiry. He was appointed a general in the British army before he resigned his post to return to London, where he died.

There have been buckets of ink expended to make Alamance the preface to Bunker Hill. But the organization and the armed resistance of the Regulators was directed against the agents of government. It was not a rebellion against the principles of the colonial regime, and in consequence it was not, in the common meaning of the word, revolution. Furthermore, however affecting it may be to write of the Regulators as the first band of Americans to defy the British, and thus of Alamance as the beginning of the Revolution, that construction is not supported by fact. The simple truth is that the Regulators employed direct action against a relatively small number of office-holders.

But indirectly the movement unquestionably contributed to the outbreak of the Revolution. To the colonies it was a graphic example, an object lesson, in armed resistance. And despite the outcome of the battle, it demonstrated that British troops were far from invincible. A completely untrained, leaderless group of some three hundred, lacking any artillery save their convictions, for more than an hour had held off Governor Tryon's force of 1,200. That was no inconsiderable feat; and it was significant that Tryon, a few months before Lexington and Concord, warned Parliament against over-confidence in forcing the colonials to terms. But even that admonition, as it developed, was an under-statement.

1769
1791

THE WAR OF THE
NEW HAMPSHIRE GRANTS

THE REDRESS OF GRIEVANCES BY DIRECT AC-
tion now was becoming traditional with the American colonial. Although past outbreaks among the colonies had been
spectacular only in action, scarcely in reforms achieved, it
was apparent that the day of polite and beguiling petitions
was over. Almost all had proved abortive. By 1769, which
may be taken as the start of Ethan Allen's Green Mountain
uprising against New York, it was clear even to the least
perceptive settler that war with England was a matter of a
few years. That conclusion among thousands of colonists
gave their leaders some extenuation for acts that, before the
law, were unquestionably incitement to rebellion, or constituted treason. If the break with the Crown was inevitable,
an uprising here or there against a discredited regime might
have the virtue of precipitating a struggle for independence
in which all the colonies would join against England.

Thus many of them argued in the taverns.

The revolt of the Green Mountain Boys, a group of farmers with positive ideas of independent land-ownership, was
the last major colonial intransigeance before the Revolution

—which, in fact, interrupted it. If Massachusetts in 1775 had not been in an even greater state of revolt, the immediate *casus belli* with England would probably have been found in the quarrel between the settlers in the New Hampshire Grants (later to become Vermont) and the colony of New York. At the height of that quarrel, the governor of New York was William Tryon, whose genius in colonial administration has been remarked in the North Carolina War of the Regulators. But his opponent here was not a man of Husbands' stamp, aware of injustice but in terror of violence. Ethan Allen embraced violence, and the Revolution gave him an opportunity for acts more valorous than the chastisement of surveyors and sheriffs by means, in his own phrase, "of a castigation with the twigs of the Wilderness."

The War of the New Hampshire Grants had its origin in the morass of conflicting charters signed away indifferently by British sovereigns. It has been suggested by the foregoing that at Buckingham Palace, from the early seventeenth century until the outbreak of the Revolution, there never existed a realistic understanding of the geographic, social and economic picture of the American colonies. They were a source of revenue; but since in the main the colonists were ungrateful children unwilling to pay for the protection of England, it was a blessing and a convenience that they were a distant source.

The indiscriminate land-granting of the kings had produced, among others, four documents confusing the geographical status of the New Hampshire Grants. Under a charter of 1664, Charles II had granted to the Duke of York (later James II) all the territory from the Connecticut River to Delaware Bay—a grant that Andros, while the ducal deputy in New York, had been unable to enforce. In subsequent negotiations the eastern boundary of the colony of New York was fixed along a line twenty miles east of the Hudson. Between that line and the Connecticut River lay the New Hampshire Grants. Between 1749 and 1764, acting in the King's name, Governor Benning Wentworth of New Hampshire granted 138 townships, each six square miles, in the territory, a labor for which he personally collected a hundred dollars 138 times.

In the last year of that span, 1764, settlers in the Grants were puzzled by the occasional appearance of travelers, evidentally well supplied with money, but with little interest in buying lands. From their dress, their boots and cocked hats, people rightly judged them to be men of New York. Most of their time was spent in the taverns, ordering punch with the air of men of means, but after they had disarmed innkeepers with their patronage they showed a persistent curiosity about the names of the neighborhood settlers. In later years, farmers in the New Hampshire Grants, then become the State of Vermont, were astonished to learn that their names had appeared on a petition to King George III praying for annexation to New York. The petition claimed that these settlers would benefit materially by selling their crops in the larger markets of the adjoining colony, and it asked that the eastern boundary of New York be advanced to the Connecticut River.

The names on the petition were forgeries, the fraud devised by land-speculators in New York City and Albany, probably with official connivance. The chief speculators are said to have been James Duane, a prominent lawyer of New York City and its future mayor, a man in whom Washington later placed confidence; John Kempe, the Attorney-General of the colony; and Walter Rutherford, a merchant.

The petition, however much a fraud, so impressed the King that he made the western bank of the Connecticut the new boundary. Governor Wentworth of New Hampshire protested vigorously, but at the outset the settlers in the Grants were indifferent over the boundary question. The majority of the hardy, unlettered settlers had emigrated from Massachusetts and Connecticut, and they cared little whether governed by one or another colony so long as they were let alone to raise their crops.

New York colony, however, had no intention of letting them alone.

Up to this point Governor Wentworth had made 138 grants west of the Connecticut River, in territory now decreed to be within the jurisdiction of New York. The phrase "to be the boundary line" in the King's decree, used with reference to the Connecticut River, was very differently interpreted by New York and by New Hampshire. Governor Wentworth was willing to concede that the river was now the boundary, but the connotation of "to be" was in the sense of "henceforth," he insisted. New York, on the other hand, argued that "to be" referred to the past as well as the present and future, that the King was clearly basing his action upon the original charter to the Duke of York, and hence all Wentworth's grants were illegal and invalid.

Suddenly the settlers in the New Hampshire Grants awoke to the full consequence of government by the colony of New York. The new administration divided the Grants into four counties, courts of justice were established, and county militia-commanders appointed. After that machinery had been erected, the Governor of New York called upon the settlers to surrender their farms, for which they had already made payment to the colony of New Hampshire, or to repurchase them under grants from New York. Their plight was brought home to them by a trickle of land-agents and other grantees from New York demanding possession of their farms and waving the New York titles in their faces.

When, in a body, the original settlers refused to budge, the new counties were deluged with eviction-writs issued by the Supreme Court at Albany.

Among those such writs affected was Ethan Allen, who with four brothers in 1766 had emigrated from Connecticut to the territory west of the Green Mountains. Ethan, with his youngest brother, Ira Allen (to become the founder of Vermont), began an energetic canvass of the settlers, urging them to form an association to combat the claims of the New York land-robbers. At the outset the association enjoyed some success—to the surprise of most of its members. There was a meeting of delegates from the districts west of the Green Mountains, and one of the delegates, Captain Samuel Robinson, of Bennington, (a town named for Governor Wentworth), was appointed their agent to go to London. There he was instructed to argue the validity of the grant establishing New York's eastern line twenty miles east of the

Hudson, and not at the Connecticut River, and to stress before the King the obvious injustice of asking the settlers to pay twice for their land. While Robinson was away, sheriffs of the new counties sought repeatedly to oust the farmers. There was no great violence: the settlers merely squatted on their acres and ignored the court officers or tore up their writs and laughed at the hopeful arrivals from New York with claims to their rich, cultivated lands.

Captain Robinson was fortunate to find friends of the American colonials at court. He presented his petition for relief on behalf of 1,000 settlers, adding that the grantees and their families in the New Hampshire Grants totalled at least twenty thousand. The result of this appeal was an order, in July 1767, by Lord Shelbourne, secretary of state for the colonies, on Governor Sir Henry Moore.

"I am to signify to you [it read] his Majesty's command that you make no new grants of those lands, and that you do not molest any person in the quiet possession of his grant who can produce good and valid deeds for such grant, under the seal of the province of New Hampshire, until you receive further orders respecting them."

But Moore, and later Tryon, read nothing in this restraining them from making grants of land not occupied in the New Hampshire Grants, although more than half of the patents they immediately issued infringed on farms already occupied.

The settlers were jubilant over their unexpected success in London, and they had no intention of permitting the governor of New York to ignore the King's order. When he persisted in making grants—he did slightly better than Governor Wentworth, pocketing between $2,000 and $3,000 with every patent—the Green Mountain men, again recognizing the futility of petitions, determined upon action. Their first move was to expel from the district a number of surveyors sent north by the New York purchasers preparatory to selling or leasing their new properties. Incidentally, the New York purchasers were, most of them, friends or dependents of the Governor, particularly after the arrival of Tryon in 1771.

The first direct resistance to the writs of eviction occurred in October 1769 on the western outskirts of Bennington, where about twenty settlers were harvesting wheat on the farm of James Brackenridge. Three New York surveyors arrived, and, without addressing Brackenridge, proceeded to run their lines across the property. Brackenridge, Silas Robinson, and the local minister, the Reverend Jedediah Dewey, ordered them off the farm, refusing to admit the surveyors were acting legally by authority of New York. A number of the harvesters had guns, and they suggested that the surveyors might find a greater degree of contentment back in Albany. A few days later indictments for rioting were returned against the trio. It is a Vermont tradition that in this mild dispute were the seeds of statehood.

Soon afterward Robinson booted a surveyor off his farm, and pursued him down the road brandishing a hoe. For this he was promptly arrested, and imprisoned two months at Albany before his case came to trial and the charge was dismissed. The farmers now realized that New York meant to seize their lands despite the King's order of two years before. They looked about for leadership and for funds.

At this moment Ethan Allen rode upon the scene. Largely by self-acclamation he was appointed leader.

Both Ethan and Ira Allen were land-speculators, as the latter's journal often artlessly attests, although not on a scale comparable to the New Yorkers' operations. Neither could assert, as could the original settlers in the New Hampshire Grants, that they had paid for their land at a time when there was no reason to expect any subsequent claim by New York. Both of them were buying up farms, after 1769, in the full knowledge that the titles were jeopardized by the judgments of the courts at Albany; indeed they were able to purchase the farms, or options, by reason only of that threat from New York, which naturally had depressed land prices.

Ethan Allen, at this time thirty-two, interested himself immediately in the trial of a number of eviction-suits scheduled for hearing at Albany. In the absence of any lawyer in the new counties, he sought one in Connecticut, and helped to raise funds for the lawyer's services. He went next to Portsmouth, New Hampshire, to obtain a copy of the commission under which Governor Wentworth had been empowered to make grants as far west as the line twenty miles east of the Hudson. This and other documents were offered by the defense at Albany, in 1770, when the cases came to trial, but were ruled inadmissible by Judge Robert R. Livingston. He held that New York, not New Hampshire, held title to the Grants, and he ridiculed the argument that the charter of Charles II was obsolete. The jury was directed to return a verdict for the New York plaintiffs. Not without reason, Ethan worked himself into a rage over the brusque dismissal of all the settlers' arguments.

Long after the trials, the Green Mountain leader wrote an account of the sessions at Albany in a book he titled "A Vindication of the Opposition of the Inhabitants of Vermont to the Governor of New York, and of their Right to Form into an Independent State, Humbly Submitted to an Impartial World, by Ethan Allen." It may be noted that the author had been educated for college by the village pedagogue of Cornwall, Connecticut, and that compared to his followers he was a man of extreme learning. "Most, if not all the judges and attorneys [he wrote], particularly Messrs. Duane and Kempe, which attended the court, were patentees under New York; and some of them interested in the very patents on trial. The plaintiffs appearing in great state and magnificence, which, together with their junta of land-thieves, made a brilliant appearance; but the defendants appearing but in ordinary fashion, having been greatly fatigued by hard labor wrought on the disputed premises, and their cash much exhausted, made a very disproportionate figure at court. In fine, interest, conviction and grandeur, being all on one side, easily turned the scale against the honest defendants, and judgments without mercy, in favor of the claimants under New York, were given against them."

Certainly the presence as prosecutor of Kempe and of Judge Livingston, whose family and friends held a New York patent to 35,000 acres in the New Hampshire Grants, was no guarantee of impartiality. At one point in the Brackenridge trial, when the documents of the defense were rejected, Allen cried out that "the gods of the valleys are not the gods of the hills." When Kempe, scenting some contempt of court in the cryptic citation, asked his meaning, Allen replied:

"If you will accompany me to Bennington Hill, it will be made plain to you."

Since the Supreme Court had upheld their claims, the New York speculators and other grantees demanded enforcement of its verdict. Meanwhile, upon Allen's return to Bennington, the settlers in convention again resolved to employ force to oppose eviction, and they made Allen's leadership official by electing him their agent. They "resolved to support our rights and property in the New Hampshire Grants against the usurpations and unjust claims of the Governor and Council of New York by force, as law and justice are denied us."

Early in 1771, when Tryon had become governor, Allen organized around himself a small force of the bolder backwoodsmen, settlers who had lost their farms by the preëmption of New York, although they still remained in possession. That group, numbering about a hundred, was the nucleus of the Green Mountain Boys, but the name was not adopted until later. Its members, similar in type to the rank and file at Lexington and Concord four years later, were adept with the musket, accomplished horsemen, and thoroughly at home in the mountains. A large number of them had fought in the French and Indian War, and powder was a familiar smell in their nostrils.

They did not altogether trust Allen. They were moved by his eloquence, (although many thought him too glib); they were often carried away by his harangues from a stump in a forest clearing, by his commanding figure, his gayety, his undoubted courage, and they appreciated his efforts in their behalf at Albany. But strictly speaking he was not one of them. Memoirs recall that "he could assume the deportment of the fine gentleman" readily, and coupled with his land-speculations this created an impression that it took Allen months to overcome. He had far less difficulty winning over their leaders, the giant Seth Warner, Robert Cockran, Remember Baker, Peleg Sunderland and Gideon Warren, who later served under him as captains, and who, most of them, lost their lives in the war with England. Governor Tryon's name for them was "the Bennington Mob."

The initial move by New York to enforce the Albany decisions was the expedition of a party of land commissioners to seize Brackenridge's farm at Bennington. The seizure was to be an example to the other settlers, a graphic lesson in the authority of New York.

From the Governor's point of view the expedition was not a success. The commissioners were met by an armed force of farmers, and were told that their brains would be scattered over the picturesque countryside if they failed to leave the neighborhood within ten minutes. They left.

At Shaftsbury, a few miles north of Bennington, a deputy sheriff, buttressed by John Munro, a peace-justice, and ten men, succeeded in ousting Isaiah Carpenter from his farm after disarming that farmer, whose musket was found to be loaded with kidney-beans. But the New York tenant, placed in possession by the sheriff, elected to leave his new property after a few hours. The opposition to the sheriffs and their deputies, in several instances expressed on their persons with the "twigs of the Wilderness," resulted in another hail of indictments for rioting.

As a deterrent the indictments proved so many meaningless slips of paper. The defendants' answer was the organization throughout the four counties of committees of safety —a clear implication that the settlers contemplated self-government. At another convention of exasperated leaders it was resolved that no New York officer could remove any citizen from the district without the approval of the local committee, nor could any surveys be made by the New York authorities. Allen, Warner and the rest were careful not to interfere with civil officers in the normal collection of debts and other matters unrelated to the land controversy.

But by far the most important outcome of the indictments was the organization of Ethan Allen's quasi-vigilante force into a military association, with himself as colonel-commandant, and Warner, Cockran, Sunderland, Baker and others as captains or lieutenants. They adopted the name Green Mountain Boys as a salute in the direction of Governor Tryon, who had threatened to drive the opposition in the Grants into that range.

The rebellious communities now had a simple government of their own: committees of safety for internal control, and a military force for external defense. In addition, the Green Mountain Boys' commandant and captains were to constitute a court to try violators of the various decrees passed by the safety committees.

Allen readily admitted the settlers were in a state of rebellion, but an unavoidable one.

With the Regulator uprising fresh in his mind, Tryon appealed to the colonial secretary overseas for troops. The request was denied. For the present he contented himself with the enactment by legislature of a law authorizing the sheriffs of Albany and Charlotte counties (the heart of the rebellion) to call out the *posse comitatus* in emergencies. Under this ruling, sheriffs might mobilize any number of civilians, who were subject to a fine of seventy-five dollars and six months' imprisonment if they refused to serve.

At Albany, in July 1771, Sheriff Henry Ten Eyck acted on this authority, and summoned a force of about three hundred—among them a former Albany mayor, several city officials and lawyers. They had readily enlisted in what they expected would prove a hilarious junket.

As the force was gathered at Albany, the Green Mountain men gave the lash to a number of under-sheriffs and peace-justices. Allen headed a party—recalling the treatment accorded Fanning's property at Hillsboro—that fired a volley into Justice Munro's house, sending him post-haste to Albany.

Another object of disciplinary instruction was one Dr. Samuel Adams, who was hoisted in a chair to the top of a flagpole outside a tavern, and left twenty-five feet in the air for a day to ponder on his misdemeanors. They varied these acts with regular drills and target practice, reports of which were relayed to the Governor.

The Governor's answer was to offer £150 reward for the capture of Allen, and £50 for Seth Warner and five others, in the hope that some poor or dispossessed settler in the Grants might turn traitor and "artfully betray them."

Allen laughed at the posted rewards, and dared Tryon to follow him into the mountains. In rebuttal, early in 1772, the seven proscribed men inserted a burlesque proclamation in New England newspapers offering a bounty of five pounds "to anyone who should take and deliver John Kempe, Esq., Attorney-General of the colony of New York, to any officer in the militia of the Green Mountain Boys." In that notice they referred to the settlers as the "honest peasants of Bennington, patriotic and liege subjects of George III."

Ten Eyck advanced with his armed posse to arrest Brackenridge and take possession of his farm, a move of which Allen was notified in good time. The colonel had difficulty mustering three hundred of the Green Mountain organization, for the men were scattered on both sides of the mountains. Nineteen of them were stationed inside the farmhouse, and the others deployed on both sides of the road down which the sheriff would march, and behind a ridge that commanded the dwelling.

With a readiness that astonished the mountaineers, the sheriff's force of three hundred walked into the ambuscade. The Green Mountain Boys did not show themselves until after Ten Eyck had hammered on Brackenridge's door, demanding entry, and been told, "Attempt it, and you're a dead man!"

Ira Allen, the colonel's young brother, who was among Allen's force at the farm, with a fine hand at understatement recalled that at this moment, "the sheriff and his posse seeing the dangerous situation, *and not being interested in the dispute,* made a hasty retreat, so that a musket was not fired on either side."

The bloodless victory at Bennington gave the settlers heart. It had the effect also of adding to their ranks. Farmers volunteered for service whose acres lay many miles north of Bennington. And Allen's confidence led to a flamboyant and dangerous gesture. Despite the price on his head, he offered a bet that he would enter Albany's most popular taphouse alone. Warner and others tried to dissuade him, and urged that such a foolhardy trip would jeopardize their cause, but he found someone to accept the wager. He rode into Albany, tied his horse, and stalked into an inn in the center of the city.

There he seated himself in the middle of the taproom, bellowed for punch, made certain that everyone present "knew Ethan Allen was in the city," downed his drink with a ringing "Huzza for the Green Mountains!" and left in a challenging burst of laughter. No move was made to capture him, although £150 was a small fortune.

This solitary foray was more than Justice Munro could stomach after Allen and his henchmen had fired at his home. If it was expecting too much to capture the colonel of the Green Mountain Boys, one of his captains might be seized and made to serve as a deterrent to the others. Among those for whom a reward had been offered was Captain Remember Baker, a first cousin of Allen's. On the night of March 12, Munro with ten armed men surrounded Baker's home at Arlington. His door was battered in with an axe, Baker wounded on the head and arms by swords, his wife cut about the head and neck, and their small son wounded on the arm. In danger of bleeding and freezing to death, Baker was tossed upon a sleigh after his clothes were stripped from him, and driven toward Albany.

Even at that early stage of the organization, the Green Mountain Boys had an intelligence system, crude but fairly effective. Bennington is fifteen miles south of Arlington. An express rider galloped over high snowdrifts, raised the alarm and a force of ten men. They set off in pursuit. After covering thirty miles, their horses on the verge of collapse, they sighted the Munro party, which believed the pursuers to be the advance-guard of a large Green Mountain force.

Munro and his men abandoned Baker and the sleigh, and fled. Their victim was unconscious from loss of blood and exposure when the mountain men rode up. But the captain survived—to lose his life three years later in an Indian skirmish.

The brutality of Baker's seizure, and the senseless attack on his wife and small son, had much the same effect, though in greater degree, as the indictments for rioting. It brought new recruits to the Green Mountain ranks, and stiffened the men's determination. In an account of the raid written by Ethan Allen, and published several months afterward at Hartford in the Connecticut *Courant*, it was claimed that Munro had attempted to set the Baker farmhouse afire, that the men had stripped the house of all its valuables and cash, and had set a vicious dog on the captain, the whole episode in Allen's eye constituting a "wicked, inhuman, most barbarous, infamous, cruel, villainous and thievish act . . . a reproach, shame, disgrace &c. on the laws, restrictions, regulations, peace, manners, good order and economy, both of the laws of God and Man."

Munro again met with no success when he attempted to arrest Seth Warner. When the justice met the Green Moun-

tain captain on a road near Bennington, he seized his bridle
and called to his ten companions to subdue Warner. The
latter knocked Munro senseless with the flat of his sword,
and escaped. The peace justice, unhurt, reported to Tryon
that the Green Mountain "rioters [are] striking terror into
the whole country." He urged the invasion of a strong militia
or regular force which, after routing the refractory Green
Mountain Boys, (assuming they could be found), would
evict those settlers who continued in contempt of court. The
jubilant farmers of Poultney, meanwhile, awarded Warner
a hundred acres "for his Valor in Cutting the Head of Es-
quire Munro, the Yorkite."

Word of such a punitive expedition as Munro urged
reached Bennington. Allen and his aides hurriedly planned
the strategy to be employed if, as was reported, Governor
Tryon was moving upstream at the head of a force of British
troops. They called another meeting of delegates at Bennington, and the convention resolved that "it is our duty
to oppose Governor Tryon and his troops to the utmost of
our power." The committees of safety were instructed to
mobilize the members of the military association in their districts, and speed them to Bennington. Without opposition
from the small garrison nearby, Fort Hoosac was stripped
of its two cannon and mortar, and the pieces set up on the
southern approach to the town.

Allen's plan was the simplest defense of Bennington, together with another ambuscade after the model of the one
employed near the Brackenridge farm. He proposed that a
few sharpshooters be concealed in a narrow pass along the
Albany-Bennington road. When the invaders reached this

point, Ira Hill related, Ethan's orders were that "the Governor was to be pointed out, and the expert marksmen were to fire, one by one at him, until he fell from his horse." Another ambuscade was planned closer to Bennington to pick off other officers, while the main body of Green Mountain Boys were to await the British troopers—presumably, by this time, leaderless and demoralized—on the outskirts of Bennington, supported by the three artillery pieces. To his followers Allen's strategy seemed flawless.

But it had one major defect. The enemy did not arrive.

A scout had been sent ahead to Albany to learn the size of Tryon's force, the time of his advance on Bennington, and to commit to memory the faces of the officers selected for sudden death by ambush. He returned from a tour of the Albany taverns to report that while a force of British troops were wind-bound a few miles below Albany, they were destined for the garrisons of Oswego, Niagara and Detroit. Moreover, he said unhappily, Governor Tryon was not with them.

Allen admitted his disappointment. He had wanted the opportunity to demonstrate to Tryon, before the Governor fell from his mount, that the Green Mountain Boys were not to be intimidated by British regulars. But even if the battle did not materialize, the mobilization of the settlers had given Tryon pause. After the fiasco at Brackenridge's farm, the Governor decided to substitute mediation for force. To Parson Dewey and other insurgents at Bennington he addressed a conciliatory letter asking that they lay before him the reasons for their rebellious behavior. These reasons, he pledged, he would discuss "with deliberation and candor."

Any delegates from the Green Mountains would be assured of immunity—excepting, of course, four gentlemen named Allen, Baker, Warner and Cockran. In the case of the first two, the reward for their capture was raised another £100.

After the safety committees discussed the letter, Allen held a council of war. There was strong opposition at first to sending any delegate or delegation to Tryon. One of the captains charged that a few minutes prior to the Battle of Alamance, the year before, Tryon had ordered the execution of a Regulator emissary who had entered the Government lines under a flag of truce. In the end Captain Stephen Fay, an innkeeper, and his son, Dr. Jonas Fay, volunteered to carry a message to the Governor.

They took two messages, or replies. One was a response by Allen and the others for whose heads there were rewards. Written by Allen, it was blunt and forthright: "If we do not oppose the sheriff and his posse, he takes immediate possession of our farms and houses . . . there being no end to indictments against us so long as we act the bold and manly part . . . Though they style us rioters for opposing them, and seek to catch and punish us as such, yet in reality themselves are the rioters, the tumultuous, disorderly, stimulating faction, or in fine the land-jobbers . . . The transferring or alienation of property is a sacred prerogative of the true owners—kings and governors cannot intermeddle therewith."

The other response, on behalf of the settlers generally, recited the sheriff's seizures, urged the Governor to halt measures against the original settlers in the Grants, stressed the validity of the titles given by the province of New

Hampshire, and demanded an end to violence until the King could decide the controversy.

The Fays at Albany conferred with a committee of Tryon's council, and the committee made a favorable report to the Governor. He adopted its recommendations in July 1772. The Governor consented to a suspension of all civil and criminal suits against the men of the Grants until the King acted upon the dispute. Before that substantial victory was known at Bennington, the settlers had been bedeviling the sheriffs as a matter of routine duty. They had burned the log-cabins of several New York emigrants, or made them uninhabitable by carrying away their roofs. When the Fays returned to Bennington with the news, the Green Mountain men fired the cannon in celebration.

But the salvo to "universal peace and plenty, liberty and prosperity," and the proposal of toasts to Tryon, were premature. The resentment against the Governor and the land-speculators soon flared again. The Fays, father and son, had not suspected a joker in the agreement at Albany, and in the courtesies of Tryon and the Council members they had read more than existed. They learned that in the agreement there was nothing to prevent New Yorkers from claiming possession of lands which had been awarded to them in past decisions of the courts, nor anything forbidding these New York grantees from sending their surveyors to the Grants. The Governor had merely agreed not to prosecute pending suits. With this realization, the settlers learned that a surveyor named Kockburn was laying lines in several northern townships. Colonel Allen, charging Tryon with bad faith, collected a small party, went after the surveyor, smashed his levelling-rod and telescope, and threatened him with hanging. For good measure they dispossessed a number of New York emigrants, burned three log-houses, and destroyed the flour-mill of Colonel Reed of New York. His miller was warned not to repair it "on pain of suffering the displeasure of the Green Mountain Boys."

Another convention was called in October. There delegates adopted a prohibition to oppose a new effort of the Governor to achieve his ends by indirection. Recently he had appointed several settlers in the Grants to relatively lucrative civil jobs. The convention voted that whipping and banishment would be the lot of anyone within the disputed territory accepting office under the authority of the colony of New York. That ended Tryon's efforts at boring from within. It also made the schism between the territory and New York complete and final. Thenceforth the Grants conducted their affairs as an independent republic, administering laws of their own making, and remaining only theoretically loyal to the Crown. That anomalous status endured for five years, until the Grants, in 1777, declared their independence formally, and enacted their own constitution.

On the site of Colonel Reed's mill a block-fort was built, stocked with arms, and a small garrison posted. Another was built on the Winooski River. The settlers raised funds to send an agent to Europe to buy munitions.

When he heard of this, Tryon's alarm was considerable. He called on General Sir Frederick Haldimand to lead an expedition of Regulars to the Grants. But that official, preoccupied with keeping order among the French-Canadian sympathizers of the American colonials, vetoed the proposal.

He could not grow excited over the petty activities of a small group of mountain farmers.

Rebuffed by the military, Tryon turned again to the New York Assembly, appealing for legislation to terrorize the settlers into submission. The Governor was authorized to issue a proclamation calling upon all settlers who had resisted the sheriffs to surrender themselves to the justices of the peace within seventy days. The punishment for disobedience was the pronouncement, *in absentia*, of sentence of death by the Supreme Court. That extraordinary measure, which may well have been borrowed by Tryon from the Inquisition, served only to provoke another laugh from Allen. "They may *sentence* us to be hung for refusing to voluntarily place our necks in the halter; but how will the fools manage to hang a Green Mountain Boy before they catch him?"

The infiltration of New Yorkers continued to meet with reprisals. The punishment suffered by Benjamin Hough was typical. Hough was one of the settlers in the Grants who had accepted office from the Governor. When he refused to heed warnings, and attempted to discharge his duties as a justice of the peace, Green Mountain men seized him, and dragged him before the Committee of Safety at Sunderland. The Committee read him the resolution prohibiting inhabitants of the territory from holding office under New York.

Hough readily confessed he had accepted the post, but in defense said he believed in the validity of New York's claim to the Grants. More damaging to his case was the admission that he had supported the passage by the Assembly at Albany of the law under which settlers were outlawed and condemned to death without trial.

Ethan Allen

The sentence upon Hough: "That the prisoner be taken from the bar of the Committee of Safety, and be tied to a tree, and then, on his naked back, receive two hundred stripes; his back being dressed, he should depart out of the district, and on return, without special permission of the convention, to suffer death."

Settlers swarmed into Sunderland, undeterred by the deep snowdrifts, to witness the execution of the sentence. They packed into the village square, stacking their guns in a circle around the oak to which Hough was bound. The icy air was filled with their shouts as the whip fell on the magistrate's bared back. He had fainted long before the two-hundredth lash. When he recovered consciousness, he displayed an astonishing concern for formalities of the law. Would the Committee give him some written attestation that he had paid his penalty? The Committee members felt that the welts on his back were a receipt in full. Hough insisted. Allen and Warner executed this certificate:

Sunderland, 30th January, 1775.
This may certify the inhabitants of the New-Hampshire Grants, that Benjamin Hough hath this day received a full punishment for his crimes committed against the country; and our inhabitants are ordered to give him, the said Hough, a free and unmolested passport toward the city of New York, or to the westward of our Grants, he behaving himself as becometh.

Given under our hands the day and date aforesaid,
Ethan Allen
Seth Warner.

Every prospect of reconciliation with New York had vanished. Much the same might be said of the likelihood of peace between the colonies and Britain. The bloodshed at Lexington was only seventy-nine days away.

On April 11, 1775, a convention was held on the east side of the mountains, at Westminister, where William French, a young farmer of Brattleborough, had been killed the preceding month in a clash between Whigs and royalists. The meeting was the last before the outbreak of the Revolution. There it was resolved "that it is the duty of said inhabitants, as predicated on the eternal and immutable law of self-preservation, to wholly renounce and resist the administration of the government of New York." Although Lexington now was but eight days distant, the resolution referred to such time as "his most Gracious Majesty in Council shall settle this controversy." The New Hampshire grantees had been so engrossed in safeguarding their farms that most of them had paid small attention to the quarrel brewing with the mother country. But not so Allen and Warner.

By early May that pair were leading a detachment of Green Mountain Boys in a successful attack on Fort Ticonderoga. The Grants' differences with New York disappeared in the common struggle against England. Ethan was captured by the British in the reckless September attempt to seize Montreal, and was taken prisoner to Falmouth. There he appeared in "a short fawn-skin jacket, double-breasted, an undervest and breeches of sagathy, worsted stockings, a decent pair of shoes, two plain shirts, and a red worsted cap . . . this was all the clothing I had in which to make my appearance in England."

He was not exchanged until May, 1778, at New York, and then was immediately breveted colonel by Washington. He was ordered home to regain his health, and soon after his arrival at Bennington Allen was given command of the "Vermont" militia, with the rank of major-general.

Home from the wars. Here was the opportunity to resume the fight against the New York settlers. In September he presented the claims of Vermont to state independence to the Continental Congress at Philadelphia—the new name of "Vermont" had been adopted the year before. Prefacing their petition, the settlers stated themselves to be "at all times ready, in conjunction with their brethren in the United States, to contribute their full proportion towards maintaining the present just war, against the fleets and armies of Great Britain."

Most of the members of the Congress knew of the feats of the Green Mountain Boys in the Revolution. Some of the Grants men had been at Bunker Hill. They had proved themselves reliable allies. The Vermont petition had the support of New Hampshire, and it was approved also by Connecticut and Massachusetts.

But the New York members were adamant against creating a fourteenth State of a fertile district, nine thousand miles square, that had been under their jurisdiction since 1764, even though that was an authority emanating from the Crown, and even though the Grants had successfully ignored or resisted the Albany government. Another and more personal reason for the hostility of the New York members was that a few had been given land in the New Hampshire Grants. And although in the War they were fighting on the same side as the Green Mountain Boys, they believed that their land claims were valid. The New York delegation proved itself strong enough to defeat consideration by Congress of the demand for independence and for seats in the national legislature.

The "independent republic of Vermont," in 1778, elected Thomas Chittenden its first governor, and Ira Allen its secretary of state. Before this, and at Ethan Allen's recommendation, the "republic" had been narrowed to contain only the territory west of the Connecticut River. That move had two purposes: to impress Congress with the geographical homogeneity of the Vermont republic, and to avoid disputes with New Hampshire.

The two Allens and Governor Chittenden now found it more difficult to lead and control the farmers than in the old days when they fought a single foe. Governor George Clinton of New York made a favorable impression on many setlers when, issuing a proclamation again claiming jurisdiction over the republic, he agreed to recognize the validity of the grants made originally by New Hampshire. Allen and others toured the countryside exhorting the farmers to hold firm to their right to self-government.

They had some success. Congress was growing nervous over the course of the war. In the emergency it did not feel it could grant statehood to Vermont at the risk of alienating New York. In a weak effort to browbeat the republic into accepting the jurisdiction of New York, the Continental Congress adopted a resolution declaring the conduct of Vermont "to be subversive of the peace and welfare of the United States"—despite the spectacular loyalty of the settlers to the Continental cause.

To that resolution General Allen and Governor Chittenden replied that if Vermont were not to be included as an independent unit, it was entitled to treat with Britain toward an end of hostilities. Of doing this, they said, they had no intention, although it was their right; but they would again apply to the Congress for admission. Although this hint of negotiations at some later time with England—a third of whose force was immediately north of Vermont—gave delegates at Independence Hall a severe attack of nerves, Congress re-tabled a consideration of the Vermont application.

The difficulties of Vermont were well known to General Haldimand, in command of the British troops in Canada. Nor was the meaning of Allen's second rebuff at the hands of a vacillating Congress in 1780 and of Governor Chittenden's reference to the republic's right to deal separately with the enemy, lost on Haldimand. He concluded that the citizens of Vermont were smarting under snubs administered by Congress, and that their leaders might be persuaded to detach the republic from the United States.

The first overture to this end was a letter to Ethan Allen, dated March 30, 1780, from one of Haldimand's aides, Colonel Beverly Robinson. This is the first of a celebrated correspondence between Allen and the British, the basis of a still-unsettled controversy as to whether he and other leaders planned to make Vermont a province of Britain.

Colonel Robinson's letter:

I have often been informed that you and most of the inhabitants of Vermont are opposed to the wild and chimerical scheme of the Americans in attempting to separate from Great Britain and establish an independent government of their own; and that you would willingly assist in uniting America to Great Britain, and in restoring that happy constitution so wantonly and unadvisedly destroyed. If I have been rightly informed, and these should be your sentiments and inclination, I beg that you will communicate to me without reserve whatever proposals you would wish to make to the commander-in-chief; and I hereby promise that I will faithfully lay them before him according to your directions, and flatter myself I can do it with as good effect as any person whatever. I can make no proposals to you until I know your sentiments; but think, upon your taking an active part, and embodying the inhabitants of Vermont under the crown of England, you may obtain a separate government under the King. If you should think proper to send a friend here with proposals to the general, he shall be protected, and allowed to return whenever he pleases.

Allen conferred with Chittenden. The invitation went unanswered. Two months later, when the British had increased their troops in Canada to ten thousand, Colonel Robinson repeated his offer to the Green Mountain general. The two letters were forwarded by Allen to the President of the Congress, on which he hoped they would exert sufficient pressure to bring Vermont into the Confederacy. He wrote:

. . . I do not hesitate to say I am fully grounded in opin-

ion, that Vermont has an indubitable right to agree on terms of a cessation of hostilities with Great Britain, provided the United States persist in rejecting her application for a union with them. For Vermont would be, of all people, most miserable were she obliged to defend the independence of the United claiming States, and they be, at the same time, at full liberty to overturn and ruin the independence of Vermont. When Congress consider the circumstances of the state, they will, I am persuaded, be more surprised that I have transmitted them the enclosed letters, than that I have kept them in custody so long; for I am as resolutely determined to defend the independence of Vermont, as Congress is that of the United States; and rather than fail, I will retire with the hardy Green-Mountain Boys into the desolate caverns of the mountains, and wage war with human nature at large.

The tone of Colonel Robinson's second letter was less warm than the first. The reason was that the British had determined upon an advance southward from Canada, and they had very little fear of opposition, since they were concentrated in great strength at the head of Lake Champlain, near the northwest corner of Vermont. The British general's plan was to invade the northern part of the confederacy while Washington was preoccupied in the south.

To slow up the advance, Governor Chittenden sent an emissary to Haldimand proposing an exchange of prisoners. This was acceptable to the enemy, and Colonel Ira Allen and Major Joseph Fay were appointed the Vermont commissioners for the exchange negotiations.

During the period of exchange, the British again suggested

that Vermont accept the sovereignty of Britain in return for autonomous provincehood. There are a good many letters and reports which show that Ira Allen and Fay gave General Haldimand the definite impression that they could lead a strong separatist sentiment in the republic, but that they did so only to keep the British at bay. With the aid of the governor, the two Allens, and five others in the secret, Haldimand was kept in Canada, awaiting from day to day favorable action by the Vermont leaders, who were fertile in reasons for one or another delay. But the eight Vermonters could not have held up Haldimand much longer when word came, October 19, of the surrender at Yorktown.

Yet Vermont maintained its independence for more than another decade. In New York there were attempts made to obtain the legislature's recognition of Vermont independence, which would have smoothed the way for admission into the Continental union. And Vermont, growing wise in politics, made a number of grants to influential New Yorkers, among them Governor Clinton and John Jay. The republic obtained the support, for example, of Hamilton, and General Philip Schuyler, who recognized the fact that, charter or no charter, Vermont was separated from New York, and had been since 1777. In 1789 New York and Vermont appointed commissioners to seek a settlement. The Albany delegation whittled down their claims to $30,000. That was precisely their nuisance value to Vermont. On March 4, 1791, after fourteen years of independent rule, the republic was received into the Union. The War of the New Hampshire Grants was over.

And Ethan Allen was dead near Burlington. He had not lived to see the Green Mountain Republic admitted into the union, but his objective was very nearly accomplished fact on that early morning of February 12, 1789, when, returning to his farm atop a load of hay, the rebel fell over, dead of apoplexy. His role had been the most spectacular in the long struggle to prevent a land-grab which, excepting the nation's thefts from the Indians and the Texas annexation, was the baldest in post-colonial history.

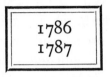

SHAYS' REBELLION

ON THE LAST TUESDAY IN THE MONTH OF
August, 1786, the somnolent town of Northampton in Massachusetts was awakened by the shouts of an armed mob that
had gathered overnight. If the uproar at that early hour were
not impious enough to this Congregational bywater, its inhabitants were subjected at breakfast-time to the cacophony
of beating drums and querulous fifes, and to the tramp of
fifteen hundred men raising clouds of dust in endless parading before the courthouse.

Drums and fifes and marching men had been common
enough during the Revolution. But that had ended with
Cornwallis' surrender five years before. The town's invaders,
some carrying muskets, swords or bludgeons, were not concerned now with the iniquities of George III. They were
concerned with preventing the opening in the forenoon of
the fall session of the Court of Common Pleas.

Shortly before noon, three men rode through the mob,
and dismounted at the foot of the courthouse steps. They
were Eleazar Porter, John Bliss, and Samuel Mather (a descendant of the Boston zealots of Andros' day), the three

justices of the court. With an air of judicial aloofness they climbed the steps to the bench. But the arch detachment of the trio was no passport beyond the entrance, which was barred by a score of men with guns. There the justices were told that the mob was in possession of the courthouse, and then they were given a petition.

The petition demanded the suspension of the court session. In his minutes of the day, the clerk reported that "the Court having considered thereof, thought proper to open the same [session] at the House of Capt. Sam'l Clark, Innholder in Northampton, & having continued all matters pending in said court . . . adjourned, without day."

After this bit of face-saving in the local tavern, the justices untethered their horses, and returned to their homes. The mob, which appeared "with less insolence and violence, and with more sobriety and good order, than is generally expected from such a miscellaneous crowd bent on such an unlawful errand," remained in the courthouse until midnight, and then dispersed.

The Court of Common Pleas was restricted to civil suits, but it had the authority to enforce payment of debts and taxes. Once judgment was obtained against a debtor, the court could levy against anything he owned. The reasoning of the band that descended on Northampton was elementary enough. If the court did not sit, the court could not levy against them: ergo, prevent the court from sitting.

The Northampton incident was the start of the epidemic uprising known to history as Shays' Rebellion, although it was led by others beside Captain Daniel Shays. Its causes followed the pattern more or less of the Regulator rebellion, but it did not arouse the same degree of sympathy as the North Carolina movement, possibly because it occurred so shortly after the colonies had won their independence in an exhausting struggle. The Constitutional Convention at Philadelphia was still a year in the future. Even Washington, whose patience and understanding were certainly phenomenal, wrote his confidant and former aide-de-camp, David Humphreys, "For God's sake, tell me what is the cause of these commotions? Do they proceed from licentiousness, British influence disseminated by Tories, or real grievances which admit of redress? . . . It was but the other day that we were shedding our blood to obtain the constitutions under which we now live—constitutions of our own choice and making—and now we are unsheathing the sword to overturn them."

The grievances of the farmers in western Massachusetts were real enough. The eight-year attritive struggle with England had been followed by the inevitable post-war depression, and its burdens fell most acutely, as had those of the war, upon the poor. Rufus King, a member of Congress from Massachusetts, in a letter to John Adams, wrote that the State taxes for 1786 would appropriate a third of the income of its citizens, a figure that was, he believed, "beyond what providence would authorize." It was largely raised by that familiar and inequitable device, the poll tax. An anonymous complainant, conveying his bitterness to the Massachusetts *Centinel*, declared that "to have the Collectors call for twenty dollars taxes at a time is more money than we ever see at once."

Aside from the State taxes—a slice of which, naturally,

went to support the insecure Washington government—the ebb-tide of war had left a morass of private debt, in the adjustment and liquidation of which the courts, unaware of the economic temperature of the day, were often inconsistent. The courts enforced the sale of farms, at times, and most often the proceeds failed to discharge the owners' indebtedness, and left farmers without means of ever discharging it—or of eating; and they went to prison, if the courts so directed. Moreover, the entire civil-court mechanism that operated in cases of non-payment of debt and taxes was wasteful and expensive. Fees were exorbitant, the salaries of court officials disproportionate. Often when a debtor possessed property sufficient in value to pay his creditors, or pay some of them, there was insufficient paper money for the transaction, and the jailing of the debtor was the only satisfaction open to the money-lender. In the year of the first scattered uprisings that compose the Shays rebellion, 1786, there were as many men in jail at Concord for debt as the total of all other convictions—even though post-war Massachusetts was noted for its indifference to the law.

The delegates of farmers held a succession of meetings and informal conventions to draft the familiar petitions, and to decide upon action. Notice of these gatherings was usually made by circulars, broadcast over the counties by mountain messengers who posted them in the town halls, the churches (if the language of the broadsheet was seemly), in the small stores and on barn walls. Occasionally two counties would join in one of these gatherings. On August 22, for example, delegates from fifty towns in Worcester and Hampshire counties assembled at Hatfield. The usual procedure, after the election of a presiding officer, was to "resolve that this meeting is constitutional." In Bristol County one such convention agreed to employ force, if necessary, to combat all courts hearing suits for debt, because such trials were involving "a great part of the people in beggary and misery." In Worcester County the delegates complained of court fees, the cost of litigation in the Courts of Common Pleas—but resolved against the employment of force for redress. But the subsequent rising at Northampton, whatever the sentiment among the moderates against mob-action, crystallized the state-wide impatience with the legislature at Boston, which had refused to act on the petitions. Dr. Jonathan Judd, a Northampton minister, noted in his diary after the raid that "all is again afloat. No law, nor order. Prison full of criminals, but none can be punished . . . What the consequences of these things, none can tell. Destruction seems to await us."

The immediate sequel to the ruckus at Northampton was a proclamation by Governor James Bowdoin calling upon all the authorities, civil and military, to suppress vigorously any further "treason," and advancing the convention of the legislature to September 17. But this was no deterrent.

In the week after the Northampton raid, a force of about three hundred descended on Worcester, and seized the courthouse: the Common Pleas Court adjourned, also *sine die*, and the Court of Sessions was similarly interrupted. On September 11 another band acted to prevent the courts from meeting in Middlesex County. An identical raid occurred at Concord several days later, after the Governor had recalled his order mustering the militia.

The dissidents went a step further at Great Barrington, where eight hundred of them not only made it impossible for the courts to sit, but, for good measure, released all prisoners in the jail for debt. And of the four judges at Great Barrington, three had to agree to hand down no decisions until the "grievances of the people" were resolved. Forcing jurists from their sworn duty, whether the judges were corrupt or not, at the point of a gun was direct action with a vengeance, and intolerable in a society with any pretense to government. Plainly a collision was a matter of time only, and of not much time.

The rioters at this juncture evidently realized that their performances constituted treason, and that the authorities might be expected to abandon further leniency. Treason against the State, then as now, was punishable by death (although the capital sentence was not mandatory). If to save their homes they had estopped the civil courts, to save their necks it seemed logical now that they must effect the suspension of the criminal courts, although up to this time no indictments finding treason had been returned against any of the insurgents.

They made no effort to keep their plans secret. The Supreme Judicial Court was scheduled to sit at Springfield, Hampshire County, on September 26. One of the leaders against the Government in that county was Daniel Shays, of Pelham. So far as is known, he had not been a member of the armed bands that had captured the courthouses at Northampton, Worcester and elsewhere.

Western view of the Armory Buildings, Springfield.

At this time Shays was thirty-nine. He was born at Hopkinton, Massachusetts, and his origins and his early life were humble. His early preoccupation was the soldiery; he armed his playmates with wooden swords and guns, and marched them up and down the village green. With the outbreak of the Revolution he was quick to answer the emergency at Lexington, where he saw action for eleven days. He was also at Bunker Hill, and was promoted and cited for his conduct there. He saw action later at Ticonderoga, Stony Point and Saratoga. He received a captain's commission in 1777 in the Fifth Massachusetts. The existing evidence is that he was generally liked by his men, who found him considerate, but there are also records of a sudden loss of popularity when he sold an elaborate sword presented to him by Lafayette. But there is credible evidence that he had to sell it in order to eat. In 1780 Shays resigned his commission in resentment over criticism of his sale of the Frenchman's gift, and he established himself and his wife at Pelham. There he held several public offices, serving on the Committee of Safety and as warden, and deriving a small income from farming.

After his Revolutionary career, he found life in a village somewhat tasteless, relieved only by the occasional companionship of the fabulous Stephen Burroughs, "The Eternal Scamp," counterfeiter, seducer and preacher-extraordinary (who, just before the Northampton raid, attempted to escape from the jail there by setting it afire). The gradually swelling movement against the Government, however, offered an outlet for Shays' energies. His first appearance as a leader, and then a reluctant one (he refused to be called "General"), was in the mob of about a thousand, about one-half of the number armed, at Springfield on that September morning when the Supreme Court was scheduled to convene.

It should be noted here that nine years before, in 1777, the Federal Government had leased ten acres from the town for a national arsenal and magazine, which now contained at least 450 tons of military stores, including 7,000 small-arms with bayonets, 300 barrels of powder, a substantial amount of shot and shell, a foundry for casting brass cannon and a strong magazine.

There had been talk among the insurgents, half in earnest and most of it irresponsible, of seizing the arsenal. General Henry Knox, the Secretary of War, in a confidential report to Congress on September 20 said that "great numbers of people in Massachusetts and the neighboring States . . . avow the principle of annihilating all debts public and private . . . It is my firm conviction unless the present commotions are checked with a strong hand, that an armed tyranny may be established on the ruins of the present constitution." He asked for eight hundred men to be added to the United States Army, which then numbered only seven hundred.

Since the insurgents had made no effort to keep their plans secret, counting on public sentiment to support them, Governor Bowdoin ordered out the Hampshire County militia under the command of General William Shephard. On September 23, three days before the court was to meet, a militia force of 120 took possession of the Courthouse to forestall any similar tactic by the farmers. By the 26th, there were fully 1,000 militia in the town, most of them gathered outside the court building. The judges took the benches, and at once were confronted with an absurd and ironic situation. The

Court could transact no business because most of the Grand Jury were in uniform, guarding the Courthouse so that it might discharge its duties. A summons for another panel proved ineffective, because no one wanted to serve while two armed forces opposed each other in the town. After three futile days the justices withdrew. Before that, a number of the militia companies had gone over openly to Shays' forces, encouraging the leader and leading him to strike a high-handed attitude to the Court. He sent the justices a "request," demanding first that no indictments be returned against his men for past or present behavior; second he said that as a condition of his withdrawing his force the Court must promise not to try civil suits unless trial were agreed to by both parties; and third that the militia at the Courthouse and stationed before the arsenal should not be paid for their present service in the field.

The Court had the courage to retort that none of these conditions would be met, that the laws would be observed as laid down in the statutes. Nevertheless—it adjourned.

The insurgents paraded continuously in front of the militia guards, challenging them, according to some of the records, with the proverbial chip. In fact, it appears Shays had difficulty making them withhold their fire; many of them were young, intemperate and frankly spoiling for a fight. At the close of the third day, General Shephard decided he would utilize his force more effectively as reinforcements at the arsenal, and he evacuated the Courthouse. The farmers promptly appropriated the building. After a day devoted chiefly, it is related, to "hurrahs for Shays," they dispersed to await the next call. It was a victory for Shays.

In leaving Springfield, the judges had announced that the next regular session of the Supreme Court would not be held, as was usual, at Great Barrington in Berkshire County. This move may have resulted from a natural desire to appear conciliatory, or it is possible that the Court had really been intimidated by Shays. In any event, the rioters believed they saw a ruse, that the Court would meet and adjourn in a shower of indictments against them. Accordingly they rode into Great Barrington on the appointed day, but found that the Court, abiding by its announcement, was not sitting, nor would it attempt to sit. But the crowd of nearly 1,500 grew obstreperous, and they gave vent to their frustration by beating State officials, firing at a number of Government supporters, searching homes and emptying the jail of men imprisoned for debt. With drawn bayonets they entered the home of Deputy Sheriff Ezra Kellogg, who had fled from his home a few minutes before, and sought to terrorize his wife into revealing his hiding-place. Shays succeeded in dissuading the men from demolishing the Courthouse, but it was becoming clear to residents of western Massachusetts, many of them sympathetic to the farmers' cause, that the authority of Shays, Luke and Elijah Day, Benjamin Ely and the other leaders over the men was far from absolute. The disorders at Great Barrington lost the insurgents considerable support of a tacit nature, and harmed the cause by provoking in county newspapers such sentiments as "Monarchy is better than the Tyranny of the Mob."

The legislature and the Governor were weaker in appearance than in fact. Secretary of War Knox feared that the State militia would be unable to smother a rebellion, and

indeed feared an attempt at secession from the Confederation. He wanted Federal military intervention, if only to
safeguard the Springfield arsenal. In the path of intervention,
however, there were two considerable obstacles; one, the
lack of funds at Washington (eventually circumvented by a
bond issue of $500,000 supported by a levy on the States, to
which a few well-to-do New Englanders were urged con-
fidentially to subscribe—at six per cent.—unless they wished
to see anarchy); second, the possibility that Shays and his
men, learning that the United States Government was raising a force for service in Massachusetts, would lose no time
in seizing the weakly-held armament-depot at Springfield.

On October 23 (1786), however, the Boston legislature
approved the raising of troops in Massachusetts for Federal
service, after a deal of oratory about the necessity of an enlarged Federal army to protect the State against hostile Indians. This was, of course, legislative shrubbery to disguise
the real reason for the additional troops. But the ostensible
nearness of another Indian War did not delude the insurgents, to judge by letters of the day. Even in the open legislature at Boston, Elbridge Gerry rose to remark, with the
suspiciousness characteristic of him, that "some of the
country members laugh, and say the Indian War is only a
political one to obtain a standing army." And Major William
North, inspector of Federal troops, who was then in Massachusetts, reported to Secretary Knox that "the people here
smell a rat, that the troops about to be raised are more for the
Insurgents than the Indians."

Nevertheless the difficult task of raising the Massachusetts
quota of the additional Federal recruits began, under the

direction of Major-General Henry Jackson of the State militia. It was slow and discouraging work, owing partly to the sympathy in many districts with the grievances of the insurgents, and partly to the recollection of former soldiers to whom the government was still in arrears for services during the Revolution.

The legislature's censure of the raids on the courts, its apparent hesitancy to rectify the most glaring injustices, and Governor Bowdoin's summoning of the militia all served further to arouse Shays, Day, Ely, Luddington, and the others. Their answer was another torrent of petitions into Boston, reciting their complaints once again. Chief among these was the existence of the Senate, which they wanted abolished, the disproportionate representation in the lower house, the lack of annual elections, the methods of tax collection, and the size of the magistrates' salaries, which in a few districts amounted to £1,100 annually.

On October 23, the same day that the legislature had approved Federal recruiting in the State, Shays at his Pelham headquarters circulated his first military order to the selectmen of Hampshire County. Since, he wrote, the legislature had resolved to punish those who had righteously sought to halt the continued travesty of justice in the courts, the sole alternative was to mobilize their adherents, to "see that they were well armed and equipped with sixty rounds each man, and to be ready to turn out at a minute's warning; likewise, to be properly organized with officers."

Daniel Shays had little education, and like most soldiers he was cynical about the value of life. As a youth, it has been noted, he marched his companions in military drills. With a few others, in the fall of 1786, he espoused a popular cause, which is an undeniable advantage to any leader.

But at this point Shays—"a man of no cultural background, little education, and not much ability," to cite the conclusion of James Truslow Adams—was seized with a kind of military *folie de grandeur*. Some small patience, some political forbearance if not finesse, might very probably have drawn satisfaction from a legislature that was, if not frightened, convinced now that the petitions were more than empty gestures, that their authors represented men who were both serious and courageous. Indeed, the legislature in Boston had at last begun to act: the costs of court processes were reduced, and because of the shortage of paper money it was decreed that back taxes could be paid in commodities. But Shays' defiance and his order to the selectmen, which was tantamount to mobilization against the State, had stiffened the backs of the legislators, and they promptly endorsed the Governor's demand for suspension of the habeas corpus act, empowered him to imprison the rebellious leaders with bail, authorized a return to public flogging as an emergency deterrent, and legalized seizure of the insurgents' property. But as a final bid for peace a full pardon was offered anyone who submitted immediately to the Government and took an oath of allegiance.

The dissidents' answer to this was to return in another raid to Worcester, where on November 21 the Court of Sessions was prevented from sitting and returning treason indictments. Bowdoin's riposte was an order to the militia for readiness for immediate action, and the issuance of warrants against the insurgent leaders. The rebellion, the Governor feared, was spreading to the eastern counties—uncomfortably close to home. So far there was comparatively little economic discontent in that end of the State, where a mercantile trade flourished. The militia were on duty when the Court of Common Pleas opened at Cambridge on November 28; no insurgents appeared, because their leaders had been promised by the town's representatives that the militia would not be mustered if they, the insurgents, agreed to stay away. Their absence encouraged Bowdoin, and he despatched a mounted detachment to arrest the leaders in the east. Three of five ringleaders were captured at Concord, and in one of these militia forays Job Shattuck (the leader of the September raid into Middlesex County) was severely wounded. The trio were jailed at Boston, and the spurt of uprising in the east appeared at an end. Both Governor Bowdoin and Secretary Knox, however, still saw the danger in the western counties, particularly to the arsenal at Springfield, only twenty miles distant from Shays' headquarters to the northeast at Pelham.

General Shephard, in charge of the militia body at Springfield, now gave notice that he felt obliged to arm his forces from the Government stores, whence he appropriated five hundred small-arms, three field-pieces and a howitzer—after baldly demanding the key from a perplexed Army representative.

But Shays preferred to march southeast to Worcester. He had with him at least a thousand men. It is indicative of the sentiment prevailing in Worcester County, at least, that he had little trouble in finding billets for this sizeable force in and around the county-seat. It appears that Shays' plan was to collect a larger force in Hampshire County before advancing upon Springfield, where, if all went·well, he could arm them at the Government's expense. News in that day, and that bitter time of year, travelled slowly, and the insurgent leader could not know how precarious General Shephard's position was at the arsenal, only forty-five miles away. Had Shays known, it is certain the outcome of the rebellion would have been very different, and the secession that Secretary Knox feared might have been declared.

But the news he did receive at Worcester was discouraging. The insurgent force there had scarcely had time to rest in the barns about the town when word came of the arrest and imprisonment at Boston of their three leaders in Middlesex County late the month before.

The weather had a marked effect on the morale of the men, but the schism that now developed also lessened the collective initiative. They split over a proposal to march immediately upon Boston and free the imprisoned men. Shays, sufficiently the military realist to know that he could not hope to take the State capital, persuaded the hotheads against a fantastic adventure.

But a good many of his men had had their fill of winter campaigning, and set off for their farms. From the news of the arrest of Shattuck and the others the leaders concluded that Bowdoin's sudden and unwonted energy would result in the expedition of a punitive force against them. With his remaining men, on December 9, Shays retired fifteen miles northeast to Rutland, in the same county, an exhausting "retreat from Moscow" in miniature.

Writing of that retreat two years later, George Richards Minot, the clerk of the Massachusetts House of Representatives, declared it was such as to reduce Shays to the point of deserting his men. The charge is unsupported, and it is not credibly mentioned elsewhere in the records dealing with the rebellion. However, thus Minot:

"The retreat of these unhappy men, though less peaceable than their assembling, was attended with such distress, as rendered them objects of pity. Some were actually frozen to death, and all of them were exposed to the inclemencies of the severest winter that had happened for many years. These difficulties were heightened by a scarcity of provisions, and, we may suppose, by an unwelcome reception among some persons, who considered them as the fomenters of sedition. Their cause during this whole expedition to Worcester must have worn an unfavorable aspect in their own view. Indeed this idea seemed to make a deep impression upon Shays himself, if he was sincere in a conversation which happened about this time, between him and a confidential officer of government. Shays was asked by this officer, who left it optional with him to answer the question or not, 'Whether, if he had an opportunity, he would accept of a pardon, and leave his people to themselves?' To which Shays answered, 'Yes—in a moment.' Upon a communication of this conversation to the Governor and Council, they empowered the officer to tell Shays that in case he would immediately leave the insurgents, and engage to conduct as a good citizen in future, he might be assured that he should be protected; and in case he should be convicted by any Judicial Court, that he should receive pardon from the Governor and Council. But the commission was afterwards returned, no opportunity having appeared for the execution of it."

Meanwhile, with Shays momentarily hibernating at Rutland, three hundred insurgents prevented the sitting at Springfield of the Court of Common Pleas and the Court of General Sessions scheduled for December 26, by warning in a message of "very disagreeable consequences . . . in case of non-compliance." In view of the 1,000 militiamen now at Springfield, well equipped from the Government arsenal, the justices' timidity is surprising, unless we think that Governor Bowdoin was still willing to arbitrate, or, as is more likely, that he was waiting until Major-General Jackson had recruited a Federal force in the State. Whatever the reason, with the reappearance of the insurgents at Springfield, Bowdoin decided he had had more than enough.

The Governor declared that Massachusetts was in rebellion—the legislature had adjourned—and he called for an army of 4,400 to serve thirty days only in suppressing sedition. The January (1787) sessions of the Worcester County courts were due to open on the 23d. The cost of paying and provisioning the force, £40,000, was advanced in twenty-four hours by a few Boston businessmen, who were eventually repaid. Bowdoin realized the unlikelihood of receiving any prompt military aid from Washington. A crisis was now at hand. To command the force he selected Major-General Benjamin Lincoln, who had served with considerable valor in the Revolutionary War.

To explain the events which had led him to call for a relatively huge militia force, the Governor published an address to citizens on January 12. Shays, Day, Thomas Grover and other leaders abandoned the drafting of any more petitions. They had no direction to go now but forward. To their officers throughout Worcester County they sent a general order mobilizing their respective commands, armed and with provisions for ten days, and summoning most of the contingents to Pelham by January 19. The time for direct action had arrived, their manifesto stated, since "the Governor and his adherents" had decided to uphold the courts "by the point of the sword . . . [and] to crush the powers of the people at one bold stroke."

Major-General Lincoln arrived with most of his force at Worcester on January 22. The courts opened without disorders the next day. Shays and his aides had realized late that their one hope for success rested in seizing the Springfield arsenal before Lincoln's force arrived there. Shays had wasted no time in attempting to prevent the court sessions at Worcester. The following day, January 24, Shays reached Wilbraham, six miles east of Springfield, with nearly a thousand men, putting himself between Lincoln and Shephard, and approaching the arsenal along the Boston Road.

Captain Day, by January 21, was at West Springfield with nearly six hundred men described as the "most resolute of the regulators"—the North Carolina word was still in popular use—awaiting a junction with Shays, bearing down on the arsenal from the other side of the Connecticut River. About three miles to the north, near the present town of Chicopee, was another insurgent force of four hundred under the command of Colonel Eli Parsons. Thus the insurgents totalled about 1,800, threatening the arsenal from the east, west and north, as compared to General Shephard's force of 1,100. Even though the latter was better armed, since he had had access to Government stores, Shays seemed in a fair way to victory, at least if he could combine forces before Lincoln arrived. General Lincoln was at least two days away.

On January 24, the day Shays and his force arrived at Wilbraham, he sent a message across the Connecticut to Day, now to the west of Springfield. He said he was advancing on the arsenal the next day, January 25, and he pressed Day to join forces with him. The message reached Day safely, but not its reply. This told Shays that Day could not effect a junction before the 26th. The response was intercepted, in some fashion falling into General Shephard's hands. Nothing could have had more serious consequences for Shays. He assumed that Day was joining him the next day, while Day for his part was elated at the prospect of merging forces the day after. Finally, to make conditions ideal for the insurgents, General Shephard knew that the next day he need defend the arsenal against only one of the three converging forces. He could therefore afford to ignore an ultimatum that reached him the next morning, January 25, from the over-confident Shays. This demanded (no longer in the form of a petition):

1. That the militia in the Springfield arsenal immediately lay down their arms;

2. That these arms be deposited in the "public stores," in the custody of authorized officers, to be returned to their owners at the "termination of the present contest."

3. That the troops be returned to their homes on parole.

General Shephard was not intimidated by the *bravura* phrases of this document, the introduction to which stated that "the body of the people assembled in arms, adhering to the first principles in natural self-preservation, do in the most peremptory manner demand——" Shays was also active as a letter-writer. To slacken Lincoln's advance to the rescue of Shephard, he wrote the former on the same day, suggesting a compromise: that if the militia were immediately mustered out of service, insurgent prisoners released and none in the rebellion punished, his followers would ground their arms and return to their homes, to await a peaceful resolution of their difficulties by legislative means. Since Shays, however, did not wait for an answer from General Lincoln before marching on the arsenal, five miles away, it may be taken that the offer was merely an attempt to waste the militia commander's time in negotiations. Lincoln was not misled.

Confident of meeting with Day's force, Shays on the 25th marched his column into Springfield, arriving at a point near the arsenal about four o'clock in the afternoon. General Shephard had been warned of the advance by Sheriff Asoph King, who had galloped from Wilbraham over the crusted snowbanks, arriving well in advance of the insurgent leader, with the legs of his mount "streaming with blood." Thus the commander at the arsenal, while he might have been in an unpleasant position had he not intercepted the Shays-Day message, now cared little when Lincoln might arrive. He was so sure of victory, if it came to an assault on the arsenal, that he sent Shays two messages warning him to advance no further.

En route over the deep snows, an icy wind full in their faces, Shays' men nevertheless seemed in high spirits, confident of victory, of securing the arsenal, of hot grog soon to be had in Springfield. Repeatedly the shout arose, "Hurrah for Shays!" One of Shephard's emissaries, Captain Samuel Buffington, who had been a fellow officer of Shays' in the Revolution, reminded the insurgent leader that he, Buffington, was engaged in the defence of his country.

Shay: "Then, sir, we're on the same side."

Buffington: "We shall take very different parts, I imagine."

Shays: "The part I will take is the hill on which the arsenal stands."

General Shephard's report to Governor Bowdoin, written the next day after the smoke had cleared, is an excellent summary of what happened:

". . . Shays, who was at the head of about 1,200 men, marched yesterday afternoon towards the public buildings in battle-array. He marched his men in open column by platoons . . . He still proceeded on his march, until he approached within 250 yards of the arsenal. He then made a halt. I immediately sent Maj. Lyman, one of my Aids, and Captain Buffington to inform him not to march his troops any nearer the arsenal on his peril, as I was stationed here by order of your Excellency and the Secretary of War, for defence of the public property; in case he did, I should certainly fire on him and his men . . .

"Shays immediately put his troops in motion & marched on rapidly near one hundred yards. I then ordered Maj. Stephens, who commanded the artillery, to fire on them; he accordingly did. The two first shot he endeavored to over-shoot them, in hopes they would have taken warning without firing among them, but it had no effect upon them. Maj. Stephens then directed his shot through the center of his column. The fourth or fifth shot put the whole column into the utmost confusion. Shays made an attempt to deploy the column, but in vain. We had one howit which was loaded with grape shot, which when fired, gave them great uneasiness. Had I been disposed to destroy them, I might have charged upon their rear and flanks with my infantry and the two fieldpieces, and could have killed the greater part of the whole army within five minutes. There was not a single musket fired on either side.

"I found three dead men upon the spot, and one wounded, who is since dead. One of our artillery men, by inattention was badly wounded.

"Three muskets were taken up with the dead, which were all deeply loaded . . . I have received no reenforcements yet, and expect to be attacked this day by their whole force combined."

But no assault occurred. The grape shot had routed Shays' force. He tried desperately to rally the men. They turned their backs, and his struggle to deploy them was futile.

Abandoned, almost alone in the echoing, snow-swept square, Shays must have realized the rebellion was over. In a few minutes a militia patrol carried away the dead to a stable, where the bodies were left to freeze . . . Shays, the Revolutionary hero at Lexington, turned and followed after his men, plunging bitterly through the deep drifts to the town of Ludlow, ten miles northeast.

Even had Captain Day's force, containing the more tough-fibred of the insurgents, met Shays before the arsenal attack, it is doubtful whether the outcome would have been different. Day, although only five miles away, was not aroused by the cannon-fire, and remained at West Springfield, waiting for the government troops' surrender demanded by him of Shephard. The next morning, January 26, the despondent Shays marched due west to Chicopee, his force reduced by two hundred desertions, and joined his men to the four hundred insurgents under Colonel Parsons.

In the paralyzing cold none of the men had stomach for a fight. Shays gave the order to fall back on Amherst, fifteen miles further north. He organized a rear-guard to slow up any pursuit by Lincoln, who, he guessed correctly, was now on the outskirts of Springfield, but his men lost their heads, and shot and killed one of their guard, mistaking the party for Government scouts.

En route to Amherst, despite Shays' exhortations, threats and warnings, the men began pillaging homes.

On January 27 an advance party of five hundred insurgents reached South Hadley, where they were fired on by government sympathizers hidden in a horse-shed. An insurgent adjutant was killed, and an acting captain badly wounded. Shays captured the nine sharpshooters, but released them at Amherst. Before his men left South Hadley there was sporadic musket fire—which at least demonstrated more spirit than was shown at Springfield—, and several homes were ransacked, chiefly for their stores of rum, which, the temperature considered, was doubtless the course of wisdom.

Shays hurried toward Amherst, where he arrived the night of the same day, and here learned of Captain Day's misfortunes from some of the latter's stragglers. Accordingly he wasted no time, and with the force remaining to him pushed on another ten miles to Pelham, his home and headquarters. Behind two high, bleak hills beyond the town he was relatively safe from pursuit. Thither he discovered the fleeing Day had preceded him.

General Lincoln, although his militia were exhausted by the forced march over the snows from Worcester, decided to advance without pause against Day at West Springfield. The Revolutionary commander, with four regiments and four pieces of artillery, crossed the Connecticut River on the ice, and Day's men, holding the ferry-head, fled without firing a volley, many of them throwing away their arms, and —an indication of their morale—"left their bread and their pork and beans baking in the ovens." They fled north by way of Southampton, thence to Northampton, to Hadley, Amherst, and, with Shays, back at last to Pelham. As Lincoln pursued them on the west bank, capturing the laggards and the sick, General Shephard pushed up the east side of the river.

General Lincoln maintained the pursuit to Pelham, which he searched for insurgent leaders, but he declined to follow Shays into the hills for a profitless game of hide-and-seek. He returned to Hadley, found billets for his men, now totalling about 3,100, and prepared to treat with Shays, to whom he wrote on January 30. If the insurgents would put down their arms, surrender to the Government and subscribe to the oath of allegiance, Lincoln promised they would be recommended for pardon by the legislature.

Shays countered with a promise that the men would return to their homes and await an answer by the legislature, if the Government troops ceased hostilities. The militia commander returned the proposal, which had been signed by Shays, Francis Stone and Adam Wheeler, saying he had no authority to negotiate an armistice.

While notes were under exchange, Shays decided that General Lincoln had a correct view of the insurgents' plight when he had written him that "your resources are few, your force inconsiderable . . . You are in a post where you have neither cover nor supplies." Shays decided to slip away to Petersham.

Two hours after he had started north, Lincoln's raw recruits were in full pursuit from Hadley, and overnight in sub-zero cold made a forced march of thirty miles, at the end of which, the General reported to Bowdoin, "the greater part of our men were frozen in some part or other." Most of Shays' supporters—if they still qualified as such—were surprised at Petersham, and 150 of them were taken prisoner, the others routed. They scattered to New Hampshire, or west into New York, or to Vermont, where Shays, at Sandgate, unsuccessfully applied to Ethan Allen for support.

For several weeks thereafter there were guerrilla outbreaks, particularly in Berkshire County, but they were easily suppressed by militia detachments or by bands of civilian vigilantes. Captain Buffington was sent to Vermont to arrest the leaders, for whose capture the legislature offered £150, but although that officer obtained warrants from the Vermont courts, the insurgent refugees had no difficulty finding places to hide among sympathizers in the neighboring State. One of the leaders, Captain Jason Parmenter, was caught February 6, and others seized were Luddington, Alpheus Colton, James White, Wheeler and Henry McCullock.

The Supreme Judicial Court, whose sessions a few months before had been prevented by the insurgents, met on April 9 at Northampton, scene of the first raid. The foregoing six were found guilty of high treason, and sentenced to death. Seven others who had been captured received sentences varying from "sitting on the gallows with a rope around your neck" to twenty stripes, and fines up to £100 were imposed. Early the next month, in May, death-warrants arrived at Northampton for McCullock and Parmenter, and their execution was set for the 24th. The other four were pardoned, and on the day before the scheduled hanging of the pair a reprieve arrived delaying the execution—atop "Pancake Plain"—until June 21.

On that day hundreds gathered outside the jail on Pleasant Street to await the prisoners' appearance and delivery to the meeting-house, where they were made to listen to a "Sound, orthodox Sermon" on the uncomfortable and somewhat debatable text (Romans II: 12), "Wherefore the law is holy, and the commandment holy, and just, and good." After the sermon the throng, now grown to several thousand, followed to the hill outside the town to witness the execution. At the foot of the gallows, the noose a few inches from the prisoners, the sheriff slowly drew another reprieve from his pocket—a harrowing anti-climax which, however, Parmenter and McCullock survived. Tales were current, incapable of proof, that the Massachusetts authorities issued another reprieve because of fear that a group of insurgents in Vermont would carry out a threat to hang two Hampshire County doctors, taken in a raid as hostages, if the two rebels went to the gallows. Whether the Government was or was not intimidated, Parmenter and McCullock, after another reprieve, were pardoned.

Luke Day was caught in New Hampshire a year after the collapse of the rebellion, and imprisoned for a brief period at Boston. Eli Parsons escaped capture, and was finally pardoned on his petition to the Government. In 1788 the legislature passed an amnesty act permitting all insurgent exiles to return to the State. In February of that year, Shays petitioned for a pardon, and it was granted on June 13. He left Massachusetts to settle in Sparta, western New York. In his old age—he lived to eighty-five (dying in 1825)—Congress awarded him a pension for his services in the Revolutionary War.

The military weakness of the central Government under the Confederation was strikingly revealed in Shays' Rebellion. It was a powerful argument to the States for a new, more closely-knit form of government, and it persuaded them also that taxes must be paid into the Treasury at Washington.

At Petersham, where Shays' force was finally routed, there is a tablet on which it is inscribed that "this victory for the forces of government influenced the Philadelphia Convention which three months later met and formed the Constitution of the United States." If it is too much to say that the Constitution was a direct result of the uprising in western

Massachusetts, still it is true that the rebellion was fresh in the minds of the drafters at Philadelphia.

The rebellion did result in certain reforms. The salaries of officials were reduced (although the Governor promptly vetoed the cut in his own compensation), all court procedure was made less expensive, and the authority of the courts of Common Pleas was curtailed.

That the abortive rebellion had served a purpose, at least as an example to the States, was the conclusion of Jefferson. A week after the Springfield fiasco, on January 30, 1787, he wrote to Madison, "I hold it that a little rebellion now and then is a good thing, & as necessary in the political world as storms in the physical. Unsuccessful rebellions indeed generally establish the encroachments on the rights of the people which have produced them. . . . It is a medicine necessary for the sound health of government."

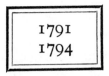
THE WHISKEY INSURRECTION

IN BACON'S REBELLION, IN THE ANDROS IN-
surrection, the War of the Regulators, and in Shays' Rebellion, the insurgents had cautious resource, at the outset, to
petitions of one sort or another. There was at least some
gesture in the direction of redress by peaceful means. In the
case of the Whiskey Insurrection in western Pennsylvania,
however, the infuriated settlers of Scotch-Irish descent acted
violently first, and turned to petitions afterward.

In their series of disorders they showed a consistent fond-
ness for the tar-barrel and a bag of feathers. To tar-and-
feather an enemy they thought infinitely more effective—
since the terror and pain provoked were presumably more
enduring—than to drill him between the eyes; moreover, the
tar-and-feather pleasantry had some special humiliation
which made the victim, they hoped, a pariah forever. After
the object of their fury had been stripped, and his body generously smeared with this paint of obloquy, it was the utmost
refinement in punishment to bind the culprit to a tree so
situated that he might witness the slow consumption of his
home by fire. It was unfortunate if the tarred one was, say,

only the inoffensive agent of a rapacious Government—but then it was well known, wasn't it, that the innocent must suffer with the guilty?

The first of a score or more of these attacks on Government agents was visited upon one Robert Johnson. He was the Federal collector of the excise tax on whiskey for Allegheny and Washington counties, and it was at Pigeon Creek in the latter county that he was seized by an armed and masked band. The particular technique employed in his chastisement was typical of all the others. He was tarred and feathered, his hair was cut off, his horse taken from him. The date was September 6, 1791. Soon thereafter the United States marshal, fearful of serving warrants himself on the guilty, deputized a civilian to bring in the guilty. The newly-sworn and doubtless unsuspecting officer was seized, flogged, tarred and feathered, his mount and money taken from him, and he was tied up and left in the woods, blindfolded, to scream five hours for help. Later the marshal unblushingly confessed he had hired a substitute because "had I gone myself, I should not have returned alive."

One more illustration of this "home-spun chastisement," as it was called occasionally in the four counties (Washington, Allegheny, Westmoreland and Fayette), before a review of the causes. Two years after the contretemps that befell Collector Johnson, another disguised party rode up at night to the home of a collector, Benjamin Wells, in Fayette County. The door was forced, and when the owner was found to be away the family was threatened and abused. Warrants were issued for the ringleaders, but the sheriff flatly declined to serve them, valuing his life above his duty

—a rational attitude which, however, did not save him from an indictment for malfeasance. The insurgents returned to Wells' dwelling, again at night, and this time found him home. He was compelled to relinquish his Federal commission and his account-books, and made to publish a resignation of his office in a Pittsburgh newspaper; otherwise, he was warned, his house would be burned to the ground.

Johnson was similarly made to resign by newspaper notice. His withdrawal from office, published in the Pittsburgh *Gazette*, says, "Finding the opposition to the revenue law more violent than I expected . . . feeling the opposition changed from dignified rabble to respectable party, I think it my duty and do resign my commission."

The primary cause of the assaults, eventually to place George Washington in armed service at the head of nearly 13,000 troops, was the Federal Government's excise tax of ten cents per gallon on whiskey, and its tax on the stills. The impost was low enough, considering the relatively enormous public debt after the Revolution, but for a variety of reasons it was immediately and energetically opposed after its adoption by Congress on March 3, 1791. It was drafted by Hamilton, the Secretary of the Treasury. Opposition in Congress itself was led by the members from Fayette and Westmoreland counties, and by Albert Gallatin, the future Secretary of the Treasury, then a resident of Fayette County and a member of the Pennsylvania legislature. The resentment over the Federal tax is easily understood. The Federal Constitution, adopted four years before at Philadelphia, stipulated that "all duties, imposts and excises shall be uniform throughout the United States." While this had a reasonable ring on first reading, the farmers of western Pennsylvania were quick to point out that a whiskey tax, for example, could be more oppressive in one part of the nation than in another. It did not bear on the economy of citizens of New Hampshire, where there were almost no stills, but it was a discriminatory tax on the western counties of Pennsylvania, where about every fifth farmer operated a still. There as elsewhere the shortage of money was acute. In large degree the farmers used their whiskey in barter for salt, iron, etcetera. Or what they did not consume themselves they sold for cash to innkeepers, to the Ohio and Kentucky markets, and to the Army, until the Government refused to buy any barrels on which the excise stamp was missing. The farmers argued that the little money brought into their counties by the sale of whiskey would be taken away again by the Government's excise. With a very limited market for their grain in bulk—freight to Philadelphia, for example, cost from five to ten dollars per hundred pounds—farmers reduced its bulk by concerting it into whiskey, which they could sell for about a dollar a gallon on the other side of the mountains. A horse could carry two kegs of eight gallons each. A still in most cases was obligatory, if the farmer was to survive. Salt cost him five dollars a bushel, and iron, procured at Pittsburgh, between fifteen and twenty cents a pound. In other States, the distilling of rye, maize and barley was negligible in quantity chiefly because it was more profitable to sell grain in bulk, to markets that were fairly near the farmers' fields.

Moreover, the farmers had the State government on their

side, at least tacitly. Various taxes "laying an excise on wine, rum, brandy and other spirits" enacted by the Assembly, in provincial days, had been invariably repealed after a few unpopular and unproductive weeks or months. After the Revolution, in 1780, the State adopted a tax on spirits which in the main was evaded, and, west of the Alleghenies, completely ignored. It became a dead letter, and was finally repealed in 1791. But the same year, after the passage of the Federal tax on whiskey, the farmers asked, "Why should we pay anything to Washington for making whiskey, when the State itself realized the injustice of its tax, and until its repeal, no longer tried to collect it?"

Although the Government had directed that offices were to be opened in June (1791) for the registration of stills, none was established by that time in western Pennsylvania. The reason was that the Government was having difficulty in finding collectors for that part of the State; the post was certain to be an unpleasant and a dangerous one. Another reason for the Federal Government's hesitancy was that many of the farmers had written to their representatives in Washington that, rather than pay the tax, they would cease distilling altogether—a post-Revolutionary variation, if you like, of the sit-down.

Apart from protests by resource to the tar-barrel, however, there was afoot a movement to bring about repeal of the despised excise by political pressure. The first public meeting was held at Red Stone Old Fort in July. Because of the harvest, the attendance was small. Gallatin, who has been credited by some with saving Pennsylvania from civil war, acted as secretary. There the right of the Federal Government to levy a commodity tax for internal revenue was recognized unequivocally—provided it was not a whiskey tax, and provided it did not fall on the four counties. It was decided to gather petitions for relief, stressing the hardships resulting from the excise, from the four counties, and to forward these to Congress. The lead was taken by Washington County, which, the next month, drew up a resolution, and published it in the Pittsburgh *Gazette*. Its threat of political reprisals is interesting. Anyone who "accepted or might accept" Federal office to execute the excise laws was to be regarded as "inimical to the interests of the country," and the county signatories to the resolution agreed to "treat every person accepting such office with contempt."

In September delegates from the four counties met at Pittsburgh to draw up resolutions for presentation to both the Federal and State legislatures.

In Hamilton's view, expressed nearly four years later in a letter to the President, these resolutions were "not less inflammatory in their tendency than those which had before passed the meeting in Washington [County]" and displayed an "unfriendly temper toward the Government of the United States." Evidence in Hamilton's own hand exists to support the belief that the Secretary of the Treasury was more eager for some pretext to demonstrate the authority of the Federal Government—and its ability to enforce that authority by military force—than interested in adding to the internal revenue. Certainly that sound-money advocate had drafted the excise-tax primarily to raise internal revenue. But the outbreaks in western Pennsylvania against the impost provided Washington, in his view, with an opportunity to demonstrate the authority of the Federal government. The hostility in the four counties to the tax-collectors, supported as Hamilton was aware by such responsible men as Gallatin, must be suppressed if the young Government was to survive. To the Secretary of the Treasury it was axiomatic that it could survive only under the strictest centralization of power, a conception over which he was at constant loggerheads in cabinet meetings with Jefferson. The opposition to the excise-tax was, to the Federalist, merely another example of the destruction inherent in the extension of excessive powers to the people.

The phraseology of the Pittsburgh resolution was not particularly reverent. Moreover, the delegates took the opportunity to express their feelings on matters other than the whiskey excise.

The delegates numbered eleven, and they, like Gallatin, were not men whose opinions could be ignored. David Bradford, district attorney of Washington County, who was to contract the messianic itch for leadership, Colonel James Marshall, Colonel Thomas Morton, and the Reverend David Phillips were four of the counties' representatives. They declare that the excise law "is deservedly obnoxious to the feelings of the interest of the people in general . . . It operates on a . . . manufacture not equal through the States. It is insulting to the feelings of the people to have their vessels [barrels and stills] marked, houses painted and ransacked, to be subject to informers . . . The excise on home-made spirituous liquors affects particularly the raising of grain, especially rye, and there can be no solid reason for taxing it more than any other article of the growth of the

United States." Besides this, the delegates tossed a brickbat at "The exorbitant salaries of officers" and the "unreasonable interest" rate of the public debt.

Hamilton considered the meeting "intemperate." It was "without moderation or prudence," and he foresaw "a point that threatens the foundations of the Government and of the Union, unless speedily and effectively subdued." The Secretary's dislike of the people—a "great beast," in the Federalist's view—was no secret, however, and the more extreme factions in the four counties, encouraged by the forthright language of the Pittsburgh resolution, continued to bedevil the collectors. Nearly a year later, in August 1792, a second meeting gathered at Pittsburgh, at which it was resolved, with respect to the collectors, to "withdraw from them every assistance, and withhold all the comforts of life . . . [to] have no intercourse or dealings with them . . . and upon all occasions treat them with the contempt they deserve." In that day, when distances were great, to "withhold all the comforts of life" could very well mean death to the traveler from exposure or hunger.

Gallatin was again present, as was David Bradford. Although the former assented to the resolution, he admitted afterward that its spirit was "violent, intemperate and reprehensible."

Tar and feathers and "intemperate" petitions were not, however, to intimidate the Treasury Department at Washington. Soon after the second Pittsburgh meeting, the Government leased the home of William Faulkner, an army officer, to use as an inspection—and collection—office in western Pennsylvania. Three months before, it should be noted,

Congress had bowed to the farmers' complaints to the extent of slightly lightening the excise tax, and permitting its payment in monthly instalments. Captain Faulkner was seized near his home, and threatened with scalping and the tar-barrel if he leased his home as a Federal tax agency. He promptly canceled the lease in a public notice in the Pittsburgh *Gazette*.

Some of the farmers, on the other hand, decided to submit to the tax, hoping that it would eventually be repealed, and believing that more violence was prejudicial to their cause. The indignities already suffered by the collectors had incited sharp criticism among many men who were generally much opposed to the excise. Across the mountains, and elsewhere among the States, there were rebukes from the pens of newspaper editors and *vox-populi* writers who did not understand the economic causes of the controversy; sneers and laughter over the right, for example, of "a parcel of drunken raggamuffins in western Pennsylvania" to drink as much whiskey as they pleased.

But the extremists turned on the moderates among them. James Kiddo and William Cochrane were two among others who had obediently recorded their stills with the inspector. In reprisal Cochrane's mills were razed. One John Lyon, whose home sheltered a collection office, was threatened with hanging, then given the tar-brush. In almost every instance of attack the victim was forced to recant publicly, or otherwise make amends in full sight of his neighbors. As for the fate of the agents, the treatment accorded Johnson and Wells was typical.

A collector's lot was not a happy one.

Late in 1792 the President realized the situation was becoming dangerous, even though his Secretary of State may have believed in "a little rebellion now and then." The want of authority that the Federal Government had shown in 1787, during Shays' Rebellion, must not recur in western Pennsylvania.

Washington's proclamation, dated September 15, referred to "certain violent and unwarrantable proceedings . . . tending to obstruct the operation of the laws of the United States for raising a revenue upon spirits," and it called upon "all persons . . . to refrain and desist from all unlawful combinations . . . tending to obstruct the operations of the laws."

The President warned that "all lawful ways and means will be strictly put in operation for bringing to justice the infractors [of the laws] thereof, and securing obedience thereto."

After its collection offices were established in the four counties, and inspectors appointed, the Government moved to seize whiskey en route to market that lacked the excise stamps. And throughout 1793 the Government seemed to make headway in enforcing and collecting the tax, partly because of the support of the larger distillers, who favored it because it had the effect of making the small farmer sell them grain at a low price.

But the Government did nothing to correct one of the most vexatious abuses. This was to make a defendant in western Pennsylvania, for example, appear in court at Philadelphia in answer to a summons for avoidance of the excise law, for the Federal court did not meet west of the mountains. The cost in time and money was ruinous. It remains inexplicable why a Federal Circuit Court judge was not assigned to that section of the State, an obvious solution which would have lessened in some degree the resentment against the national Government. It was injustice enough to have to pay the excise; to be made to lose a crop and to travel hundreds of miles to Philadelphia, to appear in court, was beyond endurance.

Finally, in June of 1794, Congress passed a law that served as the last straw to the farmers in western Pennsylvania, although the legislation was intended to ease the situation. The excise law was so amended—again—that the State courts were given concurrent jurisdiction; that is, a defendant in Westmoreland County, for example, charged with operating a still without benefit of tax, could stand trial in the Pennsylvania court in his home district. But even this belated reform, coming on the outbreak of insurrection, met with vehement opposition. For the cry now was not so much for an amended excise law as for outright repeal. Moreover, by some stupidity the amendment of June 5 was not made retroactive, so that the Federal docket at Philadelphia remained filled with indictments against farmers three hundred miles to the west, on the other side of the Alleghenies. Here was the immediate genesis of the Whiskey Insurrection, which had been brewing for more than three years.

The United States marshal in western Pennsylvania, a Major Lenox, set out early in June to serve forty writs in excise cases dated May 31, and therefore not affected by the Federal amendment of June 5. The indicted men, in other words, must trudge over the mountains at the height of the harvest season. Despite the anger against the Federal Government generally, and the marshals, inspectors and collectors particularly, Lenox had no difficulty serving his writs in Fayette County, and thence he proceeded north to Allegheny County. There he was unmolested, and by July 15 he had only one writ to serve. Possibly he knew, or feared, that his luck would not hold, because, before making service, he asked the Federal inspector of revenues for the western counties, General John Neville, stationed at Pittsburgh, to accompany him. The inspector consented, although both men must have realized that the sight of one Federal officer in the disaffected counties was nauseous enough to the residents: the spectacle of two was revolting, was incitement to rebellion. It proved exactly that in this instance. Had the marshal gone alone, the *casus belli* might not have been provided.

The pair arrived at the farm of a small distiller named Miller, at Peter's Creek, near Pittsburgh, and "without slightest insult or opposition" served the summons. Miller's neighbors were less resigned. Six of them followed the marshal and the inspector, and one of the party fired a shot at them, or, as was later claimed, merely into the air, to show their dislike of the two Federal officers and of General Neville's "effrontery" in openly supporting Captain Lenox. The inspector, recently become one of the wealthiest men in the West, had lost his one-time popularity because he supported the Government.

The marshal, or "Federal sheriff" as he was invidiously called, and General Neville rode back into Pittsburgh without further incident. By some prescience the latter knew that the firing of a shot, whether or not it had been aimed directly at him, was not to be the end of the affair. He barricaded the windows of his home, about seven miles from Pittsburgh, with heavy planks, and distributed arms to his Negroes.

The same day there had been a gathering in the meeting-house at Mingo Creek—the cradle of the insurrection, as it developed—of the regimental association, to select a militia corps to serve as the county quota of the 80,000 men required by Congress for an expedition against the Indians. The meeting was about to disperse when an excited member arrived on horse, with news of the "attack" upon the two Federal officers. Discussion continued into the night, and just before midnight (July 16) General Neville's preparations were rewarded by the arrival of thirty armed men.

The leader, John Holcroft, "Tom the Tinker," smashed fist on door. It remained unopened, but Neville from within asked his business. The retort was a demand for surrender of his Federal commission and for all the records and other documents of his office. The General made no answer. A shot was fired—by which side is unknown. The men rapidly deployed about the dwelling, and the fire became general, shots coming from the Negro quarters as well as from the manor-house. The servants were using shotgun fire, and in one volley six of the attackers fell. One died in a few minutes of his wounds. The men retreated with their casualties. Afterward the distiller, Miller, explained that the party did not rush the manor-house, the door of which had been opened, "because we were afraid that he had a swivel or big gun there."

That night a message was circulated commanding "all those who value liberty or life" to gather at the Mingo Creek meeting-house. The shedding of blood by Neville must be avenged, it was agreed, and a band of about five hundred were ordered to a rendezvous at Conche's Fort, a few miles from the Federal inspector's house. The leader elected was Major Abram Macfarlane, who had had a commission in the Pennsylvania Line during the Revolution. In the insurgent force that gathered at the appointed spot were many who answered the summons only because they did not dare refuse.

The force advanced, and a half-mile from General Neville's home they dismounted, leaving their horses with the men who had no arms. Some hours before, the inspector's guard had been reenforced by the arrival of eleven Federal troopers, commanded by Major Abram Kirkpatrick from the Pittsburgh garrison. The inspector had been warned of the insurgents' plans, and on Kirkpatrick's arrival he decided to hide in the woods, since if he were absent the farmers might withhold their fire. But General Neville before leaving ordered the major to capitulate, provided he could do so honorably, if that would save the property.

Major Macfarlane halted his men a short distance from the house, and advanced alone. He demanded General Neville.

Major Kirkpatrick replied that the Federal officer had left. The next demand shouted was for Neville's commission and other papers, with the warning that, if necessary, these would be taken from the house by force.

The army officer countered with a warning that he had

a force adequate to defend the property, and that the papers would not be relinquished.

Macfarlane spoke his last words. He said he would withhold his fire until the women and children whom he could see indoors had been sent away.

The women and children left. The firing began.

About fifteen minutes later, a shout was heard from the manor-house. Major Macfarlane, believing it signalled a request for a truce, waved to his men to cease fire, and he slipped from behind a tree and began walking toward the Neville house. He was dropped in his track by a bullet from the dwelling, killing him instantly. His infuriated men, shouting "Murder!" and "Treason!" charged the grounds, set the barn and other outbuildings afire, and the flames spread to the main structure, destroying it in turn. Major Kirkpatrick and his men were forced outside, but permitted to return to Pittsburgh.

General Neville's house was a total loss. He hurried to insert a notice in the *Gazette* that "In my house on Bower Hill, on Chartiers Creek, which was attacked, plundered and burnt, by the rioters on Thursday evening last, were four thousand, six hundred and eleven dollars and sixty cents, funded debt of the United States . . . in two certificates," and warned against their attempted sale by forgery.

The death of Macfarlane strengthened the resolve of the insurgents. Messengers again were sent throughout the four counties for another meeting at Mingo Creek to determine the most effective reprisals for the murder—in their eyes— of two citizens. At the town of Washington, seat of that county, the messengers urged the attendance of Bradford, the prosecutor, and of Colonel Marshall, both of whom had signed the forceful petition to Congress of August, 1792. Bradford, alarmed at the extremes foreshadowed, sought to excuse himself on the grounds of his office, but he changed his mind when he was threatened with the burning of his house if he did not join the insurgents whole-heartedly. Henceforth he acted very similarly to Nathaniel Bacon— here was the critical moment for the perceptive opportunist.

Colonel Marshall, who in the Pennsylvania legislature had opposed ratification of the Federal Constitution, seems to have been equally conscious of the historical potentialities of the moment. Although he was hesitant at first, the tarring and feathering of his door one midnight served to lessen his timidity. With Bradford, he threw in his lot with the growing movement against the Government. Others of responsibility attended the meeting: Edward Cook, a county judge, Benjamin Parkinson, a justice of the peace, and H. H. Brackenridge, a former member of the State legislature and one of the proprietors of the *Gazette*. The last three attended, however, in the hope that they might stifle talk of drastic revenge and of one measure in particular which the rank and file were discussing with considerable enthusiasm.

This was the burning and sack of Pittsburgh.

The Mingo Creek meeting, undeterred by the counsel of Brackenridge and the others to keep within the law, gave birth to the following notice: "By a respectable number of citizens who met on Wednesday, the 23d inst., at the meeting-house on Mingo Creek, it is recommended to the townships of the four western counties of Pennsylvania, and the neighboring counties of Virginia, to meet and choose not more than five, not less than two, representatives, to meet at Parkinson's Ferry on the Monongahela, on Thursday, the 14th of August next, to take into consideration the condition of the western country."

The insurgents, then, were making a bid for the support of farmers in northern Virginia.

But August 14 was too distant a date for the aroused Bradford. He craved immediate action, and, with Colonel Marshall, he started it. On the road near Greensburg, seat of Westmoreland County, the Washington and Philadelphia mail was seized from the postboy. Their aim was to learn what had been written of their activities to Washington and Philadelphia. They reproduced those letters which proved unfriendly to the insurgents, and their authors discreetly departed the neighborhood. The seizure of the mail, of course, was a Federal offense, but its very gravity had the effect of making the leadership of Bradford and Marshall popular with the farmers.

Soon after this Judge James Wilson, a member of the United States Supreme Court, brought to President Washington realization that the western counties of Pennsylvania were not to be quieted by anything but armed persuasion. "Sir," he wrote from Philadelphia on August 4, "from the evidence which has been laid before me, I hereby notify to you that in the counties of Washington and Allegheny, in Pennsylvania, laws of the United States are opposed, and the execution thereof obstructed by combinations too powerful to be suppressed by the ordinary course of judicial proceedings or by the powers vested in the Marshal of that district."

Hamilton was jubilant. He believed that the Government

before many weeks would be forced to show its authority in a realistic way. The day after Judge Wilson's letter to the President, in an 8,000-word review of the situation to the Chief Executive, Hamilton stressed the "disagreeable crisis" and the "existing emergency," although qualifying his thinly disguised excitement with the opinion that the "intervention of a military power . . . cannot continue a moment longer than the occasion for which it was expressly required." This last was a sop to the Jefferson he despised.

Bradford and Marshall now had the bit in their teeth. With no more authority than they had had for seizing the mail, they circulated an astonishing order to the colonels of the militia regiments in the four counties. This circular (July 28), after stating that in the correspondence seized were "certain secrets hostile to our interests," ordered each colonel "as a citizen of the western country to render your personal service, with as many volunteers as you can raise, to rendezvous at your usual place on Wednesday next, and thence you will march to the usual place of rendezvous at Braddock's Field, on the Monongahela, on Friday, the first day of August, to be there at two o'clock in the afternoon with arms and accoutrements in good order. If any volunteers shall want arms and ammunition, bring them forward and they shall be supplied as well as possible. Here, sir, is an expedition proposed in which you will have an opportunity of displaying your military talents and of rendering service to your country. Four days provisions will be wanted; let the men be thus supplied."

This scheduled concentration had no connection with the non-military meeting called at Parkinson's Ferry for August

14. That the mobilization meant action, rather than more oratory, is clear in the challenging reference by Bradford and Marshall (and by five other signatories) to the "expedition proposed in which you will have an opportunity of displaying your military tactics." If the summons itself was extraordinary, no less surprising was the number that appeared on the field, three days later; but there is plenty of evidence that many men, citizens as well as militiamen, were afraid not to appear; the dominant sentiment was that absentees were sympathizers of the Government. And the lot of Government supporters was the tar-barrel or the destruction of their homes, or both. But whatever their feelings, many of the civilians came to the field with old guns which blacksmiths had recently repaired, and they had bought flint and powder from their village stores. Brackenridge, who was present, remarked that "a breath in favor of the law [i.e., for the excise-tax] was sufficient to ruin any man. It was considered as a badge of toryism. A clergyman was not thought orthodox in the pulpit unless against the law . . . A lawyer could have got no practice without at least concealing his sentiments, if for the law; nor could a merchant at a country store get custom. On the contrary, the talk against the law was the way to office and emolument. It was the Shibboleth of safety, and the ladder of ambition." This last seems to represent accurately the conclusions of Bradford and Colonel Marshall, just as Thomas Mathews had recognized the identical calculations of Nathaniel Bacon. Nevertheless Colonel Marshall's ready enlistment with the insurgents is puzzling: he had been successively registrar, sheriff, a member of the State constitutional ratifying convention, a member

of the legislature, and a lieutenant in the militia of Washington County.

At Braddock's Field the speakers wandered far from the iniquity of the whiskey excise. There were proposals to march to Pittsburgh, then a town of about two thousand, and set it afire. There was talk of seizing the writers of the letters to the capital who had warned of treason in the counties, and treating them to a tarring, if not to the noose. Some went so far, after demanding repeal of the tax, as to call for "a new modelling of the [United States] Constitution, and there would be revolution"—thus William Findley, an eye-witness and a member of the House of Representatives. Bradford in an inflammatory harangue urged an attack upon the Federal garrison in Pittsburgh, and confiscation of the arms in the arsenal, after the plan of Captain Shays in Massachusetts seven years before.

The field, on which between four and seven thousand men were converging, is on the east side of the Monongahela, eight miles from Pittsburgh; it is named after the British general, Edward Braddock, who had been defeated there in an ambuscade by French and Indians nearly forty years before. The Washington County militia and others had to cross the river to reach the spot. There are eye-witness accounts of the meeting, all remarkable for their disagreement. Most of the men came armed, and wore the common hunting shirt with a handkerchief tied over their heads. There was constant firing in the air, presumably the result of the "unexcised" whiskey on the field. Bradford, forming his men into companies, cut a swaggering military figure. The Reverend James Carnahan, at the meeting to preach moderation, remarking that the sword-rattling Bradford had bestowed upon himself the rank of major-general, saw him "mounted on a superb horse in splendid trappings, arrayed in full martial uniform, with plumes floating in the air and sword drawn . . . Never was mortal man more flattered than was David Bradford on Braddock's field. Everything depended on his will. The insurgents adored him, and those who hated and despised him, paid him the most servile homage, in order to be able to control and manage him."

The insurgent leaders, as well as the moderates, debated throughout the night. They met with a committee of citizens from Pittsburgh, a group in part sympathetic to them but concerned primarily with saving the town from the torch. Pittsburgh, they resolved, must not be reduced to the fine ashes of another Jamestown. To proposals that the men march into Pittsburgh and seize General Neville and Major Lenox, the Federal inspector and marshal, respectively, the committee truthfully answered that the two men had fled to Philadelphia, escaping the insurgent guards on the mountain roads by a circuitous trip down the Ohio and thence north and east.

The distraught Pittsburgh committee was soon made to realize that it was not possible, the temper of the men considered, to keep them from marching to the town. With the moderates, then, the problem was to persuade Bradford and his extremists against violence there when they arrived. In this Brackenridge was partly successful by his appeals to the men.

"Yes, by all means [march on Pittsburgh]. At least to give proof that the strictest order can be observed, and no damage done. We will just march through, and, taking a turn, come out upon the plain on the banks of the Monongahela; and after taking a little whiskey with the inhabitants, the troops will embark and cross the river."

The next day the march began into the town, along the Monongahela Road, chosen to prevent the militia from coming within sight of the small and nervous Federal detachment behind their guns in the Pittsburgh garrison. Most of the men afoot and mounted halted across from the town, and were met by residents bringing out conciliatory quantities of hams, poultry, dried venison and bear-meat—and, "not forgetting the day was hot, water and whiskey." Brackenridge, who served as guide on the march, recalled that "I thought it safest to give good words and good drink, rather than balls and powder. It cost me four barrels of old whiskey that day, and I would rather spare that than a quart of blood . . . I thought it better to be employed in extinguishing the fire of their throats than of my house."

The Pittsburgh committee had consented to order the expulsion from the town of Colonel Presly Neville, son of the Federal inspector, and General John Gibson, a militia commander, both of whom had incurred the wrath of the insurgents. The two left the town, but were promptly recalled to their homes after the mob left Pittsburgh. Inevitably there was some violence, if only because the innkeepers had been ordered to serve spirits gratis to show the town's good-will. One faction determined to burn General Neville's town-house that night, the home of General Gibson, and others, and were not easily dissuaded. The entire town, chiefly wooden, might have been destroyed by that plan.

The insurgents were successful in burning down the barn of Major Kirkpatrick (the United States Army officer who had defended General Neville's country home) across the Monongahela, but were frustrated when they tried to set fire to his home in Pittsburgh. The next day most of the insurgent force dispersed to await the results of the meeting called for August 14 at Parkinson's Ferry.

In view of the temper of the rebellious force of several thousand, and of the fact that most of them were armed; in the light moreover of the quantities of whiskey consumed, and finally of Bradford's fanaticism, it was not less than miraculous that there was no bloodshed in Pittsburgh, and that the town was not burned to the ground.

No part of the march on Pittsburgh, however, was miraculous to the United States Government. President Washington took a grave view of it, and although there had been no casualties General Knox, the Secretary of War, could see nothing in the affair that was not ominous—the failure of the Federal Government to protect its arsenal at Springfield seven years before, and its humiliating dependence on the Massachusetts militia were still fresh in his mind. Hamilton saw one course only—the despatch of a punitive expedition immediately into western Pennsylvania.

But the President did not require moral or other support from his cabinet. On August 7, five days after the march on Pittsburgh, the President issued a proclamation commanding "all persons being insurgents, on or before the first day of September, to disperse and return peaceably to their respective abodes." At the same time he ordered the muster of troops "to be held in readiness to march at a moment's warning."

The total of the Federal force was set at 12,950, composed of 11,000 infantry, 1,500 cavalry, and 450 artillery men. These effectives were to be drafted from Pennsylvania, New Jersey, Maryland and Virginia, the largest quota from Pennsylvania.

The State government also grew alarmed when it received word of the disorders. Governor Thomas Mifflin assigned Chief Justice Thomas McKean, former President of the Continental Congress and a signer of the Declaration of Independence, and General William Irvine, a member of Congress, as special commissioners to establish the facts of the riots, and if practicable to "bring the insurgents to their senses." In support of the President's order raising troops the Governor also issued a proclamation urging the State militia to the utmost speed in filling the Pennsylvania quota. As a last precaution he summoned the legislature to a special session.

The President followed the example of the Pennsylvania governor. He appointed commissioners to represent the national Government in an inquiry into the causes of the disturbance. They were James Ross, a United States Senator and attorney for Washington's estates in western Pennsylvania, Jasper Yeates, a justice of the Pennsylvania Supreme Court, and William Bradford, Attorney-General of the United States.

They were instructed to hurry to the western counties, and, among other things, to inform the insurgents "that the evidence of the late transactions has been submitted to a judge of the Supreme Court [James Wilson] . . . whence a power has arisen to the President to call out the militia to suppress the insurrection." Unconditional amnesty and "perpetual oblivion" for past misdeeds were to be extended on condition that "satisfactory assurances be given that the laws be no longer obstructed in their execution by any combinations . . . Nothing will be enforced concerning the [excise] duties of former years, if they will fairly comply for the present year." (In payment for the performance of this difficult task Edmond Randolph, Secretary of State, consented to pay the commissioners eight dollars a day.)

The delegates to the gathering at Parkinson's Ferry met on August 14, unaware of the action taken by the national Government. There were 260 delegates from the four Pennsylvania counties and Ohio County in Virginia. There is no doubt that a substantial number of candidates had come intending to advocate moderation, but this faction soon recognized that if moderation was to prevail it could be achieved only by indirection and underground strategy, not by outright opposition to the majority sentiment.

Colonel Cook, who had attended the Pittsburgh meeting in 1791 as chairman, was now elected chairman, and Gallatin made secretary. The leaders against violence included the ubiquitous Brackenridge and Judge James Edgar. Gallatin was sparring for time, doing all he could to soften the language of the various resolutions. The chief aim of the moderates was to prevent the adoption of a resolution that would commit the assembly to a defensive—and certainly disastrous—war against the Federal Government.

During the sessions word came of the arrival at Pittsburgh

of the United States commissioners, and of the President's call for troops, which may have had a sobering effect on the delegates at Parkinson's Ferry. The delegates had no doubt of the Government's intentions, but the phrase "defensive war" had a righteous connotation. Gallatin later testified "that it appeared to me, from the temper of those present, that if the question had been put it would have been carried." Thanks to the efforts of Brackenridge, Gallatin and the venerable Judge Edgar that dangerous motion was sidetracked, although Brackenridge wrote, "I knew that the resolution was a favorite one with all those who had been involved in any of the outrages, and at the same time a popular one generally." The upshot of the deliberations was the selection of a committee of sixty, representing all the townships, to meet at Red Stone Old Fort on September 2; meanwhile an executive committee of twelve would treat at Pittsburgh with the Pennsylvania and the Federal commissioners.

At that meeting both groups of commissioners declared that any discussion of amnesty must be prefaced by responsible assurances from the executive committee that the insurgents possessed "a strong determination...to obey the laws of the United States." The executive committee emphasized the farmers' grievances, particularly the journeys they were forced to make to Philadelphia, but the commissioners were adamant: before redress could be discussed the submission to authority must be made.

The conference adjourned to permit the executive committee, renamed the Committee of Safety, to meet with the townships' committee of sixty at Red Stone Old Fort. There Gallatin grew eloquent in favor of giving the commissioners

the assurances they demanded. He was followed by Brackenridge. Both were savagely opposed by Bradford. Bradford
was too far committed now to back water, and he was full
of ready allusions to the creed of the Rights of Man, then
the subject of popular debate, and to the success of the Terrorists in France. He would not be satisfied short of war and
secession.

"You talk of property," he shouted, "when Liberty is at
stake! . . . We will defeat the first army that attempts to
cross the mountains. We will seize their arms and baggage,
and then organize an army that will prevent any further
attempt."

The fear which gripped the delegation shows in the fact
that the meeting had difficulty devising means of voting
secretly: they feared their handwriting would be recognized on ballots, and a simple "yea" or "nay" vote in open
meeting was an unthinkable risk. The dilemma was solved
by the distribution of slips, (two to each delegate), bearing
an affirmative and a negative—the slip not used was to be
swallowed, chewed or otherwise destroyed by the voter.
When the vote was announced as 34 to 23 in favor of presenting to the people of the four counties the question of
submission to the laws, Bradford stalked from the meeting
in disgust and fled to Louisiana, then Spanish soil. The question to go before the farmers was, "Will the people submit to
the laws of the United States upon the terms proposed by
the Commissioners of the United States?"

The results of the miniature referendum were to be in the
hands of the commissioners on or before September 11.
There was not sufficient time for the various districts to meet

and discuss the question thoroughly, and return their answers, over a territory larger than the State of New Jersey. Two of the Federal commissioners, Yeates and William Bradford, returned early to Philadelphia, leaving Senator Ross at Uniontown to follow them later with the votes.

Gallatin pleaded with the State commissioners for an extension of the deadline, pointing out the difficulties of obtaining a consensus in so short a period, and argued against the immediate expedition of troops. But the two Federal commissioners by this time had reported to the President. They had given him their impression of the dangerous temper of the people, and, creating greater apprehension in the Government's eyes, they told of groups of farmers at Parkinson's Ferry dancing around a liberty pole that bore a placard, "Liberty and no excise, and no asylum for cowards!"

And there was more from the commissioners, calculated to excite the most judicious President. "In full view of the military," they reported, the insurgents with the greatest difficulty had been restrained from hoisting aloft a flag of their own design, the symbol of secession. This was described as banner of blue with seven stars to represent the four Pennsylvania counties, the two sympathetic counties in northern Virginia, and the leadership of Bradford. (Brackenridge and other writers on the insurrection describe the flag variously, and its existence is nowhere flatly stated.) They repeated Bradford's threats to set up an autonomous government west of the mountains, and his proposal to declare war. They had not waited long enough to discover the change of sentiment which had occurred with the threat of a Federal expedition in the field against them.

The next day, September 25, Washington issued a proclamation calling out the troops. "The moment is now come when the overtures of forgiveness, with no other condition than a submission to law, have been only partially accepted." Governor Mifflin simultaneously called out the State militia, and to fill its ranks, depleted by the Federal levy, the legislature authorized bounties.

As the Federal troops began their march, the insurgents' standing committee of safety met at Parkinson's Ferry, on October 2, and passed resolutions stipulating the people's submission to the laws of the country. Two members were hurried east to intercept and interview the President, and explain that the temper of the majority of the people had changed, as shown by the hundreds of affirmative votes now coming in from districts remote from the county-seats.

They met the President at Carlisle, where he had joined the main body of the army, and where also were the Secretary of War, General Knox, and the Secretary of the Treasury, "General" Hamilton, who had dusted off his Revolutionary epaulets for the occasion. To the petition of the delegates from Parkinson's Ferry to halt the expedition, the President replied that he could not countermand the advance of the army, which was already en route to western Pennsylvania. But he promised that there would be no violence or destruction if the people showed themselves loyal to the Government, and swore allegiance.

The delegates returned to the west to find messages from almost all districts of the four counties that citizens were ready to take the oath of allegiance, and that the excise-tax collectors would no longer be molested.

But the army advanced. To many of its officers, notably in the New Jersey contingent, the junket was a magnificent opportunity to dress up and play soldier. In the column of 15,000 there were "companies of gentlemen" whose trappings were in fabulous contrast to the accoutrements at Valley Forge only sixteen years before. Friends wrote to Gallatin, then at his farm in Fayette County, that he was the favorite target of many officers who swore they would "stab the traitor." Save for such campfire histrionics there were too few ways of blowing off steam. The rank and file were more fortunate: they could filch poultry and uproot fence-posts.

After reviewing the left division of the army, at Cumberland, President Washington returned east, reaching Philadelphia nine days later. The insurgent delegates returned to meet General Henry ("Light-Horse Harry") Lee, the governor of Virginia, who had been appointed commander-in-chief. He asked the delegates to "quiet the apprehensions of all" that there would be injury to the persons or property of the peaceful and loyal.

With the advance of the army, the few remaining embers of revolt quickly fizzled. Justices of the peace in the four counties were buried in a flood of pledges of allegiance. On November 17 orders were issued for the recall of the troops, excepting a detachment of 2,500 which remained at Pittsburgh under General Daniel Morgan for the "winter defense." Five days before that order, between nightfall and dawn, cavalry detachments had been deployed across the counties, and had routed two hundred of the insurgents from their beds. The prisoners were taken to Pittsburgh and thence to Philadelphia for trial. General Hamilton, meanwhile, occupied himself with obtaining evidence against the chief defendants, and the charge has often been made that he concentrated his labors in an unsuccessful effort to build up a case against Gallatin as the Machiavelli of the Whiskey Insurrection.

Twenty-two men were indicted for treason. Four of them, among them Husbands of the Regulator uprising, who had served on the Committee of Safety, were condemned to death, but pardoned by Washington. Two others served terms of from ten to twelve months. The others, pledged to allegiance, were released. Congress was informed that the cost of the parade into Pennsylvania was $800,000.

That was, of course, a small sum to pay for a vivid demonstration to the country that the nation's supreme authority was the federal Government, and that that Government would exercise its authority by force if necessary. In a sense, then, it vindicated Hamilton's view of government. In a commonwealth, however well founded on the rights of man, local communities could not determine autonomously whether and how far they would submit to one tax. Their instrument of redress, no matter how slow, lay in their representation in Congress. Still in this case violence did lead to some relief, at least in the method of collecting the tax, as well as in bringing the federal courts nearer to litigants.

The Whiskey Insurrection provoked the first federal intervention against a State. That intervention was effective, but as a deterrent to the country at large it proved as enduring as last year's snow.

NAT TURNER'S INSURRECTION

THE SANGUINARY REBELLION LED BY A
young Negro in southeastern Virginia, in 1831, has a cabal-
istic background studded with the abracadabra beloved of
the African. There is witchcraft in it, blood on the moon,
visions, eclipses, and a good deal of the voodoo hocus-pocus
that is still to be seen and heard in Harlem. Save for its social
and political consequence, the tale might be dismissed as a
Poe nightmare come to life, horrible but scarcely of historical
importance. That consequence, however, was the postponement of the Negro's "emancipation" by perhaps as much as
a generation.

The scene of the uprising was Southampton County,
about a hundred miles south of Washington. The district
was relatively prosperous, cut into small thriving farms, its
rich lands were being rapidly cleared of timber, and in almost every direction roads were under construction. In
Virginia and elsewhere in the South manumission societies
had substantial membership, and generally the emancipation
movement was making respectable headway. In Virginia
hundreds of slaves had a degree of freedom very nearly
equal to that of their owners. Historians of the South of that
period stress the contentment, the prosperity and the feeling

of security enjoyed by whites and blacks alike. There was popular approval of the new State constitution, adopted the year before the massacre. The social and economic picture was, perhaps, as idyllic as it could be in a class society. But in Southampton County that period was the calm before the storm.

Nat Turner developed into one of those messianic Negroes who inevitably recur in the life of the race in America. The chief difficulty in evaluating the man is to judge the sincerity in his harangues against slavery. Most of the evidence suggests he was more the fanatic, confronted suddenly with a fevered vision of himself as the worshipped leader of thousands of his people, than a man sanely aware of the injustices suffered by his race. He thought of himself variously as God, or as a prophet divinely ordained. To Thomas R. Gray, who defended him at his trial, and to whom the Negro is said to have confessed, Turner was something of a puzzle —"a complete fanatic, or he plays his part most admirably." Gray spent hours with Nat before the insurrection's leader was hanged (and his corpse "delivered to the doctors, who skinned it, and made grease of the flesh." For years thereafter, Negroes in the district would not take castor oil, because of a weird conviction that the local supply had its origin, as it were, in Nat).

Turner was born in 1800, the son of a slave named Nancy, at the plantation of her owner, Benjamin Turner, in Southampton County. Nancy had been torn from Africa not many years before. Although "she later developed into a useful and faithful servant," she apparently was prone to moods of unconventional violence: she was so infuriated at Nat's birth, the memoirs say, that she had to be tied to her pallet to restrain her from murdering the infant. Nancy's fury seems to have been provoked by the decampment of the boy's father, who "was very high-spirited, and ran away . . . and was never recaptured."

On the death of her owner, Nancy and her son were inherited by Benjamin Turner's brother, Samuel Turner, a coach-builder. The latter's son, J. C. Turner, gave Nat a good deal of instruction, although in young manhood the Negro was careful to say that his considerable education came from divine instruction. Nevertheless he was certainly precocious, and it appears that he was easily reading the Bible, for example, when other and older children were lost in the fastnesses of a simple reader and speller. His new owner and Samuel Turner's neighbors were impressed with Nat's readiness at reading and writing, at the promptness with which he would spout, irrelevantly, "So saith the Lord!" and he was regarded as sufficiently truthworthy to act as an overseer. Apparently he was "very religious, truthful and honest . . . never uttering an oath, never drinking intoxicating liquors, and never committing a theft." Even at the age of five he astonished his mother, his owner and his playmates by relating in detail family anecdotes that had occurred before his birth, a faculty which, fraud or not, was sheer magic to the other slaves. His superiority over his fellows was such, he said later in prison, that it seemed certain to him he was destined to become celebrated and to serve as a leader of his people. As a boy he could read, write and talk more intelligently than some of the unlettered whites in the community. He cloaked himself in an air of religious austerity, a pose that did not draw taunts or ridicule from the neighborhood Negroes. The inspired Nat remained aloof from the other slaves, and he worked for the most part at the side of his owner.

When he reached twenty-five, however, he was seized with the itch to preach. He had behaved oddly for two years, seldom varying his response to questioners from a sonorous "Saith the Lord!" or the resounding citation become even more popular with him, "Seek ye first the Kingdom of God; and all these things shall be added unto you." He explained to the Negroes that this text had been revealed to him by the "spirit" while he was in the fields one day, kneeling in prayer in front of his plow. None of his hearers knew that Nat was plagiarizing St. Luke.

He said the holy spirit had advised him repeatedly to "Behold me in the heaven!" It is not clear whether the object to be beheld was Nat or the spirit. Among the credulous inhabitants of the Negro shacks he circulated papers covered with hieroglyphics, evidently written in blood, and otherwise decorated with a sun, a crucifix, and rows of meaningless figures.

But a few white neighbors noticed that these revelations coincided with an unwonted obstreperousness in the hitherto exemplary Nat. Shortly before 1830 he had been hired out to Joseph Travis, who with his wife admired and encouraged Nat despite a warning by Mrs. Travis' brother, Salathiel Francis, that he was "a Negro of bad character, and odd." Gradually Nat's privileges were restricted. This was intolerable to one signalled out by the "spirit," and Nat ran away to live by himself for a month in the woods before he returned. Some of the slaves, astonished that Nat went unpunished on his return, called him a fool to come back, saying that a man of his stature should labor for no one.

But after thirty days and thirty nights in the Southampton woods Nat had learned, he told his critics, that his mission was not to commune with himself and the spirit, but to take his place among his fellows. For while he was suffering the inconveniences and privations of his expedition another vision had been revealed to him. This one had unmistakable and immediate connotation: there were vast numbers of black and white spirits, in this revelation, pitched against one another in violent combat; the sun overhead was darkened ominously, there was a terrible thunder rolling in the heavens, blood stained all the waters of the world below, and there was a voice of authority repeating, "Such is your luck, and such are you called to see, and let it come rough or smooth, you must surely bear it." Those to whom he told this shivered deliciously. Surely nothing could tell the future more plainly . . .

In 1828 Nat Turner was twenty-nine. He was a stout Negro for his age, pure African in type, somewhat below average height, the nose flat and the hair thin. An existing sketch of him shows a face certainly more amiable and sympathetic than cruel. He was a facile mimic, and he had learned oratorical tricks to which he owed much of his influence over the Negroes.

In May he told a white overseer, Ethelred Brantley, that he had "heard a loud voice in the heavens, and the spirit instantly appeared to me and said the serpent was loosed and

Christ had laid down the yoke he had borne for the sins of man, and that I should take it on and fight against the serpent, for the time was fast coming when the first should be the last and the last shall be first." Brantley and Nat were both so moved by this vision that they baptized each other in a nearby mill-pond, in the sight of scores of slaves.

The precise date when "the last should be first," of the "fight against the serpent," of "blacks and white pitched in battle," was to be determined apparently by some signal from the spirit. It might materialize at any time; indeed it might be found some morning in the hieroglyphic arrangement of the dew on the leaves, in which Nat professed to find some mystic and divine Word. He began to absent himself periodically from the Travis' employ, and in these nocturnal junkets he seems to have become familiar with much of Southampton County beyond his home.

He made a few close friends among Negroes in the neighborhood, but any plans he may have had of rebellion he kept secret—until the "sign" was made manifest. But when he found drops of blood on the corn, it was plain to him that the spirit was becoming restless, and that the signal would not be long withheld.

Conveniently for him, tragically for a good many others, there was an eclipse of the sun in February 1831. Here unquestionably was the sign from the spirit . . . It will be recalled that the sun had a special significance for Nat, for it was always prominent, together with the mark of the crucifix, on the papers he circulated among the slaves.

The appearance of the eclipse, he thought, was not only the long-awaited signal, but it was a cue to divulge his plans to others. The men closest to him were four Negroes, Henry Porter, Hawk Travis, Nelson Williams, and Sam Francis, all working with Nat or on adjoining farms. He called them together, and outlined his plans. The godliness of his proposed butchery was believed implicitly by the dazed quartet, vastly flattered at their leader's confidence in them. Their series of meetings at night were noted by their several employers and overseers, but these were dismissed as the ordinary gatherings at which slaves planned chicken-raids or other normal mischief. The plan eventually adopted— and, extraordinarily, kept secret—was a surprise attack to be launched July 4. Unhappily for the slave-owners, the insurrection did not begin on Independence Day, at which time they would have been assembled in some force in the villages and towns for their various parades and celebrations, together with their women and children. Evidently the Negro saw that these concentrations might endanger the strategy by which "the last should be first." Not to lose face with his confidants, however, he explained that the divine labor of conceiving and plotting the massacre had made him ill, and that the uprising must be postponed.

Another sign of celestial encouragement occurred on August 13, and thereafter he did not hesitate. That omen of heavenly sanction was the appearance of the sun on its rising —"having a singular appearance, probably under the influence of meteoric causes which have not yet been fully explained," in the words of a contemporary historian, Robert R. Howison. Its color, the Richmond *Enquirer* asserted, was "pale green, later turning to cerulean blue, and then to a silver white." Later in the day a black spot could be seen on its surface. The Negroes everywhere were excited, and nothing that their owners advanced in explanation was convincing. Turner and his four lieutenants saw that they might more easily find recruits now among the frightened slaves. "As the black spot passed over the sun," he told them, "so shall the black pass over the earth."

A final meeting and feast was to be held Sunday, August 21, to perfect their plans. At this period of the summer the harvest was in, and most of the slaves were granted a short "jubilee" vacation. Slaves who had been obedient and industrious could, on Saturday and Sunday, tend their own crops, and even go hunting with their masters' firearms (many of the guilty were later traced by the number of guns found missing after the slaughter).

Nat Turner arranged to meet the quartet on the banks of the Cabin Ford, near the Travis place, in the late afternoon, after they had roasted a pig and opened a gallon of brandy. To divert suspicion he told Travis that he was ill and unable to go to the slaves' dining quarters for his meals. His owners' wife came to his shack herself to serve him his meals at his bedside, a kindness that tortured his conscience some time afterward.

Nat joined his conspirators the next afternoon, Sunday. With the four men was another, a slave named Will, the property of a neighbor, Nathaniel Francis. "General" Nat demanded an explanation of his presence. The slave, who in a few hours was to demonstrate a ghastly proficiency with the broad-ax, made a reply that reflects the domination Nat exercised over the hands. Will said that he valued his life no more than those of his friends, that liberty was as much cherished by him as by Nat, that if necessary he would give his life to obtain freedom for the slaves. That satisfied the "General."

They remained on the river bank until late at night, devouring the pig, which they washed down with the brandy and some cider—all of them drinking except Nat. During the evening they were joined by a Negro named Jack, who had evidently stumbled upon the band in the dark. He pleaded he was sick, but Hawk, afraid the intruder might raise an alarm, persuaded Turner to force Jack to remain with them. The band now numbered seven.

The area of "General" Nat's operations the next several hours was in one of the least settled parts of Virginia. The woods were thick in many parts of the county, affording many places of concealment. They remained in their hiding-place until ten o'clock, by which hour the surrounding countryside was deep in sleep—and the brandy and cider were finished. As the leader, Nat agreed that he would shed first blood, and they swore to spare neither age nor sex until they had seized the firearms they needed, and had raised an adequate force. Their only weapons at this hour were a broad-ax and a hatchet. As they left the woods they were joined by Austin, another slave, who was promptly impressed into service, increasing their ranks to eight.

The night was moonless

The Travis dwelling was the small frame house, with brick chimney, typical of the district. The eight men reached it without sound, and Hawk, appointed lieutenant by Nat, insisted upon breaking down the door with the ax. He was dissuaded by the leader. The lieutenant then brought a ladder, and placed it against the chimney. Nat climbed to the top window, and crept down the stairs to seize his owner's guns and to open the front and back doors. The only sound was the breathing of five sleeping persons—Joseph Travis, his wife, Sallie, Putnam Moore (Nat's young master) and Joseph Westbrook, who was apprenticed to Travis, both boys of sixteen, and the Travis' infant. A Miss Maria Pope, who also lived in the house, had been nominated as the first victim because of her dislike of Nat. However, she was away, safely visiting friends.

The eight men climbed the stairs to the sleeping quarters. The child slept with its parents and, Nat testified later, it awakened and "smiled sweetly" when he picked it up—he had often fondled it. He put it down, conscience paralyzing his arm.

"It was then observed [again]," he confessed, "that I must spill the first blood . . . It being dark I could not give a death-blow. The hatchet glanced from [Travis'] head; he sprang from his bed and called his wife. It was his last word. Will laid him dead with a blow of his ax."

Another blow from Will killed Mrs. Travis, who was spared witnessing her husband's murder. The youths sleeping in the room adjoining probably never knew what struck them. The band returned down the stairs, and gathered in the yard. Nat brought out "four guns and several muskets," which the Negroes were set to cleaning. When this was done, he marched his patrol of eight in military formation up and down the barn-yard. From the Travis' gig the men tore the scarlet lining of the top and ripped it into head-bands.

There was not enough of the fantastic headgear to go around, so the Travises' bloodsoaked sheet was employed. Behind their ears they stuck turkey- and chicken-feathers. After Nat believed the men had been sufficiently drilled, and were suitably dressed, he stole a quantity of powder and shot, several crowbars and pitchforks, three horses, and at midnight they set off.

Salathiel Francis—Mrs. Travis' brother, who had warned her against Nat—lived a quarter-mile away. En route there Nat recalled his compunctions when holding the Travis child. But "nits make lice," he told the band. Henry Porter and Will were sent back with orders to take the infant by the heels and brain it against the fireplace.

Although they numbered eight, the Negroes were afraid of Nelson, a huge slave owned by Salathiel Francis. So as not to arouse Nelson's opposition, Nat determined upon artifice. The slave Sam, one of the original quartet, and Will were owned by Francis. These two arrived at the farm, called out that they had an urgent note for his master. The farmer came unarmed to the door in his nightclothes, and was clubbed to death. Nelson, remaining loyal, was shot, but succeeded in escaping and warning his owner's wife nearby of the danger.

Their next objective, after seizing the guns in Francis' house, was a half-mile distant, the home of Captain Nevit Harris. On the way they were joined by other excited Negroes, hearing of "Old Nat's War" by some underground medium. By the time the sky was growing light in the early August dawn, the band had increased to fifteen, most of them carrying firearms. But at Captain Harris' they found that the family had fled, probably warned by Nelson. They leveled the building, and seized money and other valuables. To get recruits Nat circulated a report that the British were abroad, repeating the Hampton atrocities of 1812, and that the slaves must rise and defend themselves against the invaders.

On the march again, they stopped next at the home of Wiley Francis, who, hearing shortly before of the massacres, had concealed his family in the woods, but had refused to flee himself. His slaves warned Nat's men, when they arrived calling for brandy, that they would be shot if they advanced beyond the barn fence. Their owner called out, "Here I am, boys! I won't go from my home to be killed!" Nat's men left, their leader now realizing, he later said, that he might find unexpected opposition from Negroes loyal to their masters.

The men were growing thirsty. The sun was above the horizon. Nat gave the order to march three miles to the home of a widow, Mrs. Elizabeth Turner, who owned a small distillery. There they shot down the overseer, and with ax and sword butchered the owner and a Mrs. Sarah Newsom, her guest. Further on, at the Newsom place, a Mrs. P. Reese and her son were pitilessly murdered in their beds, and the farm manager escaped by feigning death after repeated blows on the head.

The next day Nat decided to divide his force to cover more ground, but arranged for a rendezvous every few hours. At more than twenty farms which they passed on Tuesday the murders were repeated. The slaughter at the home of Mrs. Catherine Whitehead, a well-to-do woman living a mile east of the Turner farm, was typically savage. When the Negroes, now crazed by brandy and blood, arrived here they found one of her sons, Richard Whitehead, a Methodist preacher, in the cotton patch with his slaves. As he was hacked by Will's broad-ax, he kept crying, "Why kill me? Why kill me?" The answer was a scream of "Kill him! Kill him!" Meanwhile others killed three of the Whitehead daughters and an infant boy, being given a bath by his grandmother. Mrs. Whitehead, dragged from the house by Will, wept to Nat that she did not want to live since he had murdered all her family. At a nod from the "General" she was decapitated. Of the remaining two daughters one escaped; Nat caught the other running from the house, and, finding his sword too dull, killed her with a fence-rail. This was the only murder directly charged to Nat at his trial.

The scene was even more atrocious at the home of Levi Waller, the popular meeting-place of the district, where there was a boarding-school, distillery, and a blacksmith's and wheelright's shop. Most of the countryside had been warned, but for some reason word of the terror had not reached Waller's. Nat's band, now grown to nearly forty, arrived here after consuming literally barrels of brandy, on their way to Jerusalem, the county-seat, where the leader expected to find arms and ammunition. Waller's slaves had word that the Negroes were rising almost simultaneously with the actual appearance of the raiders. Waller had time to summon the boarding-school children and their master from their building, a quarter-mile away. But before guns could be got to the loyal slaves, Nat's band was charging on the house. Waller hid in the plum-orchard.

Fifteen were murdered, more than half of them school-children, before Nat called a halt. When they rode off, the demented Waller fled to raise the alarm and raise the troops at Murfreesboro, across the North Carolina line.

"Mrs. Waller had advised the men to flee," a contemporary writes, "as she thought the negroes would not kill women and children. How mistaken, poor woman! One of her own slaves slashed her with a razor as she defended herself. Martha Waller [one of the small children] was concealed by her nurse under her large apron, but the child could not endure this reckless destruction of furniture, so arose and threatened to tell her father. One of the negroes seized her and dashed her to death against the ground."

As the Negroes left each place, they impressed as many slaves as they could into their ranks, so that as they now approached the county-seat Nat had nearly sixty men. At one of their last stops they exhibited the extent of their madness by drinking the blood of a victim, Captain John T. Barrow, to make them "more brave and encouraged"—thus "General" Turner. The Captain had stood out against the force, refusing to surrender until he fell under the fire and clubbing of twenty Negroes. "I was sorry such a man had to be killed," the leader testified, and added that his men showed their respect and admiration for Barrow by shrouding his body in a quilt and placing a plug of chewing tobacco on his chest.

The advance on Jerusalem, where some four hundred terrified women and children had sought refuge, was halted while Turner's men broke into the wine cellar of a prosperous farmer and magistrate named James Parker. They rolled the brandy barrels into the yard. The liquor was poured into tubs and sweetened with loaf sugar. Nat, heading the other party, came upon the men snoring on the grass. He aroused them, and they started off again. Without warning they were confronted by a force of twenty white men led by Captain Arthur Middleton of the county militia.

The white volunteers moved forward to meet Nat's advance-guard, which retreated into the main body of the insurgent Negroes. Although unmolested on their march of about thirty miles, during which they had killed sixty or seventy whites (the exact total remains unknown), now they lost their nerve. When the whites were within a hundred yards, Nat shouted: — "Fire, and God damn them, rush!" The farmers slowly retreated, dodging Indian fashion behind trees. The Negroes' fire was wild, since most of the men were drunk; moreover a good many of them were using fowling-pieces loaded with bird shot. In a few minutes the farmers, whose fire had killed several of the Negroes, were reinforced by another small armed party from Jerusalem. The Negroes now fled in panic back across Parker's Field toward the woods. Had they stood up to, and routed, the little party of farmers, they would doubtless have succeeded in reaching Jerusalem, confiscating the arms there, and committing a slaughter of women and children that would have compared favorably with the enlightened warfare of modern armies.

But the threat of such a massacre continued. At least twenty men remained with Nat, who now decided to try to enter Jerusalem from the rear by way of the Cypress Bridge.

From one of his deserters, however, he learned that that approach was guarded, and also that there was no hope of immediately reassembling the deserters. Most of them had fled back toward their homes, hoping to convince their owners that they had been forced to join the insurrectionists. (One of these, returning to the home of Nathaniel Francis with one arm nearly severed, asked his owner what duties he was to perform. Francis replied, "I'll show you in a minute," bound him in his gig, and drove the slave to the courthouse, near which he was promptly hanged.) Nonetheless Nat was not prepared to capitulate. With a fatalism born of desperation he sent ahead word to his home district that the men who had returned should meet him Wednesday or Thursday next.

The men continued to plunder homes, deserted by their occupants, on the way back to their own shacks. By force and by persuasion Negro hands were recruited to substitute for the desertions, and by nightfall Nat's strength had been brought up to forty. At Buckform, Nat posted guards for the night, but the men were soon aroused by a false alarm that the militia was in the neighborhood. However false, the alarm served to make twenty of the men run away. On Wednesday at dawn, seeking more recruits, Nat marched to the plantation of Dr. Simon Blunt, who with his son, his overseer and his loyal slaves had been awaiting Nat throughout the night. When the Negroes had crept—soundlessly, they thought—to within twenty yards of the dwelling, the defenders fired a volley, the women in the house rapidly reloading the guns. Hawk Travis, one of the original four supporters of Nat, was fatally wounded, another killed, and the rest again fled, pursued by Blunt and his slaves. One of the latter made the first capture. Nat raced to the woods near the home of Captain Harris, and not far from the old meeting-place, where the same day a cavalry force from neighboring Greensville County surrounded the Negroes.

All but a few were killed, including the murderous Will. For months thereafter the spot was strewn with skeletons. Those who survived melted away. At nightfall Nat stole back to the Travis farm, where the massacres had begun, and took a quantity of food back to a nearby field, remaining away from the woods, where, he guessed correctly, he was suspected of hiding. Beneath a pile of fence-rails he dug a small cave. There he remained six weeks, leaving only at night to search for water.

A vigilante force composed of young men was organized immediately, independent of the Southampton militia. It was known that the Negro survivors were in a region bound by the Blackwater, Nottoway, Chowan and Meherrin rivers, and to prevent escape the civilian detachments guarded all the bridges and fords over these streams. Other volunteers guarded the women and children gathered at depots for safety. The militia meanwhile began ascending and descending the river banks, rounding up the few insurgents who had escaped the cavalry.

Although the insurrection had ended, reports of the uprising were so alarming that even after the news reached the Governor at Richmond, patrols were organized for the protection of the capital before troops were despatched to Southampton County. The county militia and the civilian patrols, however, had suppressed the uprising many hours before offers of assistance arrived from Richmond and from North Carolina. Even close at home, where it was known that Nat's force had been routed and most of the Negroes killed, the terror continued. General W. H. Brodnax, in command of the militia at Greensville, informed the Governor on August 25 that "the consternation unfortunately was not confined to the county where the danger existed, but extended over all immediately about it. Not a white family in many neighborhoods remained at home, and many went to other counties, and the rest assembled at different points in considerable numbers for mutual protection. In numerous instances females, with their children, fled in the night with but one imperfect dress, and no provisions."

Troops began to pour into the county. From Fortress Monroe three companies and an artillery-piece were sent to Southampton, arriving the following Sunday, and these were reinforced by naval detachments from two cruisers in Hampton Roads. The Gosfort Navy Yard offered muskets, pistols, swords and ammunition, and citizens provided carts for their transportation from Suffolk. Additional troops were refused after August 24, the day Nat went into hiding. By then the militia had captured or killed all the insurgents except Nat. The heads of several of the slain Negroes were impaled on posts as a warning, in the Chinese manner. One of the marine captains bore a rebel head aloft on his sword.

A Southampton County committee of citizens wrote President Jackson, a week after the massacre, of the sentiment prevailing. This apparently was in extenuation of the killing of several innocent Negroes, mistaken for insurgents by the nervous farmers. "Most of the havoc [the President was told] has been confined to a limited section of our county, but so inhuman has been the butchery, so indiscriminate the carnage, that the tomahawk and scalping knife have now no horrors. Along the road travelled by our rebellious blacks, comprising a distance of something like twenty-seven miles, no white soul now lives to tell how fiendlike was their purpose . . . and the excitement is so great that were the justices to pronounce a slave innocent, we fear a mob would be the consequence."

The militia officers prevented a good many summary executions, although an unknown number of both innocent and guilty Negroes was shot or otherwise executed without trial. The greatest anxiety was felt over the whereabouts of Nat. Negroes did not dare to be seen off their owners' property, for fear of being mistaken for the "General." He was variously reported in Ohio, Maryland, North Carolina, Louisiana, and as distant as the West Indies.

About the time when the feeling of danger throughout the county had subsided, Nat was seen. At no time had he been more than five miles from the Travis farm. While he was absent from his cave, a dog dived into the hole and snatched a piece of dried meat. As the animal left, Nat returned and was confronted by the dog's owners, two neighborhood slaves. He begged them to hide him, declared he was insane with fear after skulking around farms at night in search of information about the trials. But the slaves ran, seeing he was armed, and raised an alarm. A civilian posse methodically and unsuccessfully searched the woods. It remained for a farmer to capture him. One Benjamin Phipps, on his way to visit a neighbor, sat beneath a tree to rest, his gun over his knees. A few minutes earlier, Phipps had heard a patrol crashing through the woods ahead of him. After the patrol passed, Nat stuck out his head from a new cave he had dug beneath a fallen tree.

Phipps ordered Nat to throw out his weapon, a rusted gun and a sword. His captor fired into the air, the pre-arranged signal. In a few minutes a hundred men had gathered. The date was October 30, 1831.

The "spirit" had failed Nat. Curiously, the possession of a hat, unusual for a Negro slave, kept his spirits buoyant throughout the whipping, and the jabbing of pins into his flesh, that he endured before he was delivered to the jail at Jerusalem, miraculously alive. There, until his trial, he spent the days in foolish grinning, in exhibiting his hat—which with seventy-five cents was all the wretched loot that remained to him—and shouting denials of repentance. In his confession, however, he warned other Negroes "against any such plots through the misinterpretation of revelations."

Fifty-three Negroes were indicted and brought before the Southampton County Court, which sat the next month. Preliminary hearings had eliminated about fifteen others; their owners vouched for their past behavior. The trials provoked editorial vehemence throughout the nation comparable to that aroused by the Scottsboro cases. Northern editors held that it was manifestly unfair to hold the trials in Southampton County. Southern editors were generally unanimous, afterward, that "the trials were conducted with a patience and care highly creditable to the magistracy of the County." Four of the defendants, who were freed

Negroes, could not be tried by the county court, and their cases were heard by the State Circuit Court. That court ordered the execution of three of them.

Of the fifty-three, seventeen were condemned to death by hanging, among them a woman; twelve were transported out of the State; and the others were discharged, except the three condemned by the Circuit Court. When the considerably subdued Nat, clothed in rags and covered with chains, heard that he was to be "hung by the neck until you are dead! dead! dead!" he "raised his manacled hands to heaven, with a spirit soaring above the attributes of man." That, in any event, was the report of his lawyer.

To say, as did most newspapers and abolitionists of the North, that the atrocities of Nat Turner's insurrection had their origin in the injustice of slavery in Southampton County seems to go considerably beyond the truth. But to say, on the other hand, that their origin lay in the over-indulgent policy of the slave-owners is the part of special pleading by the South. It seems closer to confirmable fact that the trouble lay in vast quantities of brandy and in the fanaticism of Turner, unable to find expression for his superior intelligence in any direction but violence.

Turner was apparently more interested in heading an army, with the awe and adulation that the position might bring, than in liberating his race. He may sincerely have believed himself appointed by the "spirit" to a place of leadership over the Negroes—history is full of sincere men become Moses by personal nomination; but that he was convinced his mission was to free the Negroes seems doubtful. He had a mission, but precisely what he was never certain. While his own confession need not be taken as gospel, his warning against "misinterpretation of revelations" suggests that he was never sure what the visions meant.

After 1831, both in the South and the North, the nation was extremely sensitive to any sign of restiveness among the Negroes. But such signs were few. Before the Turner massacres Negro insurrections were not uncommon—although scattered and local in character—in the slave-holding States. Most of these had occurred in Virginia and Maryland, where slaves were bred and sold to Alabama and Louisiana planters, breaking up families. One such uprising, the Gabriel insurrection, had broken out in Richmond shortly before the terrible raids in Southampton County. But the mass execution of twenty of Nat's followers discouraged further attempts by the Negro at mass revolt until the shelling of Fort Sumter. And for some time the corner abolitionist could be effectively silenced by reminders of Southampton. Less than four years after the massacres, William Lloyd Garrison narrowly escaped assassination by a mob in Boston, the center of abolitionism. If the eventual conflict that cost a half-million lives could not be averted, Nat Turner was not the least factor in its postponement for thirty years.

THE DORR WAR

"LISTEN, THOMAS WILSON DORR, TO THE SEN-
tence of the Court, which is that you be imprisoned in the
State's Prison at Providence for the term of your natural life,
and there kept at hard labor, in separate confinement."

The short and stocky People's governor, in his full face
and bearing a mild suggestion of Napoleon, turned heavily
toward the bench in the Supreme Judicial Court, and again
muttered: "I appeal to the people of Rhode Island, and to
the country. I have nothing more to say." The Newport
County sheriff led away the defendant, found guilty of high
treason. The date was June 24, 1844.

One year after the prison doors had closed behind the
life-convict, Dorr walked out, a pardoned felon, but exhausted in mind and body, grown ill in prison and old before
his time. The State legislature in 1854 annulled the verdict
of the Supreme Court, but Dorr long since had lost interest
in living. Ten months later he was dead, at forty-nine.

Rhode Island, the smallest of the thirteen colonies, fearful
that it might be annexed by one of its neighbors—as New

York had sought to swallow Vermont—was the last of the States to ratify the federal Constitution. After articles of peace were signed with Britain, it made no effort to revise its fundamental law as given in the charter of Charles II, procured by Roger Williams. When at last it ratified the Constitution, in 1790, the original charter was 147 years old; and despite its many archaic provisions, that document remained the basic law of the land, its substitute for a written constitution, for another fifty-three years.

For more than a century the suffrage restrictions in the charter of 1643 had worked no intolerable injustices. The vote was restricted to freeholders or freemen, i. e., land-owners with an estate worth $134, or renting for $7 a year, and to their eldest sons. Since the majority of the inhabitants were farmers, owning their land, it seemed that the privilege of suffrage was in the right hands. But by 1824, the economic and social picture in Rhode Island had changed. For one thing, the size and number of towns had increased substantially. Manufactures were introduced, and neither the manufacturers, some of whom were men of large means although they owned not a foot of land, nor their employes had the slightest voice in the political affairs of the State. With reason, they were jealous of the farmers, resentful of the exclusive rôle of the landowners in running the government and electing its officers.

The towns, moreover, had another complaint against the venerable charter. It had arbitrarily limited the town's representation in the Assembly, which if practical in 1643 was far from it in 1824. For example Newport, the principal community in 1660, was allotted four representatives in the lower house, while Providence was allotted two, the proportion determined by population. By 1824 Providence had grown to twice the size of Newport. Providence County, moreover, included ten of the thirty-one towns in the State, and fully three-fifths of the population of Rhode Island, but it could send only twenty-two representatives to the State capital, while the other counties returned fifty. As increasing manufactures of cotton and worsted goods swelled the towns' population, the demand for liberalization of the suffrage restrictions grew more insistent. The only answer of the government, which was to say the delegates of the land-owning class, was a contemptuous silence, or, when forced into the open, effective political opposition. The larger landowners kept the smaller ones in line by threatening to foreclose mortgages if those indebted to them did not vote as directed. The landed oligarchy also had an effective check on the property-less, even though many men who could not vote were well-to-do. The charter forbade them from suing for debt-recovery or for personal injury unless the plaintiff's writ was endorsed by a land-owner. Such endorsement was not extended to anyone who raised his voice for a more democratic suffrage law. The inevitable argument was heard that if the charter was practical in 1643 it was *ipso facto* equally desirable today.

Nevertheless, from time to time the bolder spirits had launched, or attempted to launch, movements for a radical change in the basic law. Since all the other States had adopted constitutions of their own, why not Rhode Island? As early as 1799 a member of the Assembly had moved for a constitutional convention, one delegate to represent a thousand inhabitants. The motion was passed, doubtless because at that time the threat of an invasion of non-freeholders was unseen. But the measure was promptly killed in the Senate. In 1811 the Senate adopted a law slightly modifying the suffrage restrictions, but that measure died in the lower house. Had the legislature by 1821 adopted some moderate revision of the charter, the Dorr War of eighteen years later would probably have been averted. (Shortly after the uprising Francis Bowen, editor of the *North American Review*, in an account of the "War" that is unfriendly to Dorr, admitted that "a reasonable and judicious reduction of the qualifications required of a voter, if offered early in the period . . . would have been satisfactory to the people, would have robbed the Suffrage Party of any pretence or excuse for their illegal movements, and would have obviated the necessity of a more radical change, effected a few years later amidst the tempests of a revolution.")

During 1821-23, the movement for reform began to gain impetus. People began to see that the suffrage restrictions had created a situation in which some landowners were buying the votes of men not entitled to go to the polls. A landowner, desirous of office, would grant a so-called life-lease of a piece of property to a non-freeholder, with the understanding that the property would revert to the lessor if the rent were not paid at the end of a year. In this way men whose votes were desired were made eligible at the polls, although they had purchased no property and did not intend to pay rent. Such frauds created sentiment in favor of a change to nearly universal suffrage from a system whose restrictions led to a corrupt vote.

The newspapers of Providence, about the year 1821, began to agitate for a constitution. Editors pointed out that Connecticut in 1818 and Massachusetts in 1820 had devised their own constitutions. Finally in January 1824 a bill was brought before the legislature calling for "a convention for the purpose of forming a written Constitution of Government for this State."

One of the members in the lower house, Asher Robbins, later a United States Senator, loosed an impassioned address against the bill, on the ground that since the people had not asked for a convention, it should be assumed they did not want a constitution. The Speaker of the House, Albert C. Greene, replied that if the people did not want the convention, they had only to refrain from electing delegates to it.

The bill passed. The convention met, and drew up a constitution which made provision for a somewhat fairer apportionment of Assembly members among the towns. But far from liberalizing the suffrage qualifications, the convention made land ownership also obligatory upon the eldest sons of landowners.

When this feeble amendment came before the people of the State, in October 1824, it was defeated by nearly two to one. In part the defeat was attributed to the fact that, aside from the absence of any liberalization of the suffrage laws, the demand for a constitution was centered in Providence, and had little support in the State at large. The entrenched agricultural element voted for the *status quo*.

But the leaders for reform, for any change, were generally feckless, uncertain what they wanted or how to attain it. The movement cried aloud for direction and leadership. It had in its favor the fact that the charter was falling apart of old age. By 1829 a revived movement for a constitution had became primarily a movement for enlarged suffrage. In the short period of 1820-25 the Providence population had increased from 11,745 to 15,941 — most of the increase due to the emmigration of cotton-mill operators, mechanics, factory workers and their families. By this time many non-freeholders were beginning to realize that some revision in the suffrage laws was absolutely necessary.

The legislature received petitions from Providence, North Providence, Bristol, Warren and other towns. These were referred to a legislative committee headed by Benjamin Hazard of Newport, who dismissed them in a report generously larded with denunciations of democracy as the "curse of every nation which has ever yielded to its charms."

He reported, with respect to the petitions, that "the committee has not thought it necessary to inquire particularly how many of the signers are native citizens of the State, but they are sufficiently informed to be satisfied that a very great proportion are not so, and it is ill calculated to produce a favorable opinion of their qualifications . . . that persons who have adventured, and are every day adventuring among us from other states or countries, to better their condition, who enjoy, in common with ourselves, all the protection and benefits of our equal laws, and upon whose departure there is no restraint, should be still restless and dissatisfied."

A postscript to this dismissal gave "the petitioners leave to withdraw."

For another five years the movement for a constitution and for wider suffrage remained in abeyance. Then, in 1834, the first systematic effort was made to "educate" the public to a point where it would plainly demand a change. The propaganda was launched in various ways, chiefly in speeches at the town-meetings long familiar to New England—unless, as happened in some localities, the suffrage orators were expelled. The same year two towns of Providence County, Smithfield and Cumberland, sent invitations to other towns throughout the State to name delegates to a convention "to promote the establishment of a State Constitution." Ten towns accepted—including Newport (surprisingly, since it was a conservative stronghold). Here, then, was the birth of a faction of non-voting townsmen, engaged chiefly in one or another form of manufacturing. The delegates met at Providence, and selected a committee of five to draft an "Address to the People of Rhode Island."

Enter its author, Thomas Wilson Dorr.

At that time, 1834, Dorr was twenty-nine. He was born in Providence, and was the son of a successful manufacturer whose social position was secure even though he was not of the land-owning class. The son was sent to Phillips Exeter, and at fourteen entered Harvard, graduating in 1823, second highest in honors. He went to New York to study law under Chancellor James Kent, was admitted to the bar in 1827, and returned to practice in Providence. Seven years later he was elected a member of the Rhode Island Assembly. He was scarcely a brilliant advocate, but his arguments are said to have been clear and convincing, and he built a sizeable practise because, one contemporary remarked, "He was irreproachable in morals, urbane in his manners, and mild and

unassuming in all his intercourse." Early in his career, however, it was evident that he was more the reformer than the
lawyer-statesman, and he had the reformer's unquenchable
hope. He began as a strong Whig, bitterly opposed to the
federal Government as then represented by the views of
Andrew Jackson; one of his first moves in the Assembly
was to introduce resolutions against the removal of public
funds from the Bank of the United States, against executive
control of the Treasury, and against the spoils system in
politics. But his stand for an enlarged suffrage, his opposition
to the effort to pass laws punishing abolitionists, forced him
to break with the party. His bitterest enemy, Governor
Samuel Ward King, said of him, after his conviction, that
"he was endowed with intellectual powers which, had they
been properly directed, would always have secured him a
commanding influence. Those powers, too, were disciplined
by an education more accomplished, perhaps, than any other
man of his age in Rhode Island had been privileged to obtain
. . . He might have been a true-hearted, private gentleman,
honored by the respect and confidence of the community in
which he resided."

The suffrage movement was made to order for a reformer.
Dorr's address, which opened by paying homage to "the
ancient sturdy spirit of Rhode Island patriotism," called for
organization of a party to work for a written constitution,
since "discretionary regulation of the elective right, and of
the judicial system, can never be properly and safely vested
in the legislature . . . When the American States severed
the political tie which formerly bound them to Great Britain,
all obligation to acknowledge obedience to a British charter

as a constitution of government was, of course, dissolved; and the people of each State were left free and sovereign. . . . The sovereignty of the King of England passed, not to the Government and Company of Rhode Island, but to the people at large, who fought the battle of the Revolution, and to their descendants. That the people of Rhode Island retain their inherent right to establish a constitution cannot for a moment be doubted." And "the present system is also inconsistent with itself. It excludes intelligent and upright men from the polls, because their business is such that the possession of the requisite landed qualifications is impractical. And yet, in many instances, they are bound to the soil by a species of real property consisting of houses, workshops, &c., built upon land leased to them for a term of years. A life-estate entitles a man to vote; a lease for 99 years does not. Is this consistent?"

Despite such arguments the constitution-suffrage movement again subsided of inertia. Delegates from the towns met, but the convention expired in inactivity in 1835. The chief reason for the prevailing defeatism was apparently the setbacks suffered in 1821, 1822 and again in 1824. Yet the non-freeholders of Rhode Island fully realized, to judge by newspapers of the day, that men like themselves had the ballot in almost every other State. Three years later, running as the so-called Constitutional Party's candidate for the national House of Representatives, Dorr obtained only 72 votes of a total of 7,615.

But in 1840, after the excitement of the presidential election had subsided, there appeared throughout Rhode Island a pamphlet, "Address to the Citizens of Rhode Island, Who are Denied the Right of Suffrage," under the imprint of "The First Social Reform Society of New York." It cannot be proved today that the "Society" was fictitious, but it is probable that the ingenious argument of the brochure was written by Dorr himself, printed at Providence and distributed from there. The proposal it contained was not fully adopted by the suffragists, but some of its recommendations served as the inspiration for some of the insurgents' moves.

The pamphlet set forth a plan by which a State convention should be held. At primary meetings, delegates were to be apportioned from each county and town. All male citizens of twenty-one should be qualified to vote for delegates. Lists of the voters should be preserved, "duly certified by those appointed to receive the votes, and appended to the credentials of the delegates." After the vote, the delegates in convention should count the number of ballots, "and if the whole number of votes cast exceeds the whole number of the previous general election for Representatives to Congress, then the convention will unquestionably represent the majority of the people and will, therefore, as unquestionably have the sovereign right to frame a constitution for the State."

The next step urged in the pamphlet, after the adoption of a constitution, was the election of State and Congressional officers. The new members of Congress would present their claims to seats at Washington, and the responsibility would then devolve upon Congress of deciding whether members from a majority of the people, elected under a republican constitution, framed by the people themselves, "shall have seats in the councils of the nation, or [whether] members from an incorporated body of Land *Lords*, are stockholders of the elective franchise, and of the Government."

The plan was so alluring that the suffrage advocates decided to act upon at least its preliminary recommendations. The first step, in the autumn of 1840, was an announcement by "certain inhabitants of Providence," led by Dorr, that they had organized the Rhode Island Suffrage Association. Most of its members, of course, owned no land. The idea was epidemic. Before the next spring, nearly every town in the State had a suffrage organization of the disenfranchised.

The suffrage leaders borrowed a leaf from the frenzied Harrison-Van Buren campaign of the year before, and on a smaller scale they loosed their own political fireworks. Suffrage badges and medals, with such inscriptions as "Free Suffrage and Equal Rights—the People are Sovereign," were distributed in the towns. In Providence, suffragist speeches at the Town Hall began to be noted for the regular way in which they ended in a free-for-all. There were torchlight processions through the large towns, howling bands, the parading of banners. As a means of "educating" the public to the suffrage issue, this was far more effective than more dialectics from Dorr in the form of Addresses to the People.

Among the first resolutions adopted by the Rhode Island Suffrage Association, and subscribed to by sister units throughout the State, were the following two—significant since they showed that the leaders proposed to ignore the legally constituted government:

1. That the power of the State should rest in the hands of the people, and that the people are guaranteed the right, from time to time, of assembling either by themselves, or

through their representatives, for the purpose of establishing a republican form of government.

2. That when a majority of the citizens of Rhode Island, who are recognized as citizens of the United States, shall by their delegates in convention assembled, draft a constitution, and the same shall be accepted by their constituents, it will be, to all intents and purposes, the law of the State.

By more than implication these resolutions served notice upon the Governor and the legislature that the suffrage leaders intended to effect reforms no longer by "education," but by peaceful revolution. That they alarmed the State officers, forcing them into a pretense of reform consideration, was clear at the opening of 1841. When the Assembly met in January its members were presented with a petition, bearing six hundred names, asking for a constitution, for much wider suffrage, and for greater legislative representation of the towns. The lower house, recently treated to the spectacle of suffrage parades, consented by a vote of 48 to 20 to an election of delegates to a constitutional convention, to be held ten months hence, in November, at Providence.

But it was provided that such delegates, apportioned among the towns on a population basis, could be elected only by the freeholders, not by any of the men seeking redress.

Meanwhile the suffragists, strengthening their ranks with the establishment of a lively official organ, *The New Age*, for the most part ignored the overtures of the government, satisfied that the legislature was dallying, that its members had no intention of permitting a wider suffrage than existed.

That belief was, in the main, a mistaken one, and Dorr has been criticized harshly by both friends and enemies for inciting a rebellion when a little patience would have won from the legislature most of the suffragist demands. Still, he had no more reason in 1841 to expect favorable action of the Assembly than his predecessors had had in 1821, 1822 and 1824. Indeed, when the "Landholders' Convention," as it was dubbed, met in November, its several factions wrangled for two weeks, and then adjourned to February 14 of the next year, 1842. But at that session, finally, it drafted a Constitution extending suffrage to every male citizen of the United States, past twenty-one, who had resided in the State two years, and in his district six months. It was agreed to submit the constitution to the people for ratification on March 21-23, 1842. One concession by the landowning delegates was to allow all citizens to vote in the referendum who would be entitled to vote were their constitution adopted.

But this last did not tempt Dorr nor his chief assistants, Congressman Dutree J. Pierce and Samuel Y. Atwell, a member of the Assembly. They were too far committed for anything short of unqualified approval of a constitution after their own architecture. Moreover, Dorr believed that any sign of capitulation now would see a return of the legislature to its past hostility to reform.

Between 1840 and 1842, however, during which the legislature had crept toward some concessions in the franchise restrictions, the Suffrage Party, as it had come to be called in the newspapers, had progressed rapidly in the direction of a convention to draft its own constitution, as proposed in the resolutions of 1840. In Providence the party found even the *Republican-Herald* growing friendly, observing after the national election, for example, that "there are at least 14,000 men in Rhode Island who had not the privilege of voting for President of the United States, on Monday last—men who in all respects are equal to those who enjoyed that privilege—and who, had they lived in any other State in the Union, could have exercised the inestimable right of freemen." *The New Age*, with slight variations, hammered away at the theme that "the present system of franchise in Rhode Island is unjust inasmuch as it concedes privileges to a certain wealthy class, thereby tending to build up among us an aristocratic class, with special privileges and immunities."

In the spring Dorr and his lieutenants stepped up the tempo of the campaign. They called a mass-meeting for April in Providence. After adopting resolutions more than three thousand of the gathering formed a parade, and marched to the State House. Most of the men wore badges with such slogans as "I am an American Citizen!" and carried banners that read, for example, "Worth Makes the Man, but Sand and Gravel Make the Voter," "Virtue, Patriotism and Intelligence versus $134 Worth of Dirt," and "Liberty Shall be Restored to the People." At hostile Newport, in May, a column of 1,500 paraded, a third of the men armed with guns or swords. Two militia companies which had been summoned for police duty failed to appear. Again resolutions were adopted to ignore the legislature and its constitution.

The Suffrage State Committee called for the election of delegates to attend a constitutional convention at Providence October 4th. The eighteen members of the State Committee, of whom Dorr was not one, took pains to preserve the form at least of constitutional procedure. "Every American male citizen, of twenty-one years of age and upwards, who has resided in this State one year preceding the election of delegates," was qualified to vote. The Committee directed that the delegates' credentials of election must be endorsed by their local election chairmen. Every town of a thousand inhabitants or under could return one delegate, for each additional thousand another delegate, and it was agreed that Providence could return three delegates from each ward. The election was set for August 28, three days before the freeholders were to elect their delegates to the "Landholders' Convention." Handbills were posted in all the towns, explaining to voters the reasons for the suffrage convention.

The votes cast totalled only 7,512—the day was rainy. The votes did not show a clear majority of freeholders or non-freeholders (voters were instructed to give their civil status), but Dorr estimated that at least one-quarter of the "legal" voters had expressed their desire for the suffragists' convention. It showed the support the cause received at this time that the landowners elected twelve of their number of the eighteen suffrage delegates from Providence.

The People's Convention met October 4. After deliberations lasting four days they agreed upon a constitution. "It must be considered a curious spectacle," the Providence *Journal* noted, "and one which no other country, if any other State, can present—a number of men assembled for the avowed purpose of overthrowing the Government, under which they live, without any authority from the legislative or executive powers, and yet proceeding without opposition and without hindrance."

The convention adjourned—despite Dorr's expression of fear that in so doing it might lose public interest—to November 15, to let the constitution draft become known throughout the State, and to permit general criticism. When the delegates reconvened, minor revisions in the document (conceived by Dorr) took up three days. It was voted to submit the constitution to the people during December 27-29.

Governor King, meanwhile, was growing apprehensive. Up to now he had believed that the suffragists' only means of redress lay in the slow process of winning support in the legislature. In November the landholders held their authorized convention, whose sessions the Governor was careful to attend. The delegates produced a "Landholders' Constitution" which, in many respects, answered the demands of the suffragists—but by now the latter had written their own constitution. The delegates fell to wrangling over the property qualifications for the newly enfranchised (the suffragists had no such discrimination), and they adjourned to the following February. At that meeting it was voted to submit the "legal" constitution to the people the following month— nearly three months after male citizens were asked to vote on the Dorr Constitution.

The suffragist referendum claimed a total vote of 13,944. Voters, as before when delegates were elected, were required to indicate whether they were qualified to vote under the charter. The State Committee of the People's Convention announced that in the total there were 4,960 ballots cast by landholders. "The whole number of males in this State, over the age of twenty-one years, as nearly as can be ascertained, is 26,142. Deducting, at a moderate computation, 3,000 persons who are not citizens of the United States, the remainder is 23,142, of whom a majority is 11,572. The constitution has received 873 votes more than half of all those qualified to vote for said constitution by citizenship, age and residence, and an actual majority of 4,746 . . . The Committee believe that both the voting and the returns have been as regular and as accurate as at any election ever held in this State."

From the State House, from newspapers friendly to the landowners, particularly from the inhabitants of Newport, the cry immediately rose that the suffragist vote had been a fraud and a farce, that the ballot-boxes had been stuffed with the names of missing sea-captains and sailors, of Government soldiers in Fort Adam, and of others absent from the State or unqualified to vote,—foreigners, Negroes, the insane, and the dead.

The existing evidence is insufficient to state flatly whether fraud had been committed to a degree that sensibly affected the result. If there were as many as 2,373 improper ballots, the suffragists could not claim that the vote reflected a majority. After the vote, opponents of Dorr made much of the fact that there had been no penalty attached to voting fraudulently. His supporters, on the other hand, could point to the calibre of their leaders, men who were trusted in their communities and would not tolerate any known chicanery at the polls.

But unquestionably some fraud had been committed. That was revealed when, in March 1842, the same classes of citizens were asked to vote on the "Landowners' Constitution," with a result showing 8,689 against it, 8,013 in its favor. Simple arithmetic argued that there were not in Rhode Island 14,000 qualified to vote the past December, and another 8,000 in March, even if it were assumed that some of the men who had first voted in favor of the Dorr Constitution had voted a second time against it. Samuel Atwell, one of Dorr's supporters in the Assembly, admitted after the vote that the "result had made it a great matter of doubt whether a majority of the people of the State were in favor of that [People's] Constitution, and of course whether it had been adopted."

In the Assembly Atwell moved that the People's Constitution, together with all the records of the vote which Dorr had sent to the Governor, be referred to a legislative committee of investigation. His motion was defeated 57 to 11 because, in the words of an opposition orator, "there was nothing in it." Instead the Assembly passed resolutions declaring that the suffragists' activities had been an "assumption of power," and that the legal government would continue to "promote the peace, security and happiness of the citizens."

Although the differences between the Landholders' Constitution and the People's Constitution were not profound, Dorr declared that the disenfranchised had voted against the former "not because it was made by the freemen . . . but because its leading provisions were unjust and anti-republican." He failed to particularize, but he could have criticized the document, (voted down by a margin of only 656 ballots), on four points, as did his lieutenants: the preservation of the property qualifications for suffrage (continued until

1888), the apportioned representation in the House (although scarcely differing from the suffragists' provisions), the three-fifths vote necessary for an amendment (as compared to Dorr's demand for a simple majority), and finally, the fact that the people had already voted favorably on a constitution—to wit, his own.

The charge in the Assembly's resolution of "assumption of power" was inspired by the Governor. Implicit in it was the threat of charges of treason against the suffrage leaders. Governor King was a cautious and colorless official, but he was quick to recognize that Dorr was preparing for a *coup-d'état*. He had considered calling upon President Tyler for military aid even before the "Friends of the Suffrage Constitution," meeting in April at Providence, named their ticket: Dorr for Governor, Amasa Eddy, Jr., lieutenant-governor; William H. Smith, secretary of state; Joseph Joslin, treasurer, and Jonas Titus, attorney-general. In addition there were twelve nominations to the State senate, as well as a full list of Assembly candidates.

All these candidates, as well as the men who had voted for them, were immediately exposed to the punishment provided in the new "Act In Relation to Offenses Against the Sovereign Power of the State," passed by the legislature a few days before as a warning to Dorr and his associates. This provided sentences ranging from six months to life imprisonment, and fines from $500 to $2,000, for anyone found guilty of serving as an officer in elections "other than those in accordance with the State laws." Anyone taking office as a result of such an election, or anyone supporting or contributing to such election, was guilty of treason. The meas-

ure was popularly called the "Algerine Law" after one of
the pro-suffrage newspapers stated that "the *Dey* of Algiers
had his *day*; and Rhode Island is the last place in which the
arbitrary doctrines of this ex-potentate can be revived with
success or impunity."

This proved no deterrent, however, and on April 18 the
suffragist elections were held. In all but one instance the
candidates were unanimously elected, in a total of 6,500
ballots. The leaders explained the smallness of the vote by
the fact that anyone voting for the suffrage ticket could be
prosecuted under the "Algerine Law." Two days later the
regular charter election was held, which brought out 7,080
voters, and in which King was reëlected to the governorship. It will be noticed that the electorate was about evenly
divided between Dorr and the Governor.

With the elections over, the suffragists had nothing to do
but await the coming of their inauguration day. The government did not arrest the suffrage candidates. The "Algerine Law" evidently had been planned as a warning, not as a
statute to be enforced—both the Governor and the legislature realized that 180 prominent citizens, strongly supported
by their constituencies, could not be seized by the five
county sheriffs, at least without the aid of some outside military agency.

In April the Governor appealed to President Tyler.

"The State of Rhode Island is threatened with domestic
violence [he wrote]. Apprehending that the legislature cannot be convened in sufficient season to apply to the Government of the United States for effectual protection in this
case, I hereby apply to you . . . for the protection which is

required by the Constitution of the United States." In an informal note to the White House the Governor added that "for nearly a year last past, the State of Rhode Island has been agitated by revolutionary movements . . . There is little doubt but that a proclamation from the President of the United States, and the presence here of a military officer to act under the authority of the United States, would destroy the delusion which is now so prevalent, and convince the deluded that, in a conflict with the Government of the State, they would be involved in a contest with the Government of the United States, which could only eventuate in their destruction."

But the President had no intention of issuing a proclamation threatening federal intervention, and so exposing himself to charges of interference in the affairs of a State. The State's troubles, he wrote, were to be regretted, but they were merely questions of "municipal regulation."

On May 3, 1842, the opening day of the first session of the People's legislature, the streets of Providence were crowded with visitors from every part of the State, and with hundreds of the curious from New York, Massachusetts and Connecticut. The agreeable belief was abroad that a clash might be expected between the opposed legislatures. Several full companies of militia, supporters of Dorr, the Independent Company of Volunteers, a formidable platoon of "butchers on horseback in white frocks" and the Providence Brass Band headed a column in which were all the People's officers. The escort marched through the center of town and over Weybosset Bridge, then retraced its route, and drew up before a disused wooden building used as a foundry. No attempt was made to enter the State House, which was closed, since the Charter Assembly was not to convene until the next day— and then at Newport. Five hundred of the armed men were posted about the foundry, after which the legislature began its election of officers.

"Governor" Dorr's inaugural address set forth the suffragists' views, and urged a strengthening of the militia. After this the legislators empowered him to inform the President, and the governors of the other States, of the establishment of a constitutional regime in Rhode Island.

In a burst of cheers and laughter the new lawmakers repealed the Algerine act.

The legislature adjourned to July 5, two days later. It had made a fatal hesitation. The time for caution had passed. In Providence Dorr's was the *de facto* regime. It had been the new Governor's intention to order the sheriff to open the State House so that the suffrage government might have possession of the archives and the administrative machinery. But when three-fourths of his Assembly voted, after hours of vacillation, to "request the opening of the building" from the charter authorities, Dorr did not insist on taking possession by force.

The consequence of that weakness was that the "Foundry Legislature," as it was first called, did not meet again. The session of July 3 was its first and last.

At Newport, meanwhile, the charter Assembly met to organize the government for the ensuing year. Its first move was to draw up another appeal to the President on behalf of the entire legislature—the first appeal had represented Governor King alone. The President replied as before, but he instructed army officers in the State to watch the situation closely. In a personal letter to King the President recommended a general amnesty and the calling of another constitutional convention.

Two members of the People's Legislature, returning to their Newport homes, were promptly arrested for treason. The next day Dutree Pierce, Dorr's Congressman-supporter, was also arrested, his bail set at $5,000, and deputy sheriffs, thus encouraged, began seizing suffragists by the score. The People's Government seemed to collapse with the departure of Dorr for New York and Washington to seek support. Overnight there were dozens of resignations from office; it was mistakenly assumed by many in the party that the Governor had fled the State, since his departure had been kept secret for several days.

At Washington Dorr attempted to enlist the support of a number of Congressmen and Senators with whom he had been corresponding, and who he hoped might force the issue on the floor of the national legislature.

The response was not encouraging. From the President he obtained a promise that the Chief Executive would use his offices to obtain amnesty for those convicted under the "Algerine Law," but further he would not go. Back in New York, Governor Dorr confessed to friends and supporters at Tammany Hall that he could do no more. Tammany, strong for manhood suffrage since its inception the century before, encouraged Dorr, and actually circulated a petition demanding President Tyler's impeachment if he ordered armed intervention in Rhode Island. Dorr was cheered in several tub-thumping addresses, and he was given an honorary escort to the New York pier from which he took a steamer to Stonington, Connecticut, forty miles southwest of Providence.

The Governor met a large force of guards outside the capital. There were elaborate precautions taken against his seizure; he was not for an instant without a bodyguard. With a sense of dramatic effect, he entered Providence in a barouche drawn by four white horses, in company with almost 1,200 men, of whom 250 were armed. At the home of Burrington Anthony, on Federal Hill outside the town, he established headquarters, stationed a strong guard, and sent out a summons into the country districts for his supporters. About four hundred responded, few of them with arms.

On May 17, the first act of force occurred. A party of suffragists seized two old Revolutionary pieces posted in front of the "Town Hall Lot." The militia made no protest, but the cannon were removed with such haste that the raiding party forgot to take the ball and shot with them, and the ammunition was secreted before the men returned. The seizure of the artillery caused Governor King, now thoroughly alarmed, to placard the walls of Providence with a notice summoning citizens immediately to take arms at the State arsenal, and to muster up the militia in the capital and at Newport.

Early in the evening a council of war was held by Dorr at his headquarters. Several leaders attempted to dissuade him from a suicidal plan to capture the arsenal after the manner of Captain Shays. He remained firm, deaf to prophecies that the advance meant certain bloodshed, and after the arrival of a small suffragist force from Woonsocket he announced that the advance would be made at 2 A. M. Inside the arsenal were two hundred men, most of them volunteers. Dorr's "army," which had numbered nearly five hundred the day before, had shrunk to 234 at the zero hour.

Arrived at the arsenal, Colonel John Wheeler raised a flag of truce after posting his artillery pieces. He demanded surrender of the building in the name of Governor Dorr. The arsenal commandant bellowed into the night, "I know no such name!" Upon this reply large groups were seen to desert from the attacking force, one of them including Colonel Wheeler. In the face of almost certain annihilation Dorr gave the order to fire the cannon, and to charge.

Twice the guns flashed—without firing. Touchholes had been plugged or filled with wet powder by Dorr's men.

With fewer than fifty of his followers he returned at dawn to his headquarters to devise the next move after the treachery of the night before. And there, to make his failure more humiliating, he received a message that two of the Suffrage Party's senators and nine of its representatives had resigned, giving as their reason the abortive attack on the arsenal. It was then, at the insistence of the lieutenants remaining by his side, that he agreed to flee to Connecticut, to return when another attack had better chances of success. He had left Anthony's house only a few minutes when Governor King arrived with the sheriff's posse to search the dwelling. But the head of the charter government, now that Dorr had fled, consented to hold in suspense prosecutions for treason.

Dorr would not admit he was beaten. He had some success

raising recruits along the Connecticut border, chiefly youths excited by prospects of a lark. His determination to continue in the face of the arsenal fiasco, of the legislative resignations, and the collapse generally of the suffragist movement in Providence he explained as the only honorable course left to him. "This misadventure in the city of Providence was attributable to . . . a temporary panic . . . to the pusillanimity of leading friends of the cause, from whom better things were expected, and whose hearts had failed them."

For a third time President Tyler declined to intervene on King's statement that Dorr was raising troops in Massachusetts, Connecticut and New York. Daniel Webster, then Secretary of State, sent an investigator to report on the Rhode Island situation, which that envoy declared later was calm and untroubled. But throughout June there was a succession of tales that troops and supplies were being concentrated along the Connecticut line in the northwest. Perhaps one reason for the persistence of the reports was the attitude of Governor C. F. Cleaveland, of Connecticut, who was sympathetic to Dorr, and who had refused to honor a request from King to surrender the fugitive if found in his jurisdiction. The governors of New York and New Hampshire took a similar stand. But Boston and Providence newspapers, even up to a few days before the next foray, minimized the danger, and scoffed at stories of an army on the Connecticut line. The Providence *Express* observed laconically that "there seems to be considerable excitement abroad about Governor Dorr's movements . . . without sufficient reason. There is little or no excitement at home, and there are no known grounds for any."

In New York, however, Dorr had obtained, in addition to a good deal of encouragement and pledges that a Tammany regiment would be raised, some small assistance in money and supplies. On June 22 he arrived at Norwich, Connecticut, with twenty men from New York—self-styled "The Spartan Band." There he was met by Smith, the suffragist secretary of state, and a few close friends. It was decided to call a military council immediately at Chepachet, a village in Gloucester Township five miles east of the Connecticut line and sixteen northwest of Providence. Before his officers arrived for the conference, word was received that the village had been occupied by a force of nearly five hundred suffragist sympathizers, converging on Chepachet from within a radius of fifty miles. Dorr was at North Killingly, Connecticut, when he heard this report, and he hurried across the line to take the leadership. He arrived in the hamlet June 25.

He learned that Chepachet in the past two days had been transformed into something of an armed camp. There were three pieces of artillery in the village, a fact that was soon relayed to Providence. But instead of five hundred, there were not more than two hundred men, and by nightfall the number of men in Chepachet was reduced to fifty, the others preferring to camp in the comparative safety of the woods. With this force Dorr began to fortify Acote's Hill, an elevation eighty feet high just outside the village, skirted on its south exposure by the Providence Turnpike; to the east was a pond, and a smaller hill, but the north and west were unprotected by natural barriers. The men succeeded in raising a few breastworks.

Four men, civilian travelers, were taken into custody near the hill, marched to the insurgent camp at Woonsocket, and then released. The quartet hurried to Providence with a story—told on oath before an officer of the court—of a force of 2,000 armed suffragists entrenched on Acote's Hill.

Their tale provoked Governor King into an almost hysterical plea to President Tyler. Again Tyler refused to intervene. King then summoned the militia, and by June 26 there were fully 2,500 armed men in Providence, called up from Newport, Bristol, Warren and elsewhere. With their arrival the Governor declared martial law.

A brigade was dispatched to Foster, south of Gloucester, to cut off any attempted retreat into Connecticut. On June 27 the militia column, excepting a guard left at Providence, began the march on Chepachet, arriving next morning.

By noon that day the citizens of Providence were reading in the Providence *Journal* that "news has this moment arrived that the force of Colonel William W. Brown has taken the insurgent fortification. Dorr has fled but large numbers of his men have been captured."

A few hours later the newspapers published a message identified as "Military Orders, No. 54," which said that "the village of Chepachet and fort of the insurgents were stormed at quarter before 8 o'clock this morning, and taken with about one hundred prisoners by Colonel Brown; none killed and no wounded."

The unvarnished fact was that no fort was stormed, since the suffrage forces had nothing so formidable, and on Colonel Brown's arrival the hill was without any defenders. There were no casualties because there was no fighting.

Later it was established that most of the "hundred prisoners" were non-combatants, groups of curious farmers and their hands, or suffragists who, obeying Dorr's command to disband given more than twelve hours before, were starting out for their homes. It was also established that Dorr's flight to Connecticut the night before was known to King two hours after the insurgent left Chepachet, as the result of an intercepted letter from Dorr which stated that "believing that a majority of the people who voted for the constitution are opposed to its further support by military means, I have directed that the military here assembled be dismissed." Another reason for retiring was that the suffrage Governor had artillery ammunition for fifteen minutes only, no water, and few provisions.

Martial law endured for forty days, during which about three hundred men were arrested and their homes ransacked for evidence to use against them. The majority were discharged. There was a price of $5,000 on Dorr's head on an indictment charging high treason against the State. Slightly more than a year later, on October 31, 1843, he appeared in the offices of the Providence *Republican-Herald*, and was promptly arrested by a deputy sheriff. He had written from Boston that he planned to surrender after the landowners' constitution went into effect, in May, granting almost universal suffrage—the same except in minor details as that for which he had struggled for a decade.

That was the achievement of the Dorr War. Without the threat of civil war, a constitution entitling all male citizens to vote would have been at least another generation away. While there were no casualties, and while it was farcical from a military standpoint, the Rhode Island uprising was, in fact, more revolution than rebellion—for in 1842 Dorr had tried to overthrow the existing government and substitute his own.

Most of those who have written of Dorr's War arrive at the conclusion that the suffrage leader was an admirable figure so long as he avoided strife, so long as he did not threaten a struggle which would involve bloodshed. The majority opinion is that after he returned from New York in 1842 he should have heeded the precautionary counsels of his best-informed advisers.

It is true that he ignored their warnings. But that he should have agreed with them that equal suffrage could be attained without the threat of civil war is to expect too much of legislators who had consistently refused to give an inch except under compulsion.

The party had sought relief by petition to the state legislature; it had tried for redress by provoking the national legislators to a debate on the constitutional issue; it had appealed, through Dorr, to the President of the country; and it was later to learn, in a suit arising from the arrest of one of its supporters, that the United States Supreme Court would hold that "the power to determine that a state government has been lawfully established is not one of the powers which the courts of the United States possess." Thus checked, the only alternative was a realistic threat of bloodshed. It succeeded.

1894

THE PULLMAN STRIKE

IN 1893 THE RAILROAD WORKERS OF THE NA-
tion were feeling their oats. Despite recollections of federal
military intervention to halt their bloody rebellion of seventeen years before, thousands of them believed with a good
deal of reason that the time was ripe for another and final
showdown.

There was a host of reasons for the confidence of some of
the unions' leaders, and these seemed valid even against the
panic of that year, the preface to a depression felt the next
by nearly every industry in the United States. Chief among
these reasons were two decisions handed down in federal
courts, one by Judge Henry Clay Caldwell, of the United
States Circuit Court, the other by Judge James Dundy of
the United States District Court. In the first case, affecting
the Union Pacific Railroad, it was ruled that the workers
had full liberty to organize as a group to protect their interests and to maintain wages—then the rankest heresy to
the operators, who believed in rugged individualism, if they
had yet to devise the phrase. In the second case, which concerned the same rail system, the district court ordered the

Union Pacific receivers to restore the wages of employes to their former level.

This was not the end of encouraging signs, no matter if the Stock Market collapse had provoked failures in London, whence came the foreign capital on which American railroads depended. In 1893 Eugene Debs had succeeded in forming an "industrial" type of labor organization, the American Railway Union, which brought under one head the various bodies of workers which had split apart in jurisdictional controversies. In a series of minor differences with the railroad operators, President Debs of the new union had emerged triumphant. The effect was that workers throughout the country began to have confidence in the American Railway Union, and to trust its founder, a leader who was obviously incorruptible. But he became a figure of national prominence in April, 1894, when the union members of Jim Hill's Great Northern Railroad struck when their pay was cut, and demanded higher wages. For two weeks, to the astonishment of the inflexible Hill and his stockholders, no freight-car could be moved over the system from North Dakota to the Pacific Coast, and the carrier was forced to press ancient stage-coaches into service. In less than another week the workers were back at their posts, had won their raise and most of the strikers' other demands.

Debs was the miracle man, the messiah of a new labor militancy. In 1893, on the eve of the Pullman strike, he was thirty-eight, a tall gaunt figure with a platform voice, a power of easy expression and gestures that drew thousands to him. He had been a locomotive fireman, a grocery clerk, the secretary-treasurer of the Brotherhood of Locomotive

Firemen—the "aristocrats of labor," with whom he broke—editor of its magazine, and a member of the Indiana legislature. Debs had resigned from the Brotherhood, despite pleas that he remain, because of its policy of ignoring strikes in other branches of organized labor, its want of sympathy for the unskilled laborers, and the secrecy with which the Brotherhood clothed the meetings of locals.

Engineers, conductors, brakemen and switchmen from some of the old brotherhoods clamored for admission to the American Railway Union. By mid-year its membership was 100,000. Among other workers eager to join, men who perhaps had extravagant hopes for the fledgling union, were the workers of the Pullman Company in its shops on the outskirts of Chicago.

Both Debs and George W. Howard, the A.R.U. vice-president, felt that the Union had need to grow stronger before it could win a strike against Pullman. Thus Debs testified to the United States Strike Commission, en route to prison, that after hearing of a threatened strike at Pullman "we concluded that many of our members might possibly be flushed with the [Great Northern] triumph . . . I was particularly anxious at that time to avoid any strike if it was possible to do so." Nevertheless, on May 11 the Pullman employes struck. Arrived among the men and women workers outside Chicago, Debs said he "became satisfied that the conditions under which the employes there were obliged to work fully justified them in the course they had taken. I found that the wages and expenses of the employes were so adjusted that every dollar the employes earned found its way back into the Pullman coffers."

The causes underlying the strike must be explained by a word about the "model town" established by George M. Pullman in 1880. In that year the Pullman Palace Car Company purchased five hundred acres fourteen miles south of Chicago. It built extensive shops for the construction and repair of sleeping-cars, and for the manufacture of many other types of coaches. It also erected tenements for some four thousand workers, and the necessary streets, parks, sewers, gas- and water-works, churches and other public buildings, etcetera. Here was industrial paternalism on a scale never before realized, and the model community was as much publicized here as it was in Europe—"the healthiest industrial city in the world."

At the time of the strike the total investment at Pullman, which was only one of the company's plants, was $36,000,-000, undivided profits were $25,000,000, and on July 31, 1894, the dividends for a poor year's business amounted to $2,880,000.

The head of this enormous enterprise was a philanthropist, by his own admission and in the estimation of the country at large; and also by his own confession he was a business man. One of the four chief functions of the company was "the care and management, as owner and landlord, of the town of Pullman," and by "management" was meant a reasonable profit on the model tenements, the public utilities, the post office, savings bank and the library that it offered to its employes.

George Pullman first discovered in 1889 that while labor suspected paternalism, it reviled a profitable paternalism; the workers voted for annexation of the town to Chicago.

Subsequently the Illinois courts forced him to dispose of all properties not required for industrial purposes.

Even the ministers of the town, who might be expected to have conservative and paternalistic leanings, were openly speaking and writing of Pullman as "a civilized relic of European serfdom" and speaking sympathetically of "the prevailing tendency [of the workers] to beat the Company." The handsome library (which cost its subscribers three dollars a year), the decorative Green Stone Church (renting for $300 monthly), the parks, fountains, landscaped vistas and other institutions seen by visitors and by passengers speeding by on the Illinois Central were, in the workers' minds, merely the front for a feudal system which, in the words of Debs, was "so adjusted that every dollar the employes earned found its way back into the Pullman coffers." Above all, the rents at Pullman caused criticism.

The Reverend William H. Carwardine, pastor of the model town's Methodist Episcopal Church, found considerable agreement with his written opinion that Pullman was "a sort of hollow mockery . . . We all enjoy living here because we have an equality of interest, and we have a common enemy, the Company, but our daily prayer is, 'Lord, keep us from dying here.' "

The usual and superficially reasonable answer to such criticism was that the worker was not forced to live at Pullman. The investigators appointed by President Cleveland—Carroll D. Wright, the United States Commissioner of Labor, John D. Kernan of New York, and Nicholas E. Worthington, of Illinois—found in the course of their Chicago hearings that this reply was less than a half-truth.

"The fear of losing work," they reported, "keeps them in Pullman as long as there are tenements unoccupied, because the company is supposed, as a matter of business, to give a preference to its tenants when work is slack. The employes . . . naturally feel some compulsion to rent at Pullman, and thus to stand well with the management."

If certain sanitary and aesthetic features were excluded, rents in Pullman averaged 20 to 25 per cent higher than in Chicago or for equivalent accommodations in surrounding towns—this was the finding of the federal investigators before whom Jane Addams testified as a housing expert. There also was testimony that workers lost their jobs if they moved their homes from Pullman tenements; that the workers when paid received two checks, one of which was for rent owed the company (employes told of sometimes receiving, after two weeks' work, pay checks of four cents to a dollar, after meeting their rent); and that in 1893-94, when business grew slacker daily, superintendents and foremen drove the men inhumanly to meet the production quotas that had once been achieved with a third more workers.

Before the strike was called there were nineteen impotent unions represented at Pullman—even the laundry girls had their local. The company had no open objection to unions: its position was that it would not recognize them as bargaining agents for the men and women in the shops. That attitude may appear archaic today, but the viewpoint of Thomas H. Wickes, the Pullman second vice-president, as expressed to the federal commissioners at Chicago, had a medieval flavor even in 1894—a piece with Commodore Vanderbilt's classic remark about the public.

Wickes' testimony, expressing the labor policy of the Pullman Company, is here paraphrased:

"Our objection was that we would not treat with our men as members of the American Railway Union, and we would not treat with them as members of any union. We treat with them as individuals and as men."

"Don't you think," he was asked, "that it would give the corporation a very great advantage over the men if it could take them up one at a time and discuss the question with them? With the ability that you have got, for instance, where do you think the man would stand in such a discussion?"

"The man has probably got more ability than I have. If he is not able to do that [i.e., maintain his end of the discussion], that is his misfortune."

"Then you think that you have the right to refuse to recognize a union of the men designed for the purpose of presenting, through the ablest of their members, to your company the grievances which all complain of, or which any complain of?"

"That is the policy of the company. If we were to receive these men as representatives of the unions they would probably force us to pay any wages which they saw fit, and get the Pullman Company in the same shape that some of the railroads are by making concessions which ought not to be made."

In their report to the President the three commissioners, touching on this part of the voluminous testimony, remarked that "this position secures all the advantage of the concentration of capital, ability, power and control for the company in its labor dealings, and deprives the employes of any such advantage or protection as a labor union might afford. In this respect, the Pullman Company is behind the age."

The average wage at Pullman, however, was at least equal to that paid elsewhere in the region for similar types of skilled labor, and in a few instances was above the average. During the twelve months ended July 1, 1893, workmen at the model town received $2,760,548.99, an average of $613.86 each.

By the fall of that year the business recession was such that the corporation closed its plant at Detroit. Surplus cars were on hand at Pullman, and new orders were cancelled. Between September 18, 1893, and May 1, 1894, the operating expense was declared by the company to be 3.6% above cost of materials and labor.

To attack the operating deficit Pullman officials set about cutting wages—its undivided profits, be it noted again, were $25,000,000, of which the workers were fully aware. The reductions began in September, and averaged between 25 and 30 per cent, including wages paid for piecework. There was no explanation given the workers, and no conferences with them until the employes succeeded at last—on May 7, the next year—in obtaining an interview between their committee of forty-six, representing all the Pullman departments, and Vice-President Wickes in Chicago. He heard their plea for a return to the wage-scale of June the year before. Even the least knowing of the delegation realized that this was impractical, but it was advanced as a basis of negotiation.

Among the delegates was a seamstress, Jennie Curtiss, who with others in her department, working ten and three-quarter hours daily, earned about three dollars a week, after the cuts. (The girls made the carpets, and dressed the silk, satin, plush and velvet drapings for the dining-cars, the linen for the sleepers, the seat-tapestries, etcetera.) She described the meeting with Wickes:

"We stated our grievances to Mr. Wickes, and told him we wanted our wages raised; he said it was impossible to raise them, as the company was losing money on its contracts and it could not possibly raise our wages a cent.

"We then asked if they did not think they could lower rents a little. He said, 'No, it was utterly impossible to lower the rents one penny,' as they were only receiving about three per cent on their investment now, and were losing money on contracts just to enable their men to have work . . . We went down again and saw Mr. Pullman; he said he could not raise our wages nor lower the rents."

The company offered to show its books to employes to substantiate its claim of operating at a loss. But it insisted, in the face of two appeals by the Civic Federation of Chicago, a disinterested organization, that there could be no move toward conciliation or arbitration, for "there is nothing to arbitrate." The Pullman executives were similarly unmoved by the solicitation of the Common Council of the municipality or by telegrams from fifty mayors of the country.

Reports circulated at the plant that the company had decided upon a lock-out in anticipation of the threatened strike.

The workers' meeting with Pullman occurred on May 9. The following day three members of the delegation, employed in the iron department, were laid off by the acting superintendent, who explained there was no more work. Under ordinary circumstances this would have occasioned no surprise. But it was considered an obvious "reprisal," and word of it swept over the plant. (The acting superintendent later testified he was unaware that the three men had been members of the grievance committee.) It was considered a violation of a promise made the day before by Pullman that members of the delegation would not lose their jobs for serving as the workers' emissaries.

If sooner or later the strike was inevitable, the discharge of the three men was all that was needed to set it in motion immediately, despite the advice of Debs and Howard. On the evening of the same day the nineteen local unions affiliated with the American Railway Union assembled outside the plant, and voted a walk-out of 3,100 men. The next morning, May 11, not a man or woman was in the shops; all the machinery was idle. But three hundred of the strikers were distributed around the property to act as guards. Strike history, of course, is full of instances where so-called guards were in reality armed pickets awaiting battle with scabs. To the Pullman Company the force of three hundred was an army of terrorists, but the fact remains that throughout the strike there was no violence or destruction of property at the plant.

Pullman officials immediately laid off six hundred employes who had not joined the strike. The workers had called a walk-out; the company, in effect, replied with a lock-out.

Debs hurried to Pullman, saw that the men were justified,

and promised that the American Railway Union would call a general boycott of Pullman cars if the company, after a reasonable period, still refused to arbitrate or to give other satisfaction. On May 16 the Order of Railway Conductors and the Brotherhoods of Locomotive Engineers, Brakemen and Switchmen, not associated with the A.R.U., announced they would not strike in sympathy, but the Debs union demonstrated its sincerity with an immediate levy of three cents on every member to support the Pullman men.

At this early stage of the strike the Chicago police force numbered only thirty-six hundred, but Police Chief Michael Brennan was unalarmed. He recognized that trouble might be expected if a Pullman boycott was voted, since the network of tracks, towers, switch- and freight-houses covered about 195 square miles. The authorities were also aware that the World's Fair had attracted hordes of camp-followers who would probably join any rioting, but in mid-May the strike at Pullman seemed to be a question of which side would give in first, and violence seemed remote.

But by mid-June it was apparent to the workers that the Pullman officials really meant there would be no arbitration. On June 15 and June 22 the officials even refused to open letters from the American Railway Union containing the reasonable proposal that Pullman name two arbitrators, a local court two others, and that the four select a fifth, and that that group should determine whether the issue was subject to arbitration. By then, the strike had been in progress nearly six weeks. A stalemate.

In the town of Pullman there was entire order. At outdoor and indoor meetings the several thousand strikers were warned that order would be strictly enforced, were told that destruction of property would be prejudicial to the cause (and urged, incidentally, to regard the saloons and fleshpots of nearby Kensington and Roseland as out of bounds). Questions of policy and strategy, until the entry of the A.R.U., were in the hands of a central strike committee. Public sentiment showed in the fact that the strikers' relief committee received cash donations of more than $15,000, and that all kinds of provisions poured into the town—from a bottle of bluing to a carload of flour. There were cash contributions, for example, from Chicago police and fire organizations, from department stores, political clubs, Turnverein societies and fraternal groups. Nothing created more sympathy for the strikers than the monotonously reiterated statement from the Pullman offices: "There is nothing to arbitrate."

Early in June Debs realized that the strike at Pullman was insufficient in itself to bring concessions from the employer, and that its continuance without other support meant that the men would be starved into submission. Voluntary contribution, which now cared for 2,700 families in the town, would not continue forever, and now the Pullman Company was pressing the strikers for some $70,000 arrears in rent. No evictions were made, but the tenements of Pullman belonged to the company, and it would be mandatory upon the courts to support the Pullman Medici if he demanded possession of his property.

Support for the strikers came on June 13, when Debs announced that a coalition had been brought about between the American Railway Union and the Chicago locals of the Knights of Labor (from whose ranks had sprung the Amer-

ican Federation of Labor a few years before). Two days
later the American Railway Union opened its national convention at Chicago, with delegates from 465 unions with a
membership of 150,000. The strike at Pullman was the first
topic before the convention, even though the membership
represented had no direct personal grievance with the Pullman Company. But Pullman, with its close relation to the
railroads, was a part of the common enemy.

Among the resolutions adopted was one excluding Negroes from membership, although the only Pullman employes who could qualify as railroad men were the porters;
another resolution denied membership to anyone connected
with a military body; and a third approved government
ownership of the lines. Delegates communicated with their
home locals for instructions on the Pullman issue.

Standing beside Debs on the platform, the delegates were
swayed by the story of Jennie Curtiss, the seamstress who
had gone to interview Pullman.

"My father worked for the Pullman Company for ten
years," she said. "Last summer he was sick for three months,
and in September he died. At the time of his death we owed
the Pullman Company about $60 for rent. I was working at
the time and they told me I would have to pay that rent, give
what I could every pay-day until it was paid. I did not say
I would not pay, but rather than be thrown out of work I
would pay it. Many a time I have drawn nine and ten dollars for two weeks' work, paid $7 for my board and given
the company the remaining two or three dollars on the rent,
and I still owe more than $15. Sometimes when I could not
possibly give them anything the clerks in the bank would

insult me because Mr. Pullman would not give me enough in return for my hard labor to pay the rent for one of his houses, and live."

On June 22 the American Railway Convention voted to declare a boycott against Pullman cars unless the company agreed within five days to arbitration of its differences with the strikers.

The A.R.U., following this step, voted an assessment of five cents a member. But even the ultimatum and threat of the boycott, and the prompt move to raise a war-chest, made no outward impression upon Pullman officials. There was the same communiqué, "There is nothing to arbitrate." The threatened boycott was not taken seriously anyway. Reports from the west stated that rail networks were not alarmed over any refusal by railroad men in Chicago to move Pullman cars; the convention was below the horizon, out of sight, out of mind.

As the deadline approached, nevertheless, railroad officials in Chicago listened less skeptically to the talk of men in the yards, to the switchmen and brakemen. On June 25, the third day of the ultimatum period, a meeting was called of the General Managers' Association.

That association for several years had been the chief *bête-noire* of the railroad unions, particularly those with members in the Chicago district, but the association was feared by railroad unions in every part of the country. It was a voluntary, unincorporated body, established in 1886, of the twenty-four railroads centering or terminating in the city. It had dealt chiefly with matters other than wages, but on occasion the association had entered wage disputes by announcing, for example, a "switchmen's scale for Chicago"—in this manner a carrier embroiled in a wage controversy had ranged on its side the other twenty-three roads. The effect was to flatten out the compensation of all railroad workers in the Chicago district. Usually no baggage-agent could complain with accuracy that higher wages for his work were paid by another line (or, if that proved to be true, the offending carrier's "excessive" scale was promptly brought into line by the General Managers' Association).

From labor's point of view the activities of the Association were a conspiracy to suppress a living wage. It was a viewpoint shared by many who had no stake in the roads.

The Association, in addition, concerned itself with the strategy to be employed to break strikes. Everett St. John, the Association chairman, readily testified that "arrangements were made by which agencies were established and men employed to come to Chicago in case of necessity." In the recommendations sent to President Cleveland after the strike, the federal commissioners gave their opinion that:

"The Association is an illustration of the persistent and shrewdly devised plans of corporations to overreach their limitations and to usurp indirectly powers and rights not contemplated in their charters and not obtainable from the people or their legislatures. An extension of this association . . . and the proposed legalization of 'pooling' would result in an aggregation of power and capital dangerous to the people and their liberties as well as to employes and their rights. The question would then certainly arise as to which shall control, the Government or the railroads, and the end would be inevitably Government ownership."

The intervention of the General Managers' Association took the form of a statement that it would not permit the American Railway Union to disturb traffic. Its position was that the Union was acting unlawfully in its attempt to force the carriers to break their hauling agreements with the Pullman Company, and that the A.R.U. would violate its own agreements with the roads if the boycott were called.

But the Association's attitude that "it would not permit" railroad employes to seek redress for one of their constituent union groups was a piece of intolerable patronizing to leaders. A large part of the labor rank and file regarded it as bluff. Not so Debs and his aides: they saw that the real opponent was not the Pullman Company, but the twenty-four lines in the General Managers' Association.

Overnight the strike front threatened to grow from the small town of Pullman to a territory embracing the greater part of the nation's rail network.

The Union's answer to the General Managers' Association's statement, designed also to jar the Pullman Company into arbitration, was to call out the employes of the sleeping-car company at St. Louis and Ludlow, Kentucky, altogether five hundred men. When just before noon, on July 26, the Pullman Company again announced their stand as unchanged ("There is hardly anything new to be said as to the position of the Company"), Debs declared the boycott in effect.

The practical application of the boycott meant that American Railway Union members would not operate any train with Pullmans attached. Debs described a typical example of the boycott's operation to the federal commissioners in these terms: "The employes at once, on the 26th, refused to haul Pullman cars. The switchmen, in the first place, refused to attach a Pullman car to a train, and that is where the trouble began, and then when a switchman would be discharged for that they would all quit, as they had agreed to do. One department after another was involved, until the Illinois Central was practically paralyzed, and the Rock Island and other roads in their turn.

"Up to the first day of July," he continued, "or after the strike had been in effect five days, the railway managers, as we believed, were completely defeated. Their immediate resources were exhausted, their properties were paralyzed, and they were unable to operate their trains. Our men were intact at every point, firm, quiet, yet determined, and no sign of violence or disorder anywhere."

Once the boycott had been declared, Debs telegraphed instructions to all locals west of Hammond, Indiana. The first showdown was at Chicago, and a crowd of several thousand gathered to watch the scheduled departure of the Chicago & Erie's Buffalo Express at 2:55 P. M. The train left on time, the drawbars chained together and fastened with padlocks as a safeguard against cutting out the sleeping-cars. But the Buffalo Express and several other trains permitted to leave had been made up before the noon deadline. By nightfall the Illinois Central, Michigan Central, Chicago Great Western, the Baltimore & Ohio, Chicago & Northern Pacific and the Wisconsin Central were crippled. In another twelve hours, seven more lines were immobilized in the Chicago district.

No word from the Pullman Company or the General Managers' Association.

By June 28, two days after Debs had called the boycott, more than 40,000 men on lines in the west and southwest were out on strike—that is, so far as concerned any operations that affected trains hooked up with Pullmans. Union officials, agreeing that this was insufficient, intensified the offensive by calling out men employed on lines in the Chicago district that did not use Pullmans, but were members of the General Managers' Association. That order halted the rolling stock of the Burlington, Chicago & Alton, the Chicago & Eastern Illinois, the Monon, the Fort Wayne, Wabash, and the Lake Shore.

In sympathy, employes of the Union Stockyards Transit Company joined the strike, suspending work in the Yards.

As the boycott—now become a general railroad strike—spread west Debs was overwhelmed with telegrams from locals which, distant from Chicago, were uncertain just what was expected of them. The president of the A.R.U. in his responses left no room for doubt, although he kept warning against violence and destruction of railroad property. Characteristic messages among nine thousand he sent, leaving Chicago every few minutes, were:

"Have all men stand firm. The blockade becomes more perfect every minute."

"Northern Pacific, Southern Pacific, Santa Fé and all Chicago lines out to enforce Pullman boycott. Take same action immediately."

"Chicago and all lines west are paralyzed. Adopt measures to tie up Rock Island from Topeka west and east."

"If your company [Denver & Rio Grande] refuses to boycott Pullmans, tie it up."

But hundreds of other messages added, "Commit no act of violence. Do not interfere with mail trains in any manner."

To maintain the strike effectively, and yet not to interfere with the transit of mails, was impossible. Pullmans, of course, carried no mail, but many of them were hauled by trains which did carry mails, and these were halted. The first hint that the strike might be fought by the railroads with the weapon of federal injunctions came to Debs on June 28, when Attorney-General Richard Olney—former chief counsel of the Erie Railroad—ordered the United States Attorney at Chicago to protect the mails by posting marshals on the trains. This was the sheerest optimism, since the strike at this stage involved at least 44,000 men throughout the country. Nevertheless up to that time, the third day of the strike, no violence had been reported anywhere from Hammond to the Pacific Coast.

On the 28th a crowd of a thousand strikers halted the Erie's New York and Chicago Limited at Hammond, and forced the trainmen to cut out and sidetrack the Pullmans. The following day Pullman scabs were manhandled at Ludlow, and an engineer and fireman were stoned at St. Paul—members of the old brotherhoods, as were the trainmen on the Erie Limited. On June 30, the Diamond Special of the Illinois Central was halted and its Pullman cars sidetracked at Riverdale, Illinois.

Forced to trudge over ties and cinders, their journeys interrupted, passengers began to realize that the Pullman boycott was more than a newspaper fable. Reports arrived at Union headquarters of pitched battles in Colorado and California. The A.R.U. attributed most of the violence to nonmembers who grasped an opportunity to pillage freight-cars.

On July 1, with violence on the increase throughout the country west of Hammond, the federal government made its initial move. Edwin Walker, a railroad attorney, was appointed special attorney-general at Chicago, and charged with enforcing the laws relating to the protection of the mails and various clauses of the Interstate Commerce Act. In the former case, an Act of July 15, 1866, "To facilitate . . . postal . . . communications among the States," the railroads of the country were authorized to carry mails interstate, and to receive compensation for such service. In the latter case, the Interstate Commerce Act of February 4, 1887, gave the 1866 measure enabling powers, extending national protection to the mails, and it forbade interference with interstate commerce. Finally an Act of 1890 declared that "any person who shall knowingly and wilfully obstruct or retard the passage of the mail is guilty of a crime, and will be punished." Legally Washington was strongly armed to attack the A.R.U.

The Government considered using its other weapon, the injunction, as reports continued of the spiking and misplacing of switches, the removal of rails, crippling of interlocking systems, the sidetracking and derailing of cars and engines, the placing of coupling pins in engine machinery, and the blockading of tracks with cars. The federal injunction had found its precedent some years before in the west, where the quaint practice existed of issuing restraining orders against "train-stealing" in cases where the government acted as receiver, its purpose being to make theft of railroad property a federal crime.

On July 2 federal marshals descended on Union headquarters in Chicago, and served Debs and sixteen others, "all persons combining and conspiring with them," with an injunction enjoining them from interfering with the carrying of interstate commerce or the United States mails on the lines affected. The same day the injunction was read to a mob at Blue Island, a suburb, which greeted it with cries of "To hell with the Government! To hell with the Court! We are the Government!"

The intrepid marshal who, braving a hail of brickbats, read the injunction to the mob, J. W. Arnold, telegraphed to Attorney-General Olney that "they simply hoot at it, pay no attention to it, and have made their threats that they will not allow any Pullman cars to pass through on the Rock Island road. We have had a desperate time with them here all day and our force is inadequate, and in my judgment it is impossible to move trains here without having the 15th Infantry from Fort Sheridan ordered here at once. There are over 2,000 rioters here, and more are coming. Mail trains in great danger." The day before, he had telegraphed for permission to buy a hundred riot-guns.

At this time the strike spread eastward to Toledo, Cleveland and Buffalo. Debs, Walker and the other leaders, despite the injunctions, were still convinced they were leading the union to victory. In view of the epidemic character of the boycott, and the nation's unmistakable alarm over the violence as well as the economic cost of the strike, they believed that public opinion would compel the General Managers' Association to speak the three words that would restore order—agreement to arbitrate. They were not intimidated by the injunctions at a time when they had brought about more than creeping paralysis of commerce and mail transit over two-thirds of the United States.

Between July 2 and July 10 acts of violence in which none had been seriously injured gave way to bloodshed. At Blue Island strikers and sympathizers disarmed four United States marshals, an engine was overturned, and the tracks were blocked with freight-cars toppled athwart the tracks.

Even to many sympathizers the forcible disarming of the marshals constituted insurrection.

There were similar outbreaks in Colorado, where at Trinidad the rails were soaped, and a locomotive was run off the rails. On the night of July 2 President Cleveland, the Attorney-General and Major J. M. Scofield agreed at a conference to order the garrison at Fort Sheridan, north of Chicago, held in readiness for transfer to the lake-front. The next night a plea for intervention signed by Federal Judge P. S. Grosscup of the northern district of Illinois, Walker, the special Attorney-General, and United States Attorney Thomas E. Milchrist was sent to Olney at Washington (upon the latter's request the day before); then the order was issued dispatching the garrison to Chicago.

In full war equipment the garrison arrived on the lake-front without incident on the morning of July 4. The city was quiet. General Nelson A. Miles—the veteran Indian fighter—, in command of the Military Department of Missouri, took command the same day. He was authorized by Washington to summon up six additional companies from Fort Leavenworth and Fort Brady, increasing his force to about two thousand.

On July 5 he reported to the War Department that mobs had burned a hundred freight cars, after dousing them with gasoline, in the Stock Yards and along the lake-front railroad tracks, that the strikers and sympathizers were hourly becoming more rebellious, and that "the injunction of the United States Court is openly defied."

In the west, meanwhile, there was rioting at Sacramento, quelled by the National Guard. Federal troops were called in Utah to halt burning of freight-cars, and the state militia was mustered into service in Iowa. President Cleveland declined to accede to the request of Governor John P. Altgeld of Illinois to withdraw from Chicago the federal troops, whose presence Altgeld considered an added provocation to the strikers and an insult to the citizens of the State. "It is not soldiers that the railroads need so much," he stated in an acid telegram to the White House, "as it is men to operate trains." (In 1913 the President published a small volume in justification of federal intervention at Chicago.)

The Governor ordered up the State militia, numbering about five thousand, which in his opinion was fully able to protect the citizens of Illinois. The United States Marshal was authorized to appoint as many deputies as he needed; their selection, arming and payment were assigned to the General Managers' Association. The latter grasped the opportunity to recruit a force of 3,600 men clothed with almost unrestricted federal police authority and under the direct command of the railroads. "It is a bad precedent," the federal investigators reported, putting it mildly, "that might well lead to serious consequences." Whether or not "bad precedent," the result on July 6, when the deputies were loosed over Chicago and the suburbs, was indiscriminate firing in which six of the strikers were killed.

General Miles the next day issued to his troops an order that "if any act of hostility be committed, such as firing upon railroad trains or assaulting trainmen, marshals or soldiers by throwing at them rocks, pieces of iron or other missiles, those assaults shall be repelled by the use of firearms." An identical order was issued by the commander of the state militia.

At Forty-ninth Street and the lake-front on Chicago's South Side a mob of 15,000 had gathered near the railroad tracks of the Illinois Central. The strikers aimed to prevent the passage either north or south of all trains. Company C, Second Regiment, Illinois National Guard, fearing a charge by the mob, fired three volleys into the mass. One striker was killed, seventeen others injured, including two women.

In Colorado a bridge was burned at New Castle, and the tracks dynamited.

On July 8, at Hammond again, where five lines ran through the Indiana town, strikers, sympathizers and others identified by the newspapers only as "hoodlums, women, a low class of foreigners and recruits from the criminal classes" stormed and sacked the Western Union office, overturned and burned freight-cars, and, the police charged, were responsible for the wounding of five non-striking railroad employes, one of whom died. The tracks were blocked by the method now become familiar, and a through train derailed. A riot call was sent to Chicago for federal troops, since there was no hope of immediate aid from the Indiana militia, and the handful of U. S. marshals had been disarmed.

A party of thirty-five regulars from Company B, Fifteenth Infantry, arrived at noon, and succeeded in clearing the tracks, a considerable feat since the strikers and others numbered at least a thousand. But soon afterward the crowd —composed exclusively of "Chicago toughs," the Union asserted—expanded to three thousand. The soldiers from Fort Sheridan held their post in front of the Monon depot for two hours, bayonets drawn. They repelled two rushes by scattered fire over the heads of the crowd.

At the third charge they fired into the mob. Six were killed.

The "Hammond Massacre" elicited from the General Managers' Association this statement:

"We stand exactly where we have stood since the beginning of the strike, and where we will stand to the end. We are supported in our stand by the railroad managers all over the United States. It is no time for weakness of policy. We are compelled to make this fight by the unreasonableness of the strikers. The fight must be won regardless of its consequences to any single railroad. There will be no weakening on the part of this Association."

Outside Chicago, strikers captured the railroad shops at Galveston, Texas, and expelled scabs, caused the ditching of a Big Four passenger train outside Terre Haute, Indiana, killing the engineer and fireman, and blew up a freight train south of Las Vegas, Nevada. However unbending the railroad officials were, a realistic view brought the conclusion that the strikers had the upper hand.

But a heavy blow was dealt them in Chicago on July 10. There a federal grand jury returned indictments against

Debs, Howard *et al* on charges of obstruction of the mails, conspiring to commit offenses against the United States, conspiracy in restraint of commerce among the several states, and conspiracy to "injure, oppress, threaten or intimidate citizens in the free exercise and enjoyment of their rights." About all that was omitted was high treason and barratry.

To that jury Judge Grosscup explained that "you have come into an atmosphere, and amid occurrences, that may well cause reasonable men to question whether the laws of the United States are yet supreme." Particularly debatable in his instructions to the jury was his definition of "the fact of an insurrection."

"When men gather in such force," he explained, "that the civil authorities are inadequate to put them down, and a considerable military force is needed to accomplish that result, they become insurgents, and every person who knowingly incites, aids or abets them, no matter what his motive may be, is likewise an insurgent."

Debs, Howard and two others were arrested an hour after the jury convened, and released in bail of $10,000 each. The A.R.U. president, fearing that the indictments might lead to greater bloodshed, issued an appeal to strikers "not only to refrain from acts of violence but to aid in every way in your power to maintain law and order . . . The distance from anger to vengeance is not great." A week later the quartet was rearrested on charges of contempt of court in defying the federal injunctions, and not permitted their freedom on bail. Two days afterward the jury returned indictments on the contempt charges against the four leaders and thirty-nine others.

The strikers, leaderless, could not fight the railroads, the Pullman Company, the United States troops, the state militia, the federal courts, the Chicago police, and the indifference of the old railroad brotherhoods.

Under the circumstances the end was inevitable. There were continued outbreaks throughout the country, but by July 18 trains had returned almost to their normal schedules. Federal troops remained on duty several weeks as train-guards and as details at bridges and crossings. The most gigantic strike in the country's history had lasted twenty-three days—and had failed. By August 2 the nation was back on wheels, the mail service returned to regular schedules, and the Pullman Company had begun to manufacture another succession of palatial "Hiawathas," "Pioneers," and "Claremonts."

On the charge of contempt—not conspiracy—Debs and six others, defended by Clarence Darrow, were sentenced to six months' imprisonment, their appeal denied to the United States Supreme Court.

"In going to jail for participation in the late strike," Debs said, as he was led from the courtroom, "I have no apologies to make nor regrets to express. No ignominy attaches to me on account of this sentence. I would not change places with Judge Woods [the trial judge], and if it is expected that six months or even six years in jail will purge me of contempt, the punishment will fail of its purpose."

On Debs' return to Chicago in November the next year, he was welcomed by a demonstration unlike anything known to a city which owns to a special genius in the manufacture of noise. Two years later, with what remained of the American Railroad Union, he organized the Social Democratic Party, one of the origins of the American Socialist Party, whose Presidential candidate Debs was in 1904.

In testimony before the federal commissioners, the railroad officials estimated their property loss, together with the hire of deputy marshals and incidental expenses, at $685,308. The loss in railroad earnings was given by the General Managers' Association as $4,672,916. The loss to about 3,600 Pullman workers was $350,000. Railroad workers were out of pocket about $1,389,143. The bill for the nation at large in lost earnings and property destruction was estimated at four billion dollars by Joseph Nimmo, Jr., a statistician of Washington, D. C.

No practical brake, once a strike is declared, was devised by Congress after the bitter experience of 1894; none was found after the bloodshed of 1877 nor after the "outlaw strike" of 1920. The federal commissioners recommended a strike commission at Washington with mandatory powers of arbitration, and a bill to that end came to the floor of the national legislature. When the representatives of the railroads on one side, and those of the railroad brotherhoods on the other, finished rewriting the measure it had lost its sole virtue, that of compulsory arbitration. But at a cost of four billions, or for that matter one billion, any remaining George Pullmans in the nation are a dispensable luxury.

By BARROWS MUSSEY

IT IS NOT SOUND HISTORY TO DRAW EARLY
and late parallels too close; and it is at least not conservative
history-writing to tread too closely on the heels of events.
For this reason the farmers' risings in 1932 and 1933 offer a
puzzle to the writer on American rebellions. A serious
scholar could scarcely write about so recent an affair without falling victim to charges either of seeing red or of min-
imizing something real, and probably also of being a journal-
ist rather than a historian. Hence this postscript to a book
which is certainly solid history.

The significance of the farmers' risings is still a puzzle,
whoever the classifier. There are those who saw in these
movements a straightforward repetition of Shays' Rebellion,
of the Whiskey Insurrection, of Dorr's Rebellion. The farmers were rising against low prices, low land values, high taxes
and debt burdens. Some of the rebels themselves took the
name of Seventy-Sixers.

But while the mid-Western farmers used intimidation and
some violence, there was virtually no bloodshed; they developed some new methods of passive warfare, but the war

was more against starvation than against oppression. Although the militia were called out once or twice, public sympathy was wholly with the farmers; there were really no serious repressive measures.

The troubles of American farmers go back a long way. One of the basic difficulties is the fact that for generations few Americans really expected to make a living from farming: they bought farms in order to sell at a speculator's profit. So long as land worth a dollar an acre to-day might be in downtown Cincinnati or Chicago ten years hence, this was a temptation scarcely to be resisted. In a more sensible but hardly less dangerous form this idea persisted up to the World War: farmers bought land and machinery, built houses, sent their children to the University, on the honest income of farming—but in the expectation that crop prices would stay up. Farming was still ill-paid hard work, but apparently it would enable a man in the long run to get his farm up to an economic size and state of efficiency, and eventually to pay his honest debts. In 1915, '16, '17, '18, '19 there seemed to be no catastrophic farm problem.

In 1920 the war caught up with the nation and with the farmers. Produce prices fell, but debts contracted during the boom had still to be paid; taxes rose rather than fell. For the farmers things hardly improved from 1920 to 1933. The city slickers had an intervening boom; not so the countrymen.

During the first twelve years of their decline, the farmers of the mid-West—probably the world's richest farm land—

plugged along as mid-Western farmers always had. They scraped, and retrenched, and mortgaged their property, and complained loudly to Congress. Some of them experimented with cooperatives, but what good was a cooperative when top price was below the cost of production? Congress made a few gestures to still the noise, but the shouts were so disorganized and contradictory that elective office-holders felt fairly safe without real action. There was a "farm bloc" in Congress, but President Hoover was able to veto their Mc-Nary-Haugen Bill without driving the farmers to the barricades. There were some efforts at organization—perhaps chief among them the Farmers Union, led by a man named Milo Reno—, but the traditional American farmer's stiff-necked individualism was still strong. Reno and a lot of his followers yelled loudly and vaguely about the farmer's right to a price which would guarantee him the cost of production. Everybody favored this—it was rather like the sermon Calvin Coolidge heard "against sin." But they would not, in this rock-ribbed Republican stronghold, "turn Red" by uniting for action.

Things went along like this, getting worse by slow degrees, until the fall of 1931. Many farmers who had once owned their farms were by now reduced to tenantry, and mortgage foreclosures threatened in a rising flood. So late as 1926 the average farm family's annual cash income was estimated at $603 per year; by 1931 it was $160. In 1931 the nation's farm income failed by a billion dollars to pay the merest hired-hand wages to the farmers. In 1932 it fell another $1,700,000,000. In 1931 the Federal and the Joint Stock Land Banks began foreclosing their loans in earnest;

that year they foreclosed 16,601 farms. Taxes were 266% of what they had been in 1915. In 1932 forced sales and voluntary bankruptcies involved 24% of the farms in Iowa, and more than this proportion in Nebraska and South Dakota.

The first violent kick-back came in Iowa, and not against foreclosures, but against modern agricultural methods. Tuberculin testing of cattle was made obligatory, and animals found infected were to be slaughtered. The state paid one-third of the loss, the federal government another third, and the final third fell on the farmer. The farmers complained that their cows aborted after being tested; they said the veterinarians who did the testing were dirty and inconsiderate; finally, they began to run the state men off the farms. The governor of Iowa succeeded finally in carrying through the program by turning out the militia,—a piece of hard-handedness which nearly cost him his political life.

Still prices fell and foreclosures increased. Milo Reno had been driven from control of the Farmers Union in 1930 by the more radical and better-trusted John Simpson, but he burst into prominence again in the summer of 1932 with the National Farm Holiday Association. This was a front against one of the two millstones which ground the farmer: against low prices. Reno, traveling around and making fiery speeches, kept repeating his "cost of production" slogan, and urged his hearers to sell no produce until prices rose.

On August 8, 1932, he launched a thirty-day holiday on farm selling. It started mainly around Sioux City and Omaha, but soon spread to North and South Dakota, Minnesota, Wisconsin, and Illinois. The holiday was soon extended for a longer time.

Reno, who was by no means an outstanding personality, of course had many followers, imitators, and competitors. One of the most effective was Walter M. Singler, of Wisconsin, who formed what he called the "Milk Pool," and in the northern half or three-quarters of Wisconsin succeeded for a time in preventing almost all milk shipment. In Minnesota a force of (the rebels said) 3,000 or (the local paper said) 1,000 farmers descended on the packing plant of Swift & Co. at Marshall, and forced it to close. Pickets in sharply varying numbers were the force used to stop produce shipments in several states. Of 120,000 farmers theoretically called out in Wisconsin, perhaps 15,000 were picketing night and day, and of these 10,000 were thought ready for any violence. Most of the violence actually done occurred in the holiday movement rather than in the simultaneous foreclosure revolt, to which we shall come shortly.

Actual figures, either of membership or of damage, are very hard to come by. One picket was shot dead by blockade-runners near Madison, Wisconsin; a large number of blockade-runners were badly beaten; a great deal of milk was spilled in roads; a cattle train was unloaded; five or six railroad bridges were burned; and ten Wisconsin dairies and cheese factories were dynamited. Sioux City was tied up for several days.

Reno always professed not to know the size of the Farm Holiday Association, which gave rise to well-founded suspicion that it was smaller than he claimed. The magazine *Fortune*, trying to be specific, could say only that the Iowa membership appeared to be about 2% of the 215,000 farmers in the state, and the national membership less than 100,-

ooo. The *Farm Holiday News*, Reno's paper, had a paid circulation of 6,000, but printed considerably more.

Even 100,000 farmers, militant and firmly united, could probably have swept the Middle West before them, perhaps even have carried out the secession or the nation-within-a-nation which some of the more desperate farmers predicted. But neither John Simpson, Reno, Singler, nor any other agitator had the personality or the program to make a real army of the farmers. The eventual futility of the farm strike was evident to all outside observers and to many within the movement. After all, any rise in farm prices could last only as long as the artificial scarcity induced by the strike; successful runners of the picket blockade were the only people to profit, while the strikers had produce either rotting at home or waiting to be flung on a flat market after the strike. As a matter of fact the strike had no national effect on prices or supply, and, indeed, wheat and hog prices later came down. In Sioux City the milk price to the farmer was 2c, to the consumer 8c; this the strikers did succeed in raising to 3.6c for the farmer, 9c for the consumer. The subject of milk distribution has of course long been a *casus belli* in any case, and milk strikes spread beyond the mid-Western states, and continued long after the Farm Holiday movement subsided.

Walter Singler showed his independence and that of the dairy farmers by a flank attack on Reno when the latter gave signs of softening. Twelve hours after the Milk Pool had called its strike, Reno tried to call a truce to allow the Governors of the five states chiefly affected to go to Washington and dump the matter into the Federal Government's lap. Singler led his own adherents and a thousand of Reno's into the State Assembly at Madison, Wisconsin, steamrollered through a strike vote, and forced the Farm Holiday Association back to picketing within forty-eight hours.

This was only one of many signs of division among the farmers, desperate as they were. It was this division and the lack of any genuine panacea which prevented the strikers from using their numbers and the nationwide public sympathy for their troubles. Everyone said something must be done for the farmer; everyone agreed he had enough provocation to strike; everyone (even such men as Singler) admitted that the strike could not possibly do any good except perhaps to dramatize the situation in the eyes of the country. This finally proved to be the case, despite an unsuccessful revival of the strikes in the fall of 1933, after vigorous measures by the new Roosevelt administration had raised the farmer's economic level for a few weeks, only to have it start slipping again.

It was otherwise with what may be called the defensive side of the farm revolt. Efforts to raise prices were a positive, offensive tactic; efforts to keep farmers from losing their homes, on the other hand, represented last-ditch defense.

Foreclosures by the Land Banks have been mentioned; soon the insurance companies joined the ranks of worried creditors, and began trying to collect their loans as best they could. Many former farm-owners had already slipped down to the status of tenants on the places they had built up, but now the mortgage-holders felt themselves obliged to sell off land and equipment to raise cash. Nobody could say they were not within their rights; yet the farmers, pushed to the limit, felt it more necessary to keep a roof over their neighbors' heads than to protect law and property rights.

Shays and his followers had faced the same problem with rather less intelligence and restraint by forcibly interfering with the courts; the Iowa farmers developed a method for taking care of each case as it came up. First there were protest meetings, which reached their height in early January, 1933; then came the "five-and-ten" sales.

Five-and-ten sales were an almost legal method of preserving a farmer's home and equipment. After the worst (legally) had happened to a delinquent debtor, the sheriff and auctioneer would arrive to sell off the place. Normally the creditor would expect to buy it in to protect himself; nobody else would be likely to have the money anyway. But at these sales in the mid-Western Bankruptcy Bowl all the farmer neighbors would attend, armed sometimes with sticks and pitchforks, more often only with determination and black looks. Some joker was likely to hang up a hangman's noose in the barn—a symbol of death to foreclosure. About this time the neighbors would make it plain to the creditor that his bids were not wanted; a few creditors and other outsiders who were slow of comprehension got rough treatment in some cases. Then the actual bidding would begin. A double harness would start—and be sold—for 5c; a wagon would go for a dime; a team of grays, 10c; good cows, six or eight cents; the high point at one such sale was 15c for a binder machine. At that particular sale the proceeds of the afternoon were $5.22; the owner got his property back from the buyers. They held that possession, perhaps not nine points of the law, was certainly ten points of justice.

There was a little violence of the old Shays sort—the most famous case that of Judge Bradley, of Le Mars, Iowa, whose courtroom was invaded by farmers smoking and wearing their hats. He was outraged at this lack of manners, and as a result was dragged from the court, threatened with lynching if he did not promise to sign no more eviction orders, and all but tarred and feathered. Five counties were put under martial law as a result.

Fortunately the state governments took a less stiff-necked attitude than Judge Bradley. Faced with a choice between its taxpaying (and voting!) citizens and the banks and insurance companies, the state of Iowa on February 7, 1933, passed a law which in effect declared a two-year moratorium on foreclosures. It entrusted the district courts with distributing rents, incomes, and profits of all real estate liable to foreclosure, toward tax, mortgage and insurance claims until March 1, 1935. The model was quickly followed in Kansas, North and South Dakota, Nebraska, Wisconsin, and Idaho. There was also legislation against deficiency judgments, a very sore point with the farmers.

These efforts and the concurrent farm-strike developments early in 1933 marked at once the height of the uproar and the trough of the depression for the farmers. In February of 1933 the index of farm purchasing power stood at 49% of what it had been in 1913. In March President Franklin Roosevelt assumed office, and the banks swooned (though they had been holding private holidays of their own in Iowa before this).

The farm leaders campaigned for "the honest dollar" (inflation), for government refinancing and loans at low rates, for a reduction in tax rates, for a farm-produce minimum-price law—in short, for any sort of relief. Roosevelt and his Secretary of Agriculture, Henry Wallace, hastened to give it, though not in the forms asked.

They put into effect cotton, wheat, and later, hog crop-reduction agreements, paying farmers for producing less than they had habitually done; they offered loans on certain crops which had been rotting in the farmers' bins. The purchasing-power index by July rose from 49% to 72%.

But the Administration had also to look after industry, and the NRA, which was started in July for this purpose, for a while caused a noticeable rise in general prices. The farmers felt they were losing all the ground they had gained; and in fact their purchasing-power index slipped back to 61% in September. The wheat and cotton farmers, however, still felt happier than they had.

Efforts to strike grew sharper again in the fall of 1933; but it was a last flare-up. Public opinion, even in the affected areas, began to turn against striking; some of the farmers started Law and Order Leagues. No rebellion is complete without a battle, and Iowa had its Battle of Plattsmouth Bridge. This was a conflict between Law and Order Leaguers on one side and 150 pickets on the other, and resulted, as someone said, in a victory for the tollkeeper of the bridge, who charged the pickets one toll as they crossed the bridge to advance, and a second as they retreated.

Thus, or nearly thus, ended the Farmers' Risings in the Middle West.

These risings brought to a head generations of American farmers' misery; they showed the sternest of individualists how much combined direct action might accomplish, and yet how little is the net profit of violent rebellion; they covered more territory, with perhaps less damage, than any other American rising; it may be that one day we shall see their chief new element not in the farmers getting together but in the deliberate use of lawlessness as a method of publicity.

INDEX

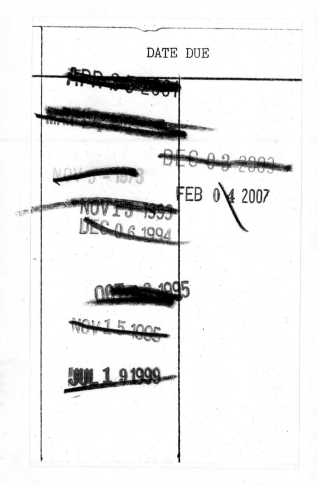